SCOTS, SASSENACHS, AND SPANKINGS

Other Works by Valerie Estelle Frankel

Henry Potty and the Pet Rock: A Harry Potter Parody
Henry Potty and the Deathly Paper Shortage: A Harry Potter Parody
Buffy and the Heroine's Journey
From Girl to Goddess: The Heroine's Journey in Myth and Legend
Katniss the Cattail: The Unauthorized Guide to Name and Symbols in The Hunger Games
The Many Faces of Katniss Everdeen: Exploring the Heroine of The Hunger Games
Harry Potter, Still Recruiting: A Look at Harry Potter Fandom
Teaching with Harry Potter
An Unexpected Parody: The Spoof of The Hobbit Movie
Myths and Motifs in The Mortal Instruments
Winning the Game of Thrones: The Host of Characters & their Agendas
Winter is Coming: Symbols, Portents, and Hidden Meanings in A Game of Thrones
Bloodsuckers on the Bayou: Myths & Tales Behind HBO's True Blood
The Girl's Guide to the Heroine's Journey
Choosing to be Insurgent or Allegiant: Symbols, Themes & Analysis of the Divergent Trilogy
Doctor Who and the Hero's Journey
Doctor Who: The What Where and How
Sherlock: Every Canon Reference in BBC's Series 1-3
Symbols in Game of Thrones
How Game of Thrones Will End
Joss Whedon's Names
Pop Culture in the Whedonverse
Women in Game of Thrones: Power, Conformity, and Resistance
History, Homages and the Highlands: An Outlander Guide
The Catch-Up Guide to Doctor Who
Remember All Their Faces: A Deeper Look at Character, Gender and the Prison World of Orange Is The New Black
Everything I Learned in Life I Know from Joss Whedon
Empowered: The Symbolism, Feminism, & Superheroism of Wonder Woman
The Avengers Face their Dark Sides: Mastering the Myth-Making behind the Marvel Superheroes
The Symbolism and Sources of Outlander

SCOTS, SASSENACHS, AND SPANKINGS

FEMINISM AND GENDER ROLES IN OUTLANDER

Valerie Estelle Frankel

Scots, Sassenachs, and Spankings is an unauthorized guide and commentary on *Outlander* and its related universe. None of the individuals or companies associated with the books or television series or any merchandise based on this series have in any way sponsored, approved, endorsed, or authorized this book.

ISBN-13: 978-0692449080 (LitCrit Press)
ISBN-10: 0692449086

LitCrit Press

For fans of fantasy and feminism

Contents

Introduction

From the extensive book series through the new Starz show, *Outlander* explores the myriad of gender roles we encounter through our lives, binding them together in a nuanced love story that's nonetheless overflowing with adventure.

Anne Helen Petersen explains the series popularity in "Outlander Is The Feminist Answer To Game Of Thrones — And Men Should Be Watching It":

> The first book, along with its seven sequels, have sold more than 25 million copies worldwide. Today, you can mention *Outlander* in a group of women, no matter the age, and chances are at least a quarter will have read it. From the beginning, they were known as "word of mouth" books, meaning that people read them not because of some marketing campaign, but because friends told them to. And it's been in this mode that these books have spread through generations and continents, weaving a web of shared narrative experience that can anchor families, friendships, and relationships. When you find someone who's read *Outlander,* in other words, you'll always have something to talk about.

The show's "core is about the emotional and cultural differences between men and women, and how their relationships have and have not changed over the centuries" (Seitz). Combined with this is an exploration of gender, from New Men to ancient warriors, modern women and those who take on classic roles of housekeeper or wife but are far from weak. While some like Geillis perform femininity, they use their gender as a mask to play at politics and rewrite history. The show bridges the gap between the novels and the conventions of cable shows, demonstrating what a feminized version of the onscreen nudity and point of view looks like.

There are also the Othered characters – those who are homosexual, disabled, or cast as minorities, who, like the women, struggle to find their place in eighteenth century culture. By exploring these many roles, readers can discover much about history and also about themselves.

Gender and Storytelling

Point of View and Voice

> Strange, the things you remember. Single images and feelings that stay with you down through the years. Like the moment I realized I'd never owned a vase. That I'd never lived any place long enough to justify having such a simple thing. And how at that moment, I wanted nothing so much in all the world as to have a vase of my very own. Somehow in my mind, V.E. day, the end of the bloodiest and most terrible war in human history, grows fainter with each passing day. But I can still recall every detail of the day when I saw the life I wanted sitting in a window.

The show starts with the blue vase, an image of potential domesticity in Claire's voiceover. Of course she abandons the "life she wanted" for an adventure in the past, giving a lie to her words. Her entire story is framed as a flashback – Claire in the future, remembering her romance with Jamie, tells the story. It also reflects the actress's own journey.

> The last of the main characters to be cast, Balfe found herself parachuted into a production already operating at full tilt to create Outlander's crammed 18th-century world. She had to scramble to keep up, an experience she likens to her character's predicament: "When Claire gets thrown

> back, she's completely clueless and it's all brand new for her, so luckily I was just able to discover things as I went along." (Virtue)

The narrator or point of view has a strong effect on the text, in this show far more than most. Narration has always been tricky onscreen, as the gendered narrator encourages the audience to identify with a male or female point of view. Simone de Beauvoir notes in *The Second Sex* that men consider themselves the subject of the world, its standard form, and thus have demoted women to the role of Other. "She is defined and differentiates with reference to man and not he with reference to her; she is the incidental; the inessential as opposed to the essential" (xxxix-xl). Thus a female point of view in *Outlander* emphasizes that historical drama, even war drama, need not be the province of only men. Of course, there's no reason men shouldn't watch it.

> When asked whether men will watch the show, Moore was adamant: "Look, I read the book, I loved the book. When my wife and producing partner gave me the book, they weren't like, 'Oh, here's a romance novel. See what you can do with it.' They said, 'Here's a really good book.' I don't see any reason why men won't watch this show." (Petersen)

Whether the preexisting female audience or the new male audience are watching, certainly Claire and her first-person story feature front and center.

Women are often silenced in fiction, so a mouthy, opinionated woman like Claire must be celebrated. Nonetheless, keeping close to her face confines the power of her voice. Most often onscreen, a disembodied male narrator, perhaps setting the prologue, is male. Female narration heavily follows a character, dictating her thoughts as her face appears. Shohini Chaudhuri, author of *Feminist Film Theorists,* explains:

> It consigns the woman to a safe place "inside" the diegesis where she can be overseen and overheard, while the man is situated in a framing space "outside," where he can identify with the functions of transcendental vision, hearing, and speech associated with the enunciator or disembodied narrator. (Chaudhuri 52)

Claire's story certainly begins with the character and her narrative. "Claire is the audience surrogate on any number of levels, not only because the audience is also clueless in the ways of Highland life, but also because the show revolves around the idea that you live and die by the feelings that Claire has, that you love whom she loves and hate whom she hates" (Hill). Though Jamie and Young Ian become viewpoint characters in time, Jenny Murray, for instance, has more conversations in front of Claire than she does privately in the point of view of any of her menfolk. Thus readers and viewers alike view Jenny for the most part through Claire's eyes.

Carol J. Clover in her essay on gender in slasher films notes:

> Some critics have wondered whether the female viewer, faced with the screen image of a masochistic/narcissistic female, might not rather elect to "betray her sex and identify with the masculine point of view." The reverse question – whether men might not also, on occasion, elect to betray their sex and identify with screen females – has scarcely been asked, presumably on the assumption that men's interests are well served by the traditional patterns of cinematic representation. Then too there is the matter of the "male gaze." As E. Ann Kaplan sums it up: "Within the film text itself, men gaze at women, who become objects of the gaze; the spectator, in turn, is made to identify with this male gaze, and to objectify the women on the screen; and the camera's original 'gaze' comes into play in the very act of filming." (235)

The voiceovers make this a rare show in which male viewers actually might "betray their genders" and empathize with the heroine. The hints of 1940s music in the past and a frequent camera on Claire fixes viewers in her mindset. Moreover, Claire is a twentieth-century woman, accustomed to gender equality and job competence. She knows history and science far beyond the eighteenth-century Scots, and in the first and third episodes, she's far more competent medically. With the Scots' foreignness of language, education, and culture, Claire is the most logical target for viewer empathy. They are engaged in a rebellion which to Claire, as well as viewers, is little more than a static page in history, while her need to return home is far more visceral.

The opening credits offer a collage of images from the early episodes: a deer, horses, the stitching of the wound, a war drum, a drawn dagger. Specifically, faces do not appear, as Jamie plays shinty from the neck down or Claire's face shows up nose to neck, her hair blowing. An anonymous hand strokes an anonymous flank. Her hand grips a pillow, Black Jack's boots and whip appear, or Frank's arm, driving. The circle dancers twirl robed and anonymous, then characters sit in profile, dim with distance. Claire runs and walks, seen only from the back. This echoes the trend of faceless women displayed neck down on bookcovers in recent times.

> Editors, according to Julianna Lee, an art director at Little, Brown & Company, often explicitly instruct designers not to show a woman's face: "A little bit of mystery allows the reader to use their imagination," she says. Furthermore, omitting individualizing details spares jacket designers from the charge (by authors and readers) that they haven't rendered characters faithfully. Even when depicted from the front, headless women are common on covers. (Schama)

Certainly, the show credits follow this pattern and may be nodding to such a literary series – the credits tell the audience, "Picture Claire and Jamie as their book counterparts if you wish, or picture yourself in their roles." By de-emphasizing faces, there's also a sensual trend here. However, by highlighting bodies, it steps away from the personality of the characters:

> Perhaps the trend is more inadvertent than pernicious. The ubiquitous book-cover back suggests to potential readers that the book is about bodies and the forces contained therein, and there's nothing wrong with that – in fact, it's a fairly accurate description of all novels. The irony is that this design has become so prevalent that it undermines the very purpose of the book cover: to whet the appetite for the real meal. As my novelist friend put it, "A book jacket seems, to me, like the single most efficient way to signal whether a book has substance or not." But these books offer only skin, which is all surface. (Schama)

The credits obviously emphasize Claire and her journey – the quick impressions of objects tie to the blue vase and the concept of telling a story by recalling the objects around her. These images are intercut with the circle dancers – also blurry and impressionistic, signaling her unclear knowledge about their natural force and the magic which carried her back. "The demanding nature of the song ('Sing me a song') and the search for identity ('All that was me is gone') suggest Claire's own personality as she tries to decide where she belongs and how she's meant to spend her life" (Frankel, *Symbolism and Sources of Outlander* 76). This all echoes against the Skye Boat Song. Composer Bear McCreary explains:

> We performed "The Skye Boat Song," one of the most famous Scottish folk tunes, one that is known to be about the Jacobite uprising, during which *Outlander* takes place. The lyrics are taken from the lesser-known Robert Louis Stevenson text, with one alteration in the gender of the speaker, which helps the song relate to Claire's character. ("Comic Con 2014 Highlights")

The song is an anachronism from a century later,

though it certainly is linked with the tale of Bonnie Prince Charlie. The original 1884 lyrics by Sir Harold Boulton, 2nd Baronet, describe his defeat at Culloden, followed by his escape with Flora MacDonald "over the sea to Skye." Stevenson's version, vaguer and more romantic in language, seems a better fit for the show:

Sing me a Song of a Lad that is Gone
Robert Louis Stevenson 1850–1894

Sing me a song of a lad that is gone,
Say, could that lad be I?
Merry of soul he sailed on a day
Over the sea to Skye.

Mull was astern, Rum on the port,
Eigg on the starboard bow;
Glory of youth glowed in his soul;
Where is that glory now?

Sing me a song of a lad that is gone,
Say, could that lad be I?
Merry of soul he sailed on a day
Over the sea to Skye.

Give me again all that was there,
Give me the sun that shone!
Give me the eyes, give me the soul,
Give me the lad that's gone!

Sing me a song of a lad that is gone,
Say, could that lad be I?
Merry of soul he sailed on a day
Over the sea to Skye.

Billow and breeze, islands and seas,
Mountains of rain and sun,
All that was good, all that was fair,
All that was me is gone.

The *Outlander* theme tune is a shorter excerpt of this, with the protagonist gender-flipped:

> Sing me a song of a lass that is gone,
> Say, could that lass be I?
> Merry of soul she sailed on a day
> Over the sea to Skye.
>
> Billow and breeze, islands and seas,
> Mountains of rain and sun,
> All that was good, all that was fair,
> All that was me is gone.
>
> Sing me a song of a lass that is gone,
> Say, could that lass be I?
> Merry of soul she sailed on a day
> Over the sea to Skye
>
> The description of a lost person who sailed away certainly alludes to Claire. The ending of the tune, focusing on her journey rather than her loss, suggests continuing adventures in the fairytale-sounding land of "Skye" (though Claire does not in fact visit the actual isle). Nonetheless, the Gaelic name for the Isle of Skye, *An t-Eilean Sgitheanach,* meaning the Winged Isle, and its Gaelic nickname, *Eilean a' Cheo,* or Island of Mist, both cast it as a place of mystery and romance. In English, the sky signifies enlightenment and spiritual ascension, something Claire cannot find as the housewife of an Oxford don, but only as a fighting, healing heroine far in the past. (Frankel, *Symbolism and Sources of Outlander* 76)

Of course, episode nine begins with Jamie's voiceover, mimicking Claire's from episode one with the line "Strange the things you remember." After the long break, this functions as a bookend to Claire's own magical journey. Jamie tells of storming Fort William to rescue Claire from his own perspective. After comes his struggle through marriage to a modern woman as he finds ways to compromise.

It's book three before Jamie becomes a point of view character (by necessity, as he spends a significant portion without Claire). Similarly, he's sidelined heavily in the *Lord John* books, at least until *The Scottish Prisoner.* His influence in the series grows, as the prologue to *The Fiery Cross,* speaking of family, war, honor, fire, and blood, sounds more like Jamie than Claire:

> I have lived through war, and lost much. I know what's worth the fight, and what is not. Honor and courage are matters of the bone, and what a man will kill for, he will sometimes die for, too. And that, O kinsman, is why a woman has broad hips; that bony basin will harbor a man and his child alike. A man's life springs from his woman's bones, and in her blood is his honor christened. For the sake of love alone, I would walk through fire again.

The final books see him going on adventures without Claire as the characters split into smaller groups.

Sex Scenes and Gaze

"No one was interested in doing those typical cable TV scenes where the sex is unnecessary," says Balfe. "So to get that positive reaction was a relief. People were clearly wanting this, they hadn't found a show that was giving them it before. So it was great that we were able to give them something new" (Virtue).

Cable shows on HBO and Starz, especially the histories and historical retellings, are famous for the nudity and explicit sex. They are, as one critic notes, "populated by dehistoricized male characters who have magnificent bodies, engage in energetic sex and commit brutal and spectacular violence. They present the erotic spectacle of female bodies being sexually abused and the violent spectacle of male bodies being physically abused" (Glynn 161). These include *Rome, The Tudors, Camelot, The Borgias, Black Sails, Da Vinci's Demons, and Spartacus.*

Certainly, Jack Randall's violence is brutal in book and show – on the latter, he threatens to cut off Claire's nipple. Menzies explains:

> They're not pulling their punches. [The whipping scene in Lallybroch is] a further unfolding of the ingredients that were sort of seeded in the first half. It just goes further; in a slightly clearer way we see his sadism at work. The precision, attention to detail, that is where the darkness really lies. Obviously the violence is unpleasant, but it's how the violence is conducted – it's not out of fury or anger or loss of control, it's actually coming out of the opposite, and I think that is all the more unnerving. We find out more about the actual behavior of this quality. (Lutes)

Rape and torture both occur through the first season, not only in Jack Randall's scenes, but also as Jenny confronts the redcoat courier of "The Search" (114) and a pair of deserters attack Claire in "Both Sides Now" (108). This violence emphasizes the harshness of life at the time and also the lengths to which Claire and Jenny will go in self-defense.

This show must be compared to *Game of Thrones*, the most popular contemporary cable show. Though the *Times* notes, "In keeping with the Starz ethos, though, [*Outlander* is] a lighter show all around – less heavy and also less substantial" (Hale). Both blend British history (or pseudo-history) with the magical and explore women's historical roles amid graphic violence and sex scenes. The violence entertains and shocks much as the nudity does, all of it celebrating the opportunity to operate without the restrictions of network television. Nonetheless, Matt Zoller Seitz calls *Outlander* "curiously gentle despite its often harsh content." He adds, "*Outlander* is punctuated with savage violence (including a flashback in the second episode to a woman's violation and a man's torture) but rarely dwells on it, often cutting away from explicit sex or violence before anyone can accuse the filmmakers of being gratuitous."

Likewise, the sex scenes serve different purposes. Mary McNamara in "HBO, You're Busted," notes that on *Game of Thrones*, "The upper frontals got so gratuitous – two women teaching themselves the tricks of prostitution while a male character, fully clothed, muses about his personal history and definition of power – that fans took to Twitter to complain." As Salon's Lili Loofborrow points out, this issue "isn't just about penises vs. breasts ... it's about situation and camera angle. It's about who has the right to be turned on. It's about whose genitals are worth catering to" (Petersen).

Outlander does not show naked females standing about with no purpose. Sam Heughan calls the sex scenes "character driven and to drive the story forward" (Nemiroff). Ron Moore adds: "Anytime we're gonna do this, it's for a reason. We're showing something about their relationship, where they are with each other. There's an emotional arc that we're watching through those scenes" (Nemiroff). Sex scenes appear in episode one and then not until the wedding episode, though topless women appear in the dressing Claire scene and in Jenny's assault. The former of these might certainly be filed under unnecessary nudity, while the scene with Jenny is meant to shock the audience as well as Jamie with Jack Randall's sadistic cruelty.

The bodies are also unrealistically presented: "History in these dramas has been populated with people who are clean, buff, and toned and who have sex at the drop of a period hat. Modern hair gels, breast implants and teeth whitening agents anachronistically exist" (Glynn 161). Indeed, *The New York Times* describes Jamie as "the kindest, buffest and cleanest of the group" (Hale).

"My marching orders for the cast and director of that episode were: 'Let's make it truthful,'" adds Moore. "None of us actually *have* TV sex, it never looks like that. So it's not about titillating the audience or seeing how much flesh we can get away with showing; it's about continuing the story of the characters" (Virtue). This *Game-of-Thrones* style violence and graphic sex thus meets a historical dram of unfolding love and relationships. As one critic notes,

> The "Outlander" books date to 1991, but it seems likely that TV executives looked at them and thought, oh, "Game of Thrones" meets "Downton Abbey." The series ... has some of ye-olde-time grimy violence and sex of "Games" and a little of the plummy accents and cozy Anglophilia of "Downton." (Hale)

Regarding the sex scenes, Jamie and Claire remain chaste until their wedding night (even their first kiss is at the wedding). Before this, they engage in the loving banter and sweet moments of gallantry that are indeed more indicative of *Downton Abbey* than of an explicit cable show. Even when they're a stable couple, they often go through separations where they exchange delightful and flirtatious letters (as in the end of *An Echo in the Bone*). Forced into chastity on an overcrowded ship, Jamie tells her "there are moments, Sassenach, when for one copper penny, I'd have ye on the spot, back against the mast" (*Voyager*, ch. 44). Unable to resist, Claire gives him a penny "on account."

Gabaldon discusses the frequent sex in her books, explaining it's relationship-centered:

> There are a great many reasons why an author may choose to include explicit depictions of sex; the least worthy is of course to provide titillation to the reader – and I suspect some of my correspondents feel that this is the *only* possible reason for including such material. It's not, though. Human beings being what they are, an interest in sex is hardwired into the genetic machinery, and thus lies behind a great deal of human behavior, whether it's explicitly recognized or not. Given that one level of the novels is devoted to an exploration of the nature of love and marriage, it seems to me that some reference to sex is likely desirable. (*Outlandish Companion* 390-391)

The book has many of these scenes, most of which show Jamie and Claire's physical and emotional spectrum in the bedroom (and other places), though other characters have special moments as well. Peering into their sex life shows the characters' willfulness, humor. and true love, along with the give and take of power. Claire rules their bedroom as much as Jamie or more as she shoves him out of bed to lecture him in "Lallybroch" (112) and holds a knife to his throat in "The Reckoning" (109).

Episode ten opens with Jamie explicitly pleasuring her, with many shots of her face as she enjoys herself. This time spent showing a woman not just submitting but actively taking her pleasure is unusual onscreen. As Jamie leads her to the standing stones, once more he insists on an encounter that's all about her, as he insists he only wants to look at her. He strokes her face, kisses her, and looks in her eyes as she experiences vast pleasure.

> Fiction by, about and for women that shows women capable of sexual satisfaction is now extremely popular. From a feminist perspective these are contradictory texts – on the one hand, the capitalist ideology that pervades them largely Ignores, on a manifest level at least, issues of class, race and gender but on the other, they problematize and prioritize active sexuality for women in ways that might be regarded as a upheaval to the exclusively male gaze of patriarchal structures. The genre differs radically from "bodice rippers" which are verv definitely located within the world of romance (Lewallen 88)

The first episode is even stronger for Claire. Moore explains that he "wanted to show her as empowered sexually as a person and having her own appetites and desires" (qtd. in Maerz). In this, she and Frank share several sex scenes, most famously one in the ruins of Castle Leoch. She doesn't undress for the audience, and as Frank kneels before her, she pulls his head down. "She's the one who makes the first move, telling Frank what she wants (even removing her own underwear ahead of time!) so she's also the one we get to see enjoying it," critic Melissa Maerz notes in her article "Let's Talk about that 'Outlander' Sex Scene." As she adds:

> Obviously, sex scenes that focus on women getting off are still generally seen as taboo. In the documentary *This Film is Not Yet Rated*, Kimberly Pierce, who directed *Boys Don't Cry*, reveals that the MPAA pressured her to cut a similar sex act from her film to prevent it from earning an NC-17 rating, even though the brutal murder at the film's end was acceptable under an "R" rating. Pierce believes the MPAA was particularly uncomfortable with a shot that featured no nudity at all – it was a close-up that lingered on Brandon Teena's ecstatic expression – because it was such a clear departure from more traditional sex scenes, which have a clear endpoint as their goal, and tend to finish whenever the guys involved do. Maybe that's why it feels somewhat radical that the camera pans upward during the *Outlander* sex scene so that we can see Claire's face.

This emphasis on her emotions rather than her bare breasts suggests a female perspective unusual for the cable dramas.

On *The Tudors*, "Henry and [his best friend] Charles seduce, cast aside, or send women running back to their husbands. They are heterosexual supermen" (Glynn 168). Thus viewers are encouraged to empathize with the men – users and choosers – rather than the women, who must attract men with their beauty and pray for the king's continued attention. *Rome, The Borgias,* and *Spartacus* have similar attitudes. As Cersei trains Sansa that "a woman's greatest weapon is between her legs" and Melisandre plays sex slave to her chosen king, *Game of Thrones* repeats these tropes. Mary McNamara notes in "HBO, You're Busted!" that these shows are terribly slanted:

> Although there is male nudity – men occasionally, though not always, appear shirtless and/or bottomless when they are having sex with women – there are no male brothels, no scenes of clothed women, or men for that matter, sitting around chatting in a room filled with naked men...For all their many functions, women's bodies are not props and prostitution is not something that should be regularly relegated to atmosphere.

The Starz show *The White Queen* and HBO shows *Sex and the City* or *True Blood* have a different flavor than the more masculine shows listed. All were originally marketed as women's books, as *Outlander* was (originally intended for the romance section before moving to mainstream fiction). Thus all not only have female protagonists but focus on the world of women and their emotions. In *The White Queen,* the heroine threatens suicide to make the king back off from his planned sexual assault (he's the king after all). He submits to her desires and offers her honorable marriage by episode end.

True Blood, originally a series of paranormal mystery romances starring Sookie Stackhouse, has Sookie and the viewers gazing at a fully nude Eric Northman, who's absolutely vampire eye-candy. "See anything you like?" he asks, inviting her gaze. The sixth season finale sees him lying on a beach chair, again fully nude with a slow pan up his body. It's clear which viewers are meant to enjoy this. Ryan Kwanten, who plays Sookie's brother, is often presented for the female gaze as well:

> Michael Martin: It's a sexy show. But what's interesting to me is that the guy playing your brother is the one who's gratuitously topless and naked, kind of like the women in '80s horror movies.
> Anna Paquin: We take his clothes off a lot. As the season goes on, the nudity gets shared around, but in the first couple of episodes, he carries the brunt of that.

> Michael Martin: What did you and the other women in the cast think of the guy playing the naked-bimbo role? Payback?
> Anna Paquin: It is kind of funny. It is a very sexy show. All of us girls are running around in shorts that barely cover our behinds. Yeah, he's naked a lot, but when you have a body like that…I mean Ryan [Kwanten] has, in all fairness, a ridiculously nice physique, so I don't think he minds too much. (M. Martin)

HBO's *Sex and the City* is the most female-driven of the shows. Carrie, the point of view character, provides the narration and focuses on relationships and relationship problems. She brings up many taboos not normally visible on television, as her period syncs with her friends or they aren't sure which sex acts they're comfortable performing. While their own body parts don't show up much, the women spend much time judging the bodies of their men. Sex scenes generally focus on the female main characters' faces, inviting viewers to empathize with them. As such, this show is unique in the world of cable.

Outlander with its "kilted beefcake fantasy object, Jamie Fraser" (Seitz) likewise seems targeted at women, as the *Times* sums it up, "They seem to be having a good time, and if you have a weakness for muskets, accents and the occasional roll in the heather, you probably will too."

Laura Mulvey pioneered the study of gender-bias in cinematic gaze, explaining: "There are three different looks associated with cinema: that of the camera as it records the pro-filmic event, that of the audience as it watches the final product, and that of the characters at each other within the screen illusion." Mulvey differentiates between the delight of admiring a figure onscreen and identifying with the character.

> In a world ordered by sexual imbalance, pleasure in looking has been split between active/male and passive/female. The determining male gaze projects its fantasy onto the female figure, which is styled accordingly. In their traditional exhibitionist role women are simultaneously looked at and displayed, with their appearance coded for strong visual and erotic impact so that they can be said to connote to-be-looked-at-ness.

Long, lingering pans over a woman's body place viewers in the mind of a heterosexual male main character with the woman as object of lust. Thus the female viewer must surrender her identity and identify with the male camera view. Such film techniques are seen in many movies from Marilyn Monroe's entrance in *Some Like It Hot* to the stripteases and flirtation in *Charlie's Angels.*

As Mulvey describes the male-centric camera:

> At first glance, the cinema would seem to be remote from the undercover world of the surreptitious observation of an unknowing and unwilling victim. What is seen on the screen is so manifestly shown. But the mass of mainstream film, and the conventions within which it has consciously evolved, portray a hermetically sealed world which unwinds magically, indifferent to the presence of the audience, producing for them a sense of separation and playing on their voyeuristic fantasy...Although the film is really being shown, is there to be seen, conditions of screening and narrative conventions give the spectator an illusion of looking in on a private world.

This appears in *Outlander* in the one scene of Claire's undressing with the audience being invited to look. Her garbing scene with Mrs. Fitz suggests an everyday activity conducted in a women's sanctuary, rather than a performance for spying males, though the heroine is briefly nude for it. Nonetheless, it is a performance with viewers looking on from their couches. Jenny's expelling unneeded breast milk in "The Search" (114) has a similar approach.

By contrast, the first episode shows Frank and

Claire both naked and enjoying sex (back in their bedroom after the castle scene). There are shots of her face as well as her body, indicating the pleasure she's taking, while her voiceover emphasizes the perspective here is hers. With the heavy voiceovers, it's difficult *not* to empathize with Claire.

In episode eight, "Both Sides Now," both Claire's consensual encounter with Jamie and her two near-rapes are shown mostly clothed, with a swirling camera to focus on her long-lasting trauma. Thus the scenes come out emotionally-based than filled with gratuitous nudity. Compared with Daenerys's glamorized fully naked rape in the second episode of *Game of Thrones*, after which she falls in love with that rapist, *Outlander* appears far more realistic.

The cable shows display almost everything – but almost never a man's genitals. Black Jack breaks this taboo however in his flashback of the assault on Jenny in "Lallybroch" (112). Leering at her, he rubs his exposed genitals, displaying them in a scene that's terribly rare for television. However, she laughs and he is unable to perform. This moment, while not a sensual one, invites women's gaze as they claim power over him, even as Jenny does.

> When Black Jack swept Jenny into Lallybroch in the flashback, he certainly intended to force sex on her. Instead, when his penis remained flaccid, Jenny laughed in his face.
>
> "It's obviously the most humiliated Jack is in the story; his weakest and most vulnerable, arguably," Menzies tells *Zap2it.*
>
> As for that nude moment where audiences get to see Black Jack's penis, the actor confirms, "I'm afraid it's all me.
>
> "You just have to sort of hold your breath and do it, but I suppose in a way I was as much involved in the decision to make it as graphic as that," he says. "I think it needs to have genuine humiliation in it. We see Jack so often in control. To have a moment when a young girl's laugh undoes him I think is really interesting." (Schwartz)

Thus Black Jack is undone as he's literally stripped for the female to gaze at and ridicule.

On a far happier note, during their wedding night, Claire and Jamie each admire the other, inviting fans of all genders and sexual preferences to join them. The voiceovers have mostly disappeared and Jamie does some recounting of *his* day, allowing a more gender-balanced point of view than typical for the series. At the ceremony, each has a moment of appearing in formal finery, in contrast with many shows in which only the heroine in her prom dress has a particular slow walk on or dramatic reveal. As Claire sucks in her breath, she notes in the book, "A Highlander in full regalia is an impressive sight – any Highlander, no matter how old, ill-favored, or crabbed in appearance. A tall, straight-bodied, and by no means ill-favored young Highlander at close range is breath-taking" (ch. 14). Both show a great deal of skin in their bedroom encounters, each takes charge, each shows their delight in their face.

The episode "Lallybroch" (112) has Jamie standing naked in the stream, first with some butt shots, then with his hand self-consciously over his crotch as he requests that his sister stop looking. He turns his back, and Jenny stares at the scars. The hero by this point has been fully objectified.

In other show moments, Claire gets a revolting invitation to look up Angus's kilt (she closes her eyes and winces). Jamie is the one to remove his shirt in episodes two and three for Claire to inspect, and he changes in front of her just before entering the Gathering. On the rent-collecting trip, Dougal strips Jamie's shirt off (generally ripping it) in *every single village* and invites everyone to stare at the spectacle, to Jamie's humiliation. In all these scenes, Claire is the gazer and Jamie the spectacle with his male physique on display.

In the books, Gabaldon lovingly describes Jamie's

tiny hairs and the curves of his muscles, emphasizing Claire's gaze on him. Claire watches Jamie often, as he lies "wearing nothing but a few dappled splotches of sunlight" (*Outlander,* ch. 16) or undresses for her amusement. Reunited with him in *Voyager,* she admires "the squared roundness of his buttocks the small muscular hollow that dented each one, and their pale vulnerability" (ch. 26).

There's also Jamie's partially-dressed state of the kilt, in contrast with the long trousers of most male characters in the world of television. Claire tells Jamie, "Actually, it's your kilt that makes me want to fling you to the floor and commit ravishment...But you don't look at all bad in your breeks" (*The Drums of Autumn*, ch. 13). She objectifies him in this garb, as many of the female audience do. On another occasion, Claire wants to watch Jamie make a spectacle of himself with the old-fashioned "feileadh breacan" or "feileadh mor" (the big kilt). Wearing one, Jamie explains:

> "It's a bit undignified to get into, but it's verra easy to take off"
>
> "How do you get into it?" I asked curiously.
>
> "Well, ye lay it out on the ground, like this" – he knelt, spreading the cloth so that it lined the leaf-strewn hollow – "and then ye pleat it every few inches, lie down on it, and roll."
>
> I burst out laughing, and sank to my knees, helping to smooth the thick tartan wool. (*Dragonfly in Amber,* ch. 36)

In *An Echo in the Bone,* Claire proposes to get a new kilt made for Jamie, commenting that she likes to look at him in all his glory (ch. 142).

When asked why a man in a kilt is such a romantic figure, Gabaldon notes that while "really tired" she said, "Well, I suppose it's the idea that you could be up against a wall with him in a minute" ("The Doctor's Balls," Kindle Locations 376-379). Everyone gleefully reprinted the interview. As she adds:

> A man who you know is running around with his dangly bits so immediately accessible is plainly a bold spirit, up for anything at the drop of a hat (or some more appropriate garment) and entirely willing to risk himself, body and soul. The English Government understood this very well; hence the DisKilting Act, passed after Culloden, which – as part of a program of cultural punishment and ethnic cleansing – forbade Highland men to wear the kilt or possess tartan. ("The Doctor's Balls" 382-385)

On the show, Jamie significantly stops wearing the kilt when he returns to Lallybroch. Dresbach reports getting enormous amounts of fan mail asking why. She replies:

> It is not the first time he has worn them, but it does have significance in this episode. ... Jamie has had essentially the same costume throughout most of the series. Now we are seeing a different side of him. He is now a married man, and as we find out, a man of substance. A Laird.
>
> Trews were worn most often by men who had the means to own a horse. It was more comfortable, for obvious reasons. We'll see his kilt again, and again. But we need to add dimension, shadow, nuance to him, and to all of our characters as they develop over the years. Even Clark Kent had two costumes to show two sides of his character. (26 Apr 2015)

As he assumes his role as Laird and even wears his father's coat, he is performing a type of authoritative masculinity, and as such, wearing the pants.

Bechdel Test and Female Friendships

The Bechdel test (named for comic strip creator Alison Bechdel) questions whether a film or show meets the following criteria:

1. It includes at least two women
2. who have at least one conversation
3. about something other than a man or men

The test articulates the principle that fictional women should be more than sidekicks to the male hero's adventure. Further, they should form bonds of sisterhood and work as a team, rather than competing over men. Early on, Claire has a single female friend - Geillis. In fact, Geillis discusses men all the time, from her husband to her lover Dougal to Claire's love life. They debate herbs and Geillis's possible witchcraft as well, but she's not an ideal candidate for the test. Likewise, Mrs. Fitz talks about Jamie, Dougal and Collum, while Laoghire is all the Bechdel test reviles, as all her interactions with Claire betray her obsession with Jamie.

Halfway through the first book and season, Claire meets Jenny, an independent woman with a life of her own, who nonetheless spends a great deal of time worrying over Jamie and only interacting with Claire within the bounds of Jamie's relationship with them both. She aids the Highlands women with waulking on the show and doctoring in the books, but these are only background characters. Not until Mother Hildegarde in France does Claire find a mentor or friend more interested in Claire's profession than her relationship.

Of course, this isolation also says a great deal about Claire, who earns a great deal of distrust from the women around her. Gabaldon notes on the CompuServe forums:

> Women, even in the 21st century, do not fall in line behind other women. Men move behind the strongest man. Women on the other hand tend to ostracize women that are stronger. I think women are afraid of their own power even now. Claire is an interesting depiction of this. She is not afraid of her power, and also I think somewhat unaware of it. She focuses on doing the job rather than that she has the ability to do that job. Claire is careful because she knows how easy it would be to be labeled as a witch and destroyed. In some respects she embraces it even telling

> others that she is a conjure woman. This is done in part so that people who need to be healed are able to find her.

There are a few aforementioned females around Castle Leoch and Lallybroch. However, Claire spends most of her time for the first three and a half books surrounded by only men. There's Dougal's raiding party and rent-collecting trip, her travels with Murtagh, the all-male abbey, Jamie's uncle's household in Paris, Jamie's groups of traveling companions in books three and four (admittedly with Marsali, though Claire has trouble bonding with the younger frivolous woman) and of course all her travels alone with Jamie. In most of these group situations, she indeed stands out as sole female. "She's a woman in a highly militarized group defined by alpha-dog posturing" (Seitz).

A similar articulation of gender roles onscreen comes from the author of "The Smurfette Principle," Katha Pollitt, who criticizes the many fictional teams with all men and a token female minority, such as the Muppets, the Ninja Turtles, and of course, the Smurfs. A strong character like Princess Leia of *Star Wars* has no female friends or acquaintances, and indeed might be the only female in the galaxy for all the film suggests. As Pollitt adds: "The message is clear. Boys are the norm, girls the variation; boys are central, girls peripheral; boys are individuals, girls types. Boys define the group, its story and its code of values. Girls exist only in relation to boys."

Claire fills this role traveling with Dougal's men. In "Rent" (104), the men make sexist jokes around the campfire. Claire explains, "I wasn't offended by the lewdness of their jokes or squeamish over the fact that my dinner looked like a shriveled Easter rabbit, nor was I too dainty to sleep on a pillow made of stone. What troubled me was that they were clearly using Gaelic to exclude me." Nonetheless, she makes her own racy jokes and finds acceptance.

> Rupert: So there I am in bed, harelip Chrissie on my left and sweaty Netty, the butcher's daughter, on my right. They get jealous of each other, start arguin' about who I'm goin' to swive first. Can you believe it?
> Claire: I believe your left hand gets jealous of your right. That's about all I believe.
> Jamie: [laughing] You're a witty one.
> Rupert: [laughing] I've never heard a woman make a joke!
> Claire: There's a first time for everything.

Meanwhile, they consider her something of a mascot. The brawl in the tavern is started by Claire's companions because patrons at a nearby table called her a "whore," and Murtagh explains: "You're a guest of the MacKenzie. We can insult you, but God help any other man that does."

Claire certainly doesn't have many female friends – Geillis is certainly problematic, and she and Jenny never truly become close, or spend more than a few weeks together, for that matter. Claire notes later:

> Jenny Murray had been the nearest thing I had ever had to a sister, and by far the closest woman friend of my life. Owing to circumstance, most of my close friends in the last fifteen years had been men; there were no other female doctors, and the natural gulf between nursing staff and medical staff prevented more than casual acquaintance with other women working at the hospital. As for the women in Frank's circle, the departmental secretaries and university wives.... (*Voyager,* ch. 32)

Her moments in an all-female space are delightful, but jarring in their rareness, as the women of the show invite her into the wool waulking, or the prostitutes of Edinburgh in book three welcome her. In the books, Claire learns about wool waulking in an all-women's community:

> "Hot piss sets the dye fast," one of the women had explained to me as I blinked, eyes watering, on my first entrance to the shed. The other women had watched at

> first, to see if I would shrink back from the work, but wool-waulking was no great shock, after the things I had seen and done in France, both in the war of 1944 and the hospital of 1744. Time makes very little difference to the basic realities of life. And smell aside, the waulking shed was a warm, cozy place, where the women of Lallybroch visited and joked between bolts of cloth, and sang together in the working, hands moving rhythmically across a table, or bare feet sinking deep into the steaming fabric as we sat on the floor, thrusting against a partner thrusting back. (*Dragonfly in Amber*, ch. 34)

On the rent-collecting trip of the show, the original script called for the local women to invite Claire for tea and cards – Gabaldon pointed out that in the remote Highlands neither of these were available, and suggested waulking wool, which became the new scene (Loughlin). The women share their work, music, and lifestyle in an all-female space, as they offer her a special drink and add, "It's our little secret. Not a word to the menfolk." She is even about to add to their urine supplies when Angus bursts in, and intruder into their women's world. Gabaldon notes on the CompuServe forums:

> Most women of her age would be very much house-bound, and social only in the context of church (where churches existed) or the occasional community thing like quilting or barn-raising. It wasn't a culture where women had either the leisure or the mobility to zip around to each other's houses for a cup of coffee.
>
> Claire *does* move around a lot, calling on patients, checking on people – so she'd know everyone (and they her), but she'd seldom have a lot of time to spend developing deep friendships, particularly with women whom she undoubtedly respects, but has little in common with, beyond the Eternal Feminine Concerns, men and babies. <g> She had much more in common with Mother Hildegarde, and the occasional hour of leisure to spend in conversation – and Malva was working with her, most days, thus sharing both time and mutual interest.

On Fraser's Ridge in the later books, Claire

becomes surrounded by women as leader of a growing settlement. Still, she's annoyed by the bickering and catfighting, as she thinks:

> Fond as I was of individual women – Bree, Marsali, Lizzie, and even Mrs. Bug – I had to admit that taken en masse, I found men much easier to deal with. Whether this was the fault of my rather unorthodox upbringing – I had been raised largely by my Uncle Lamb and his Persian manservant, Firouz – my experiences in the War, or simply an aspect of my own unconventional personality, I found men soothingly logical and – with a few striking exceptions – pleasingly direct. (*The Fiery Cross,* ch. 22)

Fraser's Ridge develops a women's community by the fifth book. One woman beings Claire dacau seeds but tells her "her grannie told her it was women's magic; ye dinna need to mention it to men" (*The Fiery Cross,* ch. 10). After finding herself a few female mentors like Nayawenne, she views the young woman Malva Christie as a protégé...though that turns sour. In both centuries, she seems to relate better to men and spends more time in job and war-related fields than the indoor world. Gabaldon concludes on the CompuServe forums:

> Claire is just one of those women who gets on better – by and large – with men. Partly a matter of occupation; as someone just suggested, she's not really a domestic goddess <g>, and she's usually either seeing people in her surgery or traveling to tend someone or take care of war casualties – this in a time when almost all women stuck very close to home, rarely going outside their small communities. Probably also partly a matter of personality; her very crisp, blunt style is not the way most women communicate.

Several times, Claire manages to rile her female neighbors. On the Ridge, Ute McGillivray attacks Claire and tries to tear her to pieces when Claire diagnoses her son as having syphilis. After Claire fights back in a panicked rage, Ute exiles her from town, announcing that no one will trade with her ever again.

> All of Ute's numerous relatives in and around Wachovia, Salem, Bethabara, and Bethania of course believed her version of the story, and tongues wagged busily. All of Salem did not cease trading with us – but many people did. And more than once, I had the unnerving experience of greeting Moravians I knew well, only to have them stare past me in stony silence, or turn their backs upon me. Often enough that I no longer went to Salem. (*A Breath of Snow and Ashes,* ch. 46)

Thus Ute bars Claire from the community of respectable women.

Locked up in a women's prison with a single cellmate plus the jailor's wife, Mrs. Tolliver, Claire is capable but uncomfortable, and clearly unaware of the rules. Bribing the jailor's wife with alcohol gets her no news of Jamie. She delivers a slave's baby only to be told the slave can now be executed for killing her others. She lets her cellmate trade crimes with her but discovers she might have evaded her own sentencing through right of clergy while the other, a forger, will be executed for treason no matter what. Meanwhile, her fellow prisoner is interested in a lesbian encounter, telling Claire it would make them both forget and Claire, startled, must refuse. Claire's discomfiture in the all-female space emphasizes how badly she fits into such communities.

Overcoming Rape

> It's wish-fulfillment fantasy from the point of view of a woman – but undercut with the cold horror of taking the conceit seriously. The bygone era of tartan dresses and skirling bagpipes look and sound lovely – but what if someone from the modern era was actually transported to that time period? What would she do? How would she survive? (Saraiya)

In Claire's first episode, first she's shot at, then Black Jack Randall grabs her, holds his sword to her neck and tries to rape her. Then Murtagh knocks him out and knocks her out when she tries to scream. Then she's forcibly carried to a cottage where the inhabitants address her in menacing sounding Gaelic and debate whether to rape her. It's a brutal introduction to the violence of the past, even for a war nurse. "So far I'd been assaulted, threatened, kidnapped, and nearly raped. And somehow, I knew that my journey had only just begun," she says as episode one concludes.

Claire also mentions that "While such crimes as theft and insubordination were common among the Highland army, rape was virtually unknown" (*Dragonfly in Amber,* ch. 40). The English Redcoats are far more brutal – one rapes a teenaged Lord John, and several try to rape Claire through the course of the first book.

Dougal, as he attempts to rape Claire at the Gathering and propositions her on her wedding night, is more than a little repellent. Before his arrival to save Claire at the Gathering, then turn on her himself, the men who accost Claire speak only Gaelic and are bestial, snatching at her from the shadows. With ominous music and brutal gestures, none of these men invite empathy. Fully clothed, Claire bludgeons several, including Dougal, taking complete control of the scene in a way men and women can both admire.

After, Jack Randall tries to rape her again, but Jamie rescues her at Fort William in "The Reckoning" (109). Jack Randall (who is framed as a sadist with unnatural urges to torture others) rips Jenny's dress, baring her to the waist and forcing a horrified Jamie to watch, as he tries to avert his eyes. Thus his attempted rape of Claire, as he reveals her bare bottom to the audience and she chokes with terror has a similar emphasis, focusing on Jack's destroying of all that's decent. He stares at women's bodies and invites (or rather compels) the audience to look, but he is a desecrator not a hero, and no viewer cares to empathize with him.

Violence against women is common onscreen, as it provokes a visceral terror in both genders.

> As slasher director Dario Argento puts it, "I like women, especially beautiful ones. If they have a good face and figure, I would much prefer to watch them being murdered than an ugly girl or a man." Brian De Palma elaborates: "Women in peril work better in the suspense genre. It all goes back to the *Perils of Pauline*...If you have a haunted house and you have a woman walking around with a candelabrum, you fear more for her than you would for a husky man." Or Hitchcock, during the filming of *The Birds:* "I always believe in following the advice of the playwright Sardou. He said 'Torture the women!' The trouble today is that we don't torture women enough." (Clover 234)

Jenny and Claire both manage to escape Jack Randall's assault in the first book, mostly by refusing to scream in terror or give him power over them. Frustrated, he finds he can't perform. Menzies explains of his encounter with Jenny in "Lallybroch" (112):

> Obviously one of the main, terminal things was the issue that he wasn't able to get it up and she laughs at him and getting the picture of that right. I didn't want it to be about the homosexuality or about the fact that he was only turned on by men, I wanted it to be something about the fact that it was almost a schoolground humiliation. That she sort of plugged into something ancient in him and it's a sort of, the odder the better, really. It needed to be that he really wasn't, necessarily, unmanned or weakened by it – it was just that he almost failed but it still had a danger in it; we didn't want to diminished Jack too much in terms of what he represents for everyone. I think it turns out *[laughs]* relatively creepy. (Lutes)

Every time, the women escape, but by book's end,

Jamie is not so fortunate himself.

Brownmiller observes: "A world without rapists would be a world in which women moved freely without fear of men. That some men rape provides a sufficient threat to keep all women in a constant state of intimidation, forever conscious of the knowledge that the biological tool must be held in awe for it may turn to weapon with sudden swiftness borne of harmful intent" (229).

The romance, which is never simply a love story, is also an exploration of the meaning of patriarchy for women. As a result, it is concerned with the fact that men possess and regularly exercise power over them in all sorts of circumstances" (Radway 75). Romances often depict the heroine in positions of weakness in order to explore how she might cope with her plight and how readers in a similar situation (actual or emotional) might do likewise.

The rapists in the book and in "Both Sides Now" (108) smirk that they'll make Jamie watch as they assault Claire. Black Jack makes a similar threat in Wentworth Prison. Likewise, the scheming Lord Lovat threatens Jamie with Claire's safety:

> He shot a quick look at me, seeing nothing more than another counter to be put into play. "Your oath for your wife's honor, how's that? ... How many men are there in Beaufort, Jamie? How many, who'd be of a mind to put your thathenach wench to the only uth thee's good for? You cannot guard her night and day." (*Dragonfly in Amber,* ch. 40)

All these times, an assault on her is a threat by the men in power against her husband and Claire is only a pawn in the struggle.

Disturbingly, Jamie responds to Randall's attack on Claire by blaming her and making it all about himself:

> "What's the matter wi' me? I'll tell ye what the matter is,

> since ye want to know!" he said through clenched teeth. "I'm tired of having to prove over and over that you're no an English spy. I'm tired of having to watch ye very minute, for fear of what foolishness you'll try next. And I'm verra tired of people trying to make me watch while they rape you! I dinna enjoy it a bit!"
>
> "And you think I enjoy it?" I yelled. "Are you trying to make out it's my fault?!" At this, he did shake me slightly.
>
> "It is your fault! Did ye stay put where I ordered ye to stay this mornin', this would never have happened! But no, ye won't listen to me, I'm no but your husband, why mind me? You take it into your mind to do as ye damn please, and next I ken, I find ye flat on your back wi' your skirts up, an' the worst scum in the land between your legs, on the point of takin' ye before my eyes!" His Scots accent, usually slight, was growing broader by the second, sure sign that he was upset, had I needed any further indication.
>
> We were almost nose to nose by this time, shouting into each other's face. Jamie was flushed with fury, and I felt the blood rising in my own face.
>
> "It's your own fault, for ignoring me and suspecting me all the time! I told you the truth about who I am! And I told you there was no danger in my going with you, but would you listen to me? No! I'm only a woman, why should you pay any attention to what I say? Women are only fit to do as they're told, and follow orders, and sit meekly around with their hands folded, waiting for the men to come back and tell them what to do!" (*Outlander,* ch. 21)

One critic notes the importance of point of view in the show's portrayal of this scene as "Jamie not only accuses Claire of getting captured to punish him but also needling her about how hurtful it was for him to see her nearly raped by his archenemy" (Hill). The problem is Jamie's priorities here: "Much more time is spent on Jamie's anger than is spent on his relief that no real harm has come to his wife" (Hill).

Rape that affects the husbands and boyfriends of the story rather than the actual victims can be a disturbing trend (known as the Women in Refrigerators trope in comic books). The books narrowly avoid this, yet as Jamie emphasizes that Claire's trauma reflects on his competence as her protector and Jenny's near-rape at Randall's hands drives much of Jamie's pre-*Outlander* story, it's awfully close to the line. Claire's assailants in Paris are likewise hired to kill her in order to throw Jamie into despair and thus end his Jacobite plotting. Rape as entertainment and titillation appears around the world in a truly disturbing current of patriarchal violence.

> Critical representations of the harsh reality of sexual violence, as in feminist films such as *Dust* and *Cruel Embrace,* are particularly pertinent in the context of systematic rape of women in wars. Feminists have disclosed the frequent use of rape as a weapon in war (cf Brownmiller 1975). At the time of writing this chapter, news was reported about rape camps in Bosnia, about enforced pregnancies and the Catholic interdiction on abortion even in those extreme circumstances. Most horrifying of all, it is purported that some rapes were filmed on video and distributed as pornography for the soldiers. (Smelik 192)

By contrast, "Most feminist films about sexual violence give a lucid analysis of the predicaments and contradictions of women's experiences in a male dominated culture, without the fetishism, voyeurism and sadism of traditional Hollywood cinema." Feminist films don't treat rape as entertainment but as a violent, traumatic experience from which the victims must recover and discover the way to peace. "On the contrary, they evoke a deep sympathy with the plight of the female victims" (Smelik 90-91).

After Claire stabs her assailant and Jamie kills the other in "Both Sides Now" (108), she goes into shock. The rape is filmed and described as an attack, without nudity or salaciousness. "I knew he was worried about me, Knew he wanted to talk about what had happened, but I knew if I did, if I started giving rein to my feelings, things would pour out of me that I wanted to keep locked away forever" she thinks on the show.

Other characters surviving rape include Margaret Campbell in *Voyager*, though after her attack by the Redcoats, she's incoherent, subject to screaming fits and bursts of catatonia, to the point where she can't care for herself. Claire tries to help her, but it's unclear how much she can do. The same book offers a Jack the Ripper character who murders women of "easy virtue" and often dismembers them. Both stories emphasize women's vulnerability in the perilous times and the permanent nature of assault.

More ambiguous is the treatment of prostitutes in the short story "Virgins." Early on, one of the most violent mercenaries, Mathieu, rapes a prostitute in an inn courtyard. Though Ian and Jamie are outmatched, both feel guilty about not intervening. Jamie especially is caught in worry about his sister who was treated similarly, as he thinks, by Jack Randall. At story's end, when Mathieu begins abusing a barmaid Jamie admires "and was boosting her toward the hallway with a hand on her bum, despite her protests," Jamie attacks and kills him. However, the barmaid is accidentally shot in the fight. Both women are presented in an uncertain manner, as they strongly affect Jamie but have little life outside those roles. They are a strong lesson for the protagonist that morality is not always clear, and even when it is, there may be unexpected consequences.

Mary Hawkins, a sweet, naïve friend of Claire's, is raped in book two, though Claire is saved when the rapists decide she's a powerful sorceress and run in terror. Those rapists, a gang of highborn men, attack women just for the entertainment of it. Alexander Randall, who loves Mary, helps to save her in a romantic rescue from rape – but this is subverted as it comes too late. Jamie notes, "It isna right, Sassenach, but it's how it is. Let it be known that she's a maid no more, and no man will take her –

she'll be disgraced and live as a spinster to the end of her days" (*Dragonfly in Amber,* ch. 18). The healer Master Raymond and Claire discuss her rape:

> "There's nothing I can do about her reputation at this point. All I can do is try to help her to heal."
>
> A sardonic black eye peered over the rim of the metal goblet he was holding.
>
> "Most physicians of my acquaintance would say, 'All I can do is try to heal her.' You will help her to heal? It's interesting that you perceive the difference, madonna. I thought you would." (*Dragonfly in Amber*, ch. 20)

Though her healing mostly takes place offscreen, she fights through it and emerges strong enough to choose her own destiny, running away to find the man she loves.

In a scene as disturbing as the spanking scene, Jamie accuses Brianna of lying that she was raped, adding, "Ye're no the first lass to make a slip and try to hide it" (*The Drums of Autumn,* ch. 48). As he explains, "Well, I'm thinkin' – are ye maybe playin' wi' the truth a bit, lass? Perhaps it wasna rape at all; perhaps it was that ye took a mislike to the man, and ran – and made up the story later. Ye were not marked, after all. Hard to think a man could force a lass of your size, if ye were unwilling altogether" (*The Drums of Autumn,* ch. 48).

Thus provoked, Brianna and Jamie fight with a great deal of violence and bruising:

> "You fucking bastard!" she screamed. She braced her feet and yanked down on his arm as hard as she could, bringing it into biting range. She lunged at his wrist, but before she could sink her teeth in his flesh, she found herself jerked off her feet and whirled through the air.
>
> She ended hard on her knees, one arm twisted up behind her back so tightly that her shoulder joint cracked. The strain on her elbow hurt; she writhed, trying to turn into the hold, but couldn't budge. An arm like an iron bar clamped across her shoulders, forcing her head down. And farther down.

> Her chin drove into her chest; she couldn't breathe. And still he forced her head down. Her knees slid apart, her thighs forced wide by the downward pressure.
>
> "Stop!" she grunted. It hurt to force sound through her constricted windpipe. "Gd's sk, stp!"
>
> The relentless pressure paused, but did not ease. She could feel him there behind her, an inexorable, inexplicable force. She reached back with her free hand, groping for something to claw, something to hit or bend, but there was nothing.
>
> "I could break your neck," he said, very quietly. The weight of his arm left her shoulders, though the twisted arm still held her bent forward, hair loose and tumbled, nearly touching the floor. A hand settled on her neck. She could feel thumb and index fingers on either side, pressing lightly on her arteries. He squeezed, and black spots danced before her eyes.
>
> "I could kill you, so."
>
> The hand left her neck, and touched her, deliberately, knee and shoulder, cheek and chin, emphasizing her helplessness. She jerked her head away, not letting him touch the wetness, not wanting him to feel her tears of rage. Then the hand pressed sudden and brutal on the small of her back. She made a small, choked sound and arched her back to keep her arm from breaking, thrusting out her hips backward, legs spread to keep her balance.
>
> "I could use ye as I would," he said, and there was a coldness in his voice. "Could you stop me, Brianna?"
>
> She felt as though she would suffocate with rage and shame.
>
> "Answer me." The hand took her by the neck again, and squeezed.
>
> "No!" (*The Drums of Autumn,* ch. 48).

He releases her, having made his point that she couldn't have killed her assailant or stopped the attack. Jamie explains after that Brianna hadn't really accepted this concept when he told her, so he must prove it to her. Nonetheless, the lesson is abusive and disturbing.

In the sixth book, Jamie comforts Claire after an attack, while she is appalled by the savagery of the men wanting her just because of her gender: "What bothers me – bothers! What a stupid word! What drives me absolutely mad is that I might have been anyone, anything – a convenient warm spot with spongy bits to squeeze – God, I was no more than a hole to them!" (ch. 29). She insists that she won't let the trauma overcome her. More time is spent on the recovery than the act itself and Jamie helps her through it, though his sympathy turns Claire violent rather than withdrawn. Through the later books, she and Jamie both suffer from flashbacks and nightmares, learning to comfort each other as sources of constant support.

The different perspectives on rape, generally sympathetic and focusing on the women's recovery and empowerment rather than titillation emphasize this as a series of women's issues, meant to comfort and strengthen.

Performing Femininity

> As the girl opened her mouth, I opened mine as well. And screamed as loudly as I could. The butler, taken unprepared, took a step back, tripped on a settee, and fell over sideways like a bowls pin. I could hear the startled noises of the soldiers outside, coming up the steps.
>
> I picked up my skirts, shrieked "A mouse! A mouse!" and fled toward the parlor, yelling like a banshee.
>
> Infected by my apparent hysteria, Mary shrieked as well, and clutched me about the middle as I cannoned into her. I bore her back into the recesses of the parlor with me, and grabbed her by the shoulders.
>
> "Don't tell anyone who I am," I breathed into her ear. "No one! My life depends on it!" I had thought I was being melodramatic, but it occurred to me, as I spoke the words, that I could very well be telling the exact truth. Being married to Red Jamie Fraser was likely a dicey proposition. (*Dragonfly in Amber,* ch. 44)

While women's wearing trousers as a path to power makes logical sense, women flaunting their femininity as a path to power is less obvious. Above, Claire uses clichéd feminine terror as a cover, of course. On other occasions, she pretends to faint to hide her identity at the ball of *Voyager*. She faints more authentically when Jamie meets Alexander Randall in Paris, but this manages to divert him from his murderous course. She and the other women of the story use their femininity as a tool, exploring its possibilities as a route to achieve their goals.

For critic Joan Riviére, the masquerade of femininity is a kind of reaction-formation against the woman's trans-sex identification. Womanliness is "assumed and worn as a mask, both to hide the possession of masculinity and to avert the reprisals expected if she was found to possess it" (Riviére 38). Riviére describes a housewife who deliberately hides her knowledge of building when anyone comes to work on the house and gives suggestions "in an innocent and artless manner, as if they were lucky guesses" in order to appear nonthreatening to the male ego (39). Another woman, this one a university lecturer, wears feminine clothes and jokes about her topic, again, to subvert her power in the male arena. As she adds, "The reader may now ask how I define womanliness or where I draw the line between genuine womanliness and the masquerade. My suggestion is not, however, that there is any such difference; whether radical or superficial, they are the same thing" (38).

"The very fact that we can speak of a woman 'using' her sex or 'using' her body for particular gains is highly significant – it is not that a man cannot use his body in this way but that he doesn't have to" (Silverman 139). Geillis in particular, turns sweet and coaxing to persuade her husband to be lenient with a boy caught stealing. While she summarizes this scene in the book, the show sees her putting on a deliberate masquerade as she moves from Claire to her husband. While she rolls her eyes at her friend, her manner towards her husband turns adoring and simpering:

> Arthur... Imagine if our own union had been blessed, then how would you feel if your son were taken so? Oh. Surely it was but hunger that made the lad take to thievery. .... Can you not find it in your heart to be merciful, and you the soul of justice? ("The Way Out," 103)

Claire also has such moments. On the show, she makes up a tale to explain her original encounter with Captain Randall, a tale that casts her as fallen woman with a severe lack of judgment. She emphasizes her shame and moral laxness to try to pressure the captain into leaving her alone.

> Claire: Captain, you force me to reveal things that no woman should say out loud. It was an affair of the heart. I met him in England. An officer of infantry. He swore to me that I held his affections like no other. So when he was stationed in Scotland, I...I followed him.
> Randall: Please. Carry on.
> Claire: It was then I discovered he was a most licentious man, a rake and whoremonger. It was not love he felt for me. It was lust. When I refused him, he attacked me. I fled, dressed only in my shift. I can only hope you prove yourself the gentleman you claim to be and not pry any further.
> Randall: What is the man's name?
> Claire: With all due respect, Captain, I do not wish to lower myself to this gentleman's level. By revealing his name as well as his indiscretions to you, I risk ruining both his career and his reputation. ("The Garrison Commander," 106)

More moments of feminine performance appear, most particularly in how Claire is forced to dress. Preparing for her wedding of the book, Claire puts on her beautiful gown somewhat unwillingly. She stands there "like a dressmaker's dummy," barely participating in the proceedings.

> As such, she comes across like *The Hunger Games*' Katniss, gowned and perfumed against her will, for an event she has agreed to under duress. As various critics have noted in different works of literature, greedily wanting the beautiful gown (and in this case the handsome Scot that

> comes with it) would be immoral of the heroine. If however, she's forced to accept all this, she's allowed to remain the "good girl" entrapped by circumstances.
>
> She's finally ready "complete to white asters and yellow roses pinned in my hair and a heart pounding madly away beneath the lacy bodice," as she says. She feels "quite regal, and not a little lovely" but the point is that she's been forced to primp and wear expensive satin. The story builds on this, as Dougal demands that Jamie and Claire consummate their marriage properly – if they do not, Jack Randall could still claim Claire. "Six weeks ago, I had been innocently collecting wildflowers on a Scottish hill to take home to my husband. I was now shut in the room of a rural inn, awaiting a completely different husband, whom I scarcely knew, with firm orders to consummate a forced marriage, at risk of my life and liberty," she notes (*Outlander,* ch. 15). Thus the following romance, sex, and disloyalty to Frank are also forced on Claire and she must submit to save her life...no matter how much she might also relish it. As she notes, "I supposed it would be harder if I found him unattractive; in fact, the opposite was true." (Frankel, *Symbolism and Sources of Outlander* 20)

"Not only was I a bigamist and an adulteress, but I'd enjoyed it," she adds on the show. However, as she's forced into it, she can be excused from her cheating, as she can be let off for enjoying the beautiful gowns if only a little, because they're forced on her. In France she dresses up again, allowing viewers and readers to enjoy the period drama. However, as before, Claire must wear the luxuriant gowns to establish her status and honor or impress others like the French court – she is never seen purchasing them through greed or vanity.

Her ornate wedding gown of the show is silver and white with a pattern of acorns and falling leaves and pieces of glittering mica, in contrast with the simple suit she chooses for her twentieth-century wedding. "It was as if I stepped outside on a cloudy day and suddenly the sun came out," Jaime says sweetly. As Dresbach describes the wedding gown:

> I had really had gotten directions from Ron that this needed to be a fairy tale; a beautiful moment that cements and entire book series and an entire television series. It's a series about a marriage and the foundation is this moment, but it's two people who didn't know each other and who didn't plan to be married and are being forced into this. And yet, we had to make it so impossibly romantic that we could believe that our heroine and our hero could just fall in love so completely at that moment.
>
> So, I wanted a dress that would be incredible in candlelight. And in the 18th century, metallic fabrics were made with actual metal woven into the fabrics. When you put them in a room filled with candles, they just glow. They're quite remarkable. There are museum exhibits that actually show the dresses in candlelight so you can see the effect...But that dress took us – we calculated it out at about, I think if one person had done it, it would have been about 3,000 hours' worth of work. We did a technique of embroidery that was done hundreds of years and is no longer used. The embroidery is done with metal. (Friedlander)

At Lallybroch in the first book, Jenny and Mrs. Crook make her a dress for Quarter Day. It's "primrose yellow silk" that fits her like a glove, "with deep folds rolling back over the shoulders and falling behind in panels that flowed into the luxuriant drape of the full skirt" (ch. 31). However, Claire's only input is the refusal to add a corset. Later on, Jenny dresses Claire up for a military interview:

> "That's ... tight enough."
>
> "Mmm." She was already deep in the armoire, picking through my gowns. "What about this one? It's got a deep décolletage, and your bosom's still verra good."
>
> "I'm not meaning to seduce the man!"
>
> "Oh, yes, ye are," she said matter-of-factly. "Or at least distract him. If ye're no going to tell him the truth, I mean" (*Written in My Own Heart's Blood,* ch. 6).

Jenny inflicts the performance on her, leaving Claire duty-bound to dress finely.

For a ball at the Palace of Versailles, Jamie

specifically asks Claire to have a dress made that will make her stand out, so he can attract business contacts. When she gets herself a low-cut red gown in the latest fashion, Jamie is horrified that the white charmeuse lining under transparent lace looks like Claire's skin and from his height, he can see all the way to her navel (*Dragonfly in Amber*, ch. 9). While he admits he thinks crude thoughts about the under-dressed court ladies, he doesn't want the men thinking such thoughts about his Claire.

On several other occasions, Jamie asks Claire to dress up and appear "fine" or "respectable." Their trip to Edinburgh is no exception:

> I had on brown today, an open jacket of brown velvet the color of ripe cattails, with a narrow grosgrain ribbon in gold down the edges, over my new gown – this a heavy coffee-colored silk with a close-fitted bodice and three lace-edged petticoats to show at the ankle. We would not be long in Edinburgh, owing to the exigencies of getting the brigadier to his final resting place and Jamie's eagerness to be away to the Highlands – but we did have business to conduct here. Jamie had said firmly that we could not appear as ragamuffins and had sent for a dressmaker and a tailor as soon as we reached our lodgings. (*An Echo in the Bone,* ch. 74)

By contrast on the show, Claire wears Jamie's plaid over her ripped gown for half of episodes eleven and twelve after the witch trial. This ensemble is surprisingly bulky and asexual for television. Costumer Terry Dresbach gushes on her blog over the nontraditional dress:

> I was so excited to get to do this.
>
> It went against everything that you are supposed to do on a lead actress, any actress, any woman, really. A GIANT piece of tartan wrapped around a GIANT plaid skirt that is worn over a padded roll designed to make your hips look wider???????? And then you belt it all in the middle with a man's belt?

> I mean, look at Claire, even she looks wide. I could NEVER EVER get away with that on network television. I had my fingers and toes crossed that I would get away with it on cable!!!
>
> BUT look at her. She looks amazing. Sexy and kind of wild, stunningly beautiful. Someone said, it the 18th century version of "the boyfriend shirt"! I thought that was great. I always loved it in the book when Jamie rescues her, and wraps her in his plaid, and I really wanted to keep that. I thought it was such a small, protective and loving act.
>
> OMG a woman who is not squeezed into a size zero bandage dress so we can see every bone, and she is still sexy and insanely beautiful???? How is that possible.
>
> Well it is. We did it, and the world kept spinning. Maybe Hollywood creaked a tiny bit on its axis. Was that the cracking sound I heard last Saturday? (25 April 2015)

Claire has a single sensual indulgence chosen for herself, as she lets her hair fall free instead of binding it under a cap in the eighteenth century. Gabaldon notes on the forums that there's a sexual component to a woman's hair:

> A woman's loose hair was considered very sexual by Christians, too – still is, among some sects; Amish and Mennonite women wear caps – and ought not to be on public view. A lot of the Ridge people undoubtedly would have held this view; Tom Christie certainly did.
>
> So...here's Claire, who goes to a lot more trouble than the average woman, in order to keep her hair clean and attractive (she makes her own shampoo from sunflower oil, rather than washing it with lye soap every three or four months), and then flaunts this great curly mass under the nose of every male she meets. *Of course* the other women think she's being deliberately provocative, and while they aren't going to call Himself's wife (and the local healer/midwife) a hussy, they'd certainly try to force, persuade, or inveigle her into covering her hair.
>
> Claire is, btw, certainly not unaware of this. But part of her survival strategy (emotional, that is) depends on her preserving her sense of independence and behaving according to her own values, rather than those of the time in which she finds herself. She *knows* she pisses off the other women by not wearing a cap, and she really doesn't

> care – which in turn makes them even pissier. But she needs to preserve her sense of herself, much more than she needs female friends.

The other women of the community wear mobcaps, but this display of modesty and wifely conformity is not for Claire. After many unsubtle gifts of these caps, she still dresses as she chooses.

> "Grannie Bacon's sent ye a present," she explained proudly, as I unfolded the material, which proved to be an enormous mobcap, liberally embellished with lace and trimmed with lavender ribbons. "She couldna come to the Gathering this year, but she said as we must bring ye this, and give ye her thanks for the medicine ye sent for her...roo-mah-tics." She pronounced the word carefully, her face screwed up in concentration, then relaxed, beaming in pride at having gotten it out properly.
>
> "Why, thank you. How lovely!" I held the cap up to admire, privately thinking a few choice things about Grannie Bacon. (*The Fiery Cross*, ch. 10)

Even when her hair is cut off, she walks about proudly, skull gleaming under an "unattractive crewcut" as she calls it.

The cap also suggests her emotional state. When she thinks she has lost Jamie, she allows her hair to be tucked under a cap. When she discovers he's alive, however, she throws it off, noting, "I had a feeling that my status as a respectable woman wasn't going to be important for much longer" (*An Echo in the Bone,* ch. 101).

In *An Echo in the Bone,* soldiers dismiss Claire and her basket of smuggling as a harmless, respectable grannie. Thus she continues to spread Revolutionary War propaganda, mobcap firmly in place. This moment emphasizes that the feminine role *is* a performance; Women in society must become the characters men believe they are. Simone de Beauvoir explains: "One is not born, but rather becomes, woman. No biological, psychic, or economic destiny defines the figure that the human female takes on in society; it is civilization as a whole that elaborates this intermediary product between the male and the eunuch that is called feminine" (283).

In fiction, this often takes the form of women playing seductress as the men expect. Yet in a clever subversion of this trope, Claire masquerades successfully as harmless old granny. While she is by this point a grandmother, readers who began with feisty young Claire certainly don't see her as old or harmless. Nonetheless, she finds it a valuable tool. "Womanliness is a mask which can be worn or removed" as the woman deliberately uses her own body as a disguise (Doane 6).

In "The Search" (114), Claire repeatedly dresses as a boy and sings a bawdy song. Murtagh notes that this spectacle – of a Sassenach woman as Highlander boy – will attract gossip better than anything. Though she could be said to perform masculinity here, it's actually a strange androgyny, a hybrid of gender, nationality, and even time, as she sings the Highland lyrics to the tune of "Boogie-Woogie Bugle Boy." The unusual spectacle entertains beyond anything the crowds have seen.

One of her more significant performances comes from her identity as witch and White Lady, both an expression of the powerful feminine. In France, Claire becomes known as La Dame Blanche ("white lady"). As the French butler describes her in the second book:

> "The White Lady," he murmured. "She is called a wisewoman, a healer. And yet...she sees to the center of a man, and can turn his soul to ashes, if evil be found there." He bobbed his head, turned, and shuffled off hastily in the direction of the kitchen. I saw his elbow bob, and realized that he was crossing himself as he went. (*Dragonfly in Amber,* ch. 20)

"A White Lady can strike ye blind or shrivel a

man's balls," Jared adds ("The Space Between," 201). Jamie actually invents this in a type of disguise for himself – he tells his drinking pals that being faithful to Claire isn't just a whim – if he cheated on his wife, a White Lady, she'd "shrivel [his] private parts" (*Dragonfly in Amber,* ch. 20). Nonetheless, this identity serves to protect her. Protecting his wife from rape, Jamie invokes the same protection around Lord Lovat:

> "Oh, I think I needna worry, Grandsire," he said softly. "For my wife's a rare woman. A wisewoman, ye ken. A white lady, like Dame Aliset."
>
> I had never heard of Dame Aliset, but Lord Lovat plainly had; his head jerked round to stare at me, eyes sprung wide with shocked alarm. His mouth drooped open, but before he could speak, Jamie had gone on, an undercurrent of malice clearly audible in his smooth speech.
>
> "The man that takes her in unholy embrace will have his privates blasted like a frostbitten apple," he said, with relish, "and his soul will burn forever in hell." (*Dragonfly in Amber,* ch. 40)

His strategy proves effective. Gabaldon comments: "Given Claire's naturally pale complexion, her healing arts (and the ruthlessness which is a natural part of them), and her supernatural connections (both real and perceived), it seemed only reasonable to endow her" with the title (*Outlandish Companion* 195).

> In French, Dutch, and Germanic folklore, White Ladies were a type of vicious fairy. Thomas Keightley describes the Dames Blanches as a type of Fée known in Normandy "of a less benevolent character" who lurk in narrow places like ravines or bridges and make travelers show respect or block them from passing. ...Like many fairies and like Claire herself, La Dame Blanche makes a formidable friend or enemy and expects respect from the men who want her aid. Also like many fairies, White Ladies are most likely pre-Christian place guardians, spirits of lakes or mountains. An

> ancient statue of Bride (or possibly predating Bride) features early in *Voyager* as Jamie hears the tale of a White Lady, ventures there, and discovers a hidden treasure. (Frankel, *Symbolism and Sources of Outlander* 186)

In the Dutch, *witte* means both white and wise, emphasizing that the White Lady may be a human wisewoman rather than ghostly spirit. She could heal and knew much of life and death, dispensing spells and charms. Gabaldon adds:

> Generally speaking, the White Lady is the dryad of death; she is often identified with Macha, Queen of the Dead, and sometimes as the Crone aspect of the Goddess (the Goddess is said to have three forms: Maiden, Mother, Crone – which signify the chief phases of female life). Looking more particularly, though, legends of "white ladies" don't always portray these as figures of death and destruction – though this depiction is common – but in some places as figures of healing and sorcery. Macha, one of the mythic figures identified as the White Lady, is also the Mother of Life and Death – she (and all lesser white ladies, presumably) presides over both birth and death – which, it struck me, was pretty much what a doctor does. (*Outlandish Companion* 195)

Claire's reputation as White Lady comes to a forefront when King Louis of France calls on her to make a judgment as La Dame Blanche. Unwillingly, she must free her enemy or condemn him to death. As she says:

> I didn't know that the Comte was guilty. I didn't know that Raymond was innocent. I didn't know whether the pursuit of an honorable cause justified the use of dishonorable means. I didn't know what one life was worth – or a thousand. I didn't know the true cost of revenge. I did know that the cup I held in my hands was death. (*Dragonfly in Amber,* ch. 27)

As White Lady, she gives him the poisoned cup and learns to live with her deed after.

Later, Jamie insists that if he dies, Claire must return to the twentieth century. He tells Roger, "She is an Old One. They will kill her if they know" (*The Fiery Cross*, ch. 94). Roger reflects later that if Jamie had said this in Gaelic, he'd know whether Jamie "truly thought his wife was one of the fairy-folk, or only a thoroughly human wisewoman," as the English words might suggest either. In *An Echo in the Bone,* Jamie notes that at Lallybroch, the locals called Claire a witch "frequently to your face, Sassenach...But ye didna have enough Gaelic then to know it" (ch. 76). He adds that it wasn't meant as an insult, "Only that Highlanders call a thing as they see it."

He himself seems to believe – he knows Claire is from the future, but her healing skills and foreknowledge still seem miraculous to him. She is already Other, and he emphasizes this in every conversation by calling her "Sassenach," the teasing term that emphasizes she's an outsider. On the show, Claire thinks:

> Even though I wasn't going by my own choice, I still felt a heaviness leave my breast. And for the first time since I passed through the standing stones at Craigh na Dun, I found myself surrounded by my own people. They might be called Redcoats instead of Tommies, but they were still the British Army I had been a part of for six long years. And somehow it felt liberating to be looked upon with sympathy and respect instead of hostility and suspicion. I knew only too well what Dougal was feeling. A Scottish village it may be, and on Mackenzie land at that, but for Dougal, it was now enemy territory, and he was the outlander. ("The Garrison Commander," 105)

While her status as Englishwoman, time traveler, and fairy woman all add romance and magic to Jamie's life, he's seeing her through a romantic lens rather than as she truly is. Frank too is faced with a mystery he cannot explain – a tale of ghosts and time travel and standing stones that he never truly accepts. He gently tells Mrs. Graham on the show that he can't share her beliefs. Thus to both men, Claire's life becomes a performance as they perceive her as a magical creature. Brianna and Roger by contrast, share equal magical gifts and a twentieth-century upbringing. Their skills as scholar and engineer are complimentary and neither finds the other mysterious or otherworldly.

Weddings and Marriage

Women of the eighteenth century expected to fall in love before marriage, thus Laoghire's lovestruck plans for Jamie and Jamie's own choice, born of his feelings for Claire, fit logically into the times. "In the eighteenth century, new ideas of individual freedom and the hitherto unknown opportunity for people to meet beyond the family circle led to the acceptance by many that love should precede marriage" (Marshall 186).

King Henry VIII had arguably began the custom of divorce in England, one that continued in Edinburgh, though it was unusual there. "During the period from 1708 until 1800, 347 people sued for divorce in the court" (Marshall 196). Some of these were marriage of love with hasty elopements, or mixed marriages from different social circles which soon crumbled. Infidelity was another cause. Jamie and Claire are wed by Catholic tradition, not the Church of England. In the first book, he offers her several escapes, from an annulment of the grounds of non-consummation to separate living arrangements. He also offers to return her to her other husband.

Of course, Jamie and Frank are not alive at the same time. Claire treats her two marriages as consequences of widowhood – she and one husband are alive, while the other is dead. Her husbands seem to think similarly, as Jamie accepts Frank's death or even the possibility of causing it as regrettable but no more than that. Both believe that having been chosen by Claire, Claire's full duty is to them, and she feels likewise. She never willingly leaves either man, only parting with Jamie as he goes to his death (as he thinks) and only parting with Frank two years after his.

Claire and Jamie obviously come from very different worlds and must reconcile them, especially in the spanking scene. In the episode "Lallybroch" (112), Jamie reminds Claire that they should act as the estate's lord and lady, so she shouldn't contradict him in public. When they squabble, all the servants will hear. Balfe notes:

> "I think the thing they're learning within the confines of their marriage is that you don't always have to accept what the person does, but if you can understand where they're coming from, then you can build a bridge to forgive and move forward. And he also realizes, 'okay, I can't treat you as everyone else treats everyone else in this time, and I'm willing to change, and to grow, and to meet you halfway.'" (Prudom, "Spanking")

After marriage too women of the eighteenth century had power as Jenny for instance rules her household and her husband. "In *Capital of the Mind,* (2003) a popular history of eighteenth-century Edinburgh, James Buchan asserts that 'the eighteenth century was the women's century in Scotland,' citing the decline in religious superstition, improvements in public health, increased economic prosperity, and the emergence of domesticity" (Carr 73).

In 1741, *Scots Magazine* reprinted an article from *The Universal Spectator* that offered advice to young women. It said:

> When you marry, you must not be afraid of *daring* to contradict your husband's whims and humors; what you have a mind to do yourself, you must *dare* do. We should have a fine time of it if indeed we were to *obey* all our dear spouses' solemn commands. You may say at church that you'll *obey* and be *obedient* and I don't know what, but that is only a matter of form and perhaps not ten women in England pay any regard to it. (Marshall 189)

During the Scottish Enlightenment, male fidelity was praised, as social critics believed that the increasing influence and equality of women might draw men "to direct their sexual passions to the marriage bed" (Carr 130). Nonetheless, it was accepted at the time that Scottish men might commit adultery, Dougal being the most prominent example. He is joined by Lord Lovat, the Old Fox. By contrast, Geillis is basically the only "bad woman" – Letitia only commits adulatory to give her husband an heir, in a decision Colum makes for her.

Prostitutes appear among scenes of army life as "a transgression of the Enlightenment ideal of the virtuous and increasingly domesticated woman" (Carr 131). Nonetheless, Fergus (who as a French boy brought up in a house of prostitution might be deemed immoral by nature), brings the Murray boys to houses of ill-repute – though only before marriage.

In France, things are more immoral still, with King Louis, Prince Charles, and even Uncle Jared having affairs with married women. There the men laugh at Jamie for his refusal to do likewise.

Jamie specifically stands out for his virginity before marriage and fidelity afterwards. Ian shares these values, as does Jamie's father. As Jamie notes: "He told me that a man must be responsible for any see he sows, for it's his duty to take care of a woman and protect her. And if I wasna prepared to do that, then I'd no right to burden a woman with the consequences of my own actions" (*Outlander,* ch. 15). He admits this to Claire and says he doesn't mind wedding a woman with experience.

For an adapted scene that keeps so many original lines, the book and show wedding nights have different attitudes in Jamie's behavior. His offer to undress her is delivered as the least clever and wily scheme on the planet while in the books Claire notes it's coming from "his usual practical manner." On the show, he appears to be a teen desperate for sex and not particularly sensitive about it. While the show keeps most of the sexual and romantic dialogue, it omits Jamie's most sensitive insights.

In the book, Jamie's nearly first line to her upstairs isn't a toast to her beauty, quite the opposite, as he tries to discuss her feelings, not her outward appearance:

> "Tell me about your husband," said Jamie, as though he had been reading my mind. I almost jerked my hands away in shock.
>
> ...
>
> "Well, I knew ye must be thinking of him. Ye could hardly not, under the circumstances. I do not want ye ever to feel as though ye canna talk of him to me. Even though I'm your husband now – that feels verra strange to say – it isna right that ye should forget him, or even try to. If ye loved him, he must ha' been a good man."
>
> "Yes, he... was." My voice trembled, and Jamie stroked the backs of my hands with his thumbs.
>
> "Then I shall do my best to honor his spirit by serving his wife." He raised my hands and kissed each one formally.

While book Jamie tries to unravel Claire's issues, show Jamie appears to only trying to distract her from them and seduce her back into bed – when she's lost in thought, he doesn't ask what's troubling her but charms her, calling her *ma nighan donne* and giving her the pearls. As he toasts her as a woman of astonishing beauty and promises her the protection of his body, he seems more to be saying cheap come-ons than approaching her from a place of honesty. As Claire thinks in the book, "the protection of my body" is not insinuation – it's an honorable pledge from a warrior, to be redeemed quite soon.

> "You *are* safe," he said firmly. "You have my name and my family, my clan, and if necessary, the protection of my body as well. The man willna lay hands on ye again, while I live."
>
> "Thank you," I said. Looking at that strong, young, determined face, with its broad cheekbones and solid jaw, I felt for the first time that this preposterous scheme of Dougal's might actually have been a reasonable suggestion.
>
> *The protection of my body.* The phrase struck with particular impact, looking at him – the resolute set of the wide shoulders and the memory of his graceful ferocity, "showing off" at swordplay in the moonlight. He meant it; and young as he was, he knew what he meant, and bore the scars to prove it. He was no older than many of the pilots and the infantrymen I had nursed, and he knew as well as they the price of commitment. It was no romantic pledge he had made me, but the blunt promise to guard my safety at the cost of his own. I hoped only that I could offer him something in return.

As he follows this by toasting "Mrs. Fraser" and she by toasting "honesty," they're beginning their relationship as a partnership.

Likewise, in the book scene, Jamie tells Claire straightforwardly that he won't tell her all his reasons for marrying her, while on the show he simply tells her he was trying to save her. In fact, the secret he's hiding in the books is that he loves her, but he realizes with customary book-tact that telling her so while she's married him unwillingly would only make her uncomfortable. There's more happening than their relationship in the chapter: Claire wakes from a nightmare to discover Jamie's taken a knife to bed with him and "wondered again, what threat would make a man sleep armed and watchful in his bridal chamber." Thus the book emphasizes the danger rather than only romance.

Various weddings and marriages appear in the later books. There's also Marsali's beautiful destination wedding in the West Indies, though somewhat farcical.

> Laoghaire was not going to be pleased at hearing that her eldest daughter had eloped with a one-handed ex-pickpocket twice her age. Her maternal feelings were unlikely to be assuaged by hearing that the marriage had been performed in the middle of the night on a West Indian beach by a disgraced – if not actually defrocked – priest, witnessed by twenty-five seamen, ten French horses, a small flock of sheep – all gaily beribboned in honor of the occasion – and a King Charles spaniel, who added to the generally festive feeling by attempting to copulate with Murphy's wooden leg at every opportunity. The only thing that could make things worse, in Laoghaire's view, would be to hear that I had participated in the ceremony.
>
> Several torches were lit, bound to stakes pounded into the sand, and the flames streamed seaward in tails of red and orange, bright against the black velvet night. The brilliant stars of the Caribbean shone overhead like the lights of heaven. While it was not a church, few brides had had a more beautiful setting for their nuptials. (*Voyager,* ch.. 52)

Echoing this are the sweet romance and awkward public consequences of Lizzie's romantic midnight wedding and Brianna's own spontaneous handfasting. Old Alec tells Claire the story of Jamie's mother and her elopement: betrothed to one of Colum's allies, she insulted the man during their romantic meeting in the rose garden, then ran off with Brian Fraser – an illegitimate son who was "so handsome; tall and sturdy ... with hair like a black silkie's and eyes like a cat."

Claire replies that "Ellen MacKenzie sounds as though she were rather free with her opinions" (*Outlander,* ch. 24). In fact, she only returned to her family when heavily pregnant, and that was to demand her marriage be acknowledged.

In each of these stories, the woman makes her own choice in the face of opposition and makes a love match, however ill-advised. Claire notes of Marsali:

> So she had done it. One fifteen-year-old girl, with nothing but stubbornness as a weapon. "I want him," she had said. And kept saying it, through her mother's objections and Jamie's arguments, through Fergus's scruples and her own fears, through three thousand miles of homesickness, hardship, ocean storm, and shipwreck. (*Voyager,* ch.. 52)

Mary Hawkins is introduced to Claire in the French salons as a girl so shy and stuttering that she's desperate to meet another Englishwoman. She's there for an arranged marriage to a rich old man she's never met. Nonetheless, she has surprising backbone. She is the only lady to stay with Claire as others are put off by the horrors of the hospital. At age sixteen, she falls in love with an unsuitable clerk and is raped by a gang of thugs. While rather naïve about sex, politics, and other things no one has taught her, she's brave, clever, and above all, determined. She tricks her family into sending her to Edinburgh and bribes a servant to escort her to her lover each day, pawning her jewels for his comfort. When she's sent south to stay with the Duke of Sandringham and marry properly, she's already pregnant. When Claire arrives, she bribes her way into Claire's room and demands to be taken back to Edinburgh instead of settling for a respectable marriage.

Though she seems innocent and childlike (even to sucking her thumb) she knows what she wants: "I'm going with you!" she said fiercely. "If you don't take me, I shall run down the corridor, screaming as loudly as I can. So there!" (*Dragonfly in Amber*, ch. 44). In a comic interlude, she scratches Jamie's face, making her the third woman to viciously beat Jamie that night as he sneaks through the grand estate in search of his wife. He concludes, "I'll tell ye, Sassenach; if ever I feel the need to change my manner of employment, I dinna think I'll take up attacking women – it's a bloody hard way to make a living" (ch. 44).

In similar fashion, Dorothea Grey (Dottie) grows up the adored daughter of the Duke and Duchess of Pardloe with every luxury. Despite this, she falls in love with Quaker Denzell Hunter and builds a complex scheme, convincing her cousin William to insist he's ruined her and beg for permission to marry her, all to arrange her passage to America so she can find her real love and propose to him on the spot. Despite family opposition, Dottie refuses to give up her Quaker, and abandons a life of wealth to assist with battlefield surgeries in shapeless homespun gowns. She continues to be a force of strength, exploring America in search of her brother even while married and pregnant.

Rachel Hunter, Denzell's sister, accompanies her brother to war as his nurse, and refuses to ever be left behind. Though a pacifist, she is capable of taking care of herself. She knees a man in the balls and tells Ian, "discouraging a man from committing the sin of rape wasn't violence" (*Written in My Own Heart's Blood,* ch. 115). While her brother doesn't contest her choice of husband, her own ethics do, as Ian is a man of war. Nonetheless, she tells him, "Thy life's journey lies along its own path, Ian…and I cannot share thy journey – but I can walk beside thee. And I will" (*Written in My Own Heart's Blood,* ch. 57). Upon hearing he's committed murder, she resolves to marry him straightaway to be a more fervent support in his life.

The Quaker double marriage ceremony is conducted as a meeting, and gives all those involved a chance to air their worries over leading their families into danger and compelling them from the paths of peace. Somewhere between family therapy and a wedding, it lets the young people face their problems before committing.

Among the Kahnyen'kehaka and other Mohawk tribes, the woman chooses a man and invites him into her house. Young Ian describes the role the "mothers and grandmothers and aunties" often take in arranging the match. However, he defies convention and marries Works With Her Hands for love. Well dressed and accompanied by their parents, the young couple celebrate their wedding by exchanging baskets, "his containing the furs of sable and beaver, and a good knife, symbolizing his willingness to hunt for her and protect her; hers filled with grain and fruit and vegetables, symbolizing her willingness to plant, gather, and provide for him" (*A Breath of Snow and Ashes,* ch. 70). If a woman wants to dissolve the marriage, she can, simply by piling his things outside her home. Young Ian finally departs when Works With Her Hands chooses someone else and her grandmother tells Ian it's time for him to leave without looking back. While the story follows him in his grief and lack of purpose, their story emphasizes how all the choices are hers.

In "Lord John and the Succubus," Princess Louisa tries to seduce John in her nightgown, long hair down her back. She murmurs to him, "You will protect me, protect my son" emphasizing her priorities. Lord John thinks, "He had sufficient experience to see what she was about - he was a handsome man, of good family, and with money; it had happened often enough - but not with royalty, who tended to be accustomed to taking what they wished" (ch. 5). This is meant as a practical arrangement, as Lord John often finds in London society. There, mothers often try to matchmake him with their daughters.

Though preferring men as sexual partners, Lord

John finally weds Lady Isobel Dunsany, noting to several skeptical friends that their families are very close and they need his strength and management skills. He respects and cares for his wife, though he keeps somewhat distant in their relationship. As he observes later:

> To live with someone you love, knowing that they tolerate the relation only for the sake of obligation – no, I wouldn't do it, either. Were it only a matter of convenience and respect on both sides, then yes; such a marriage is one of honor. As long as both parties are honest –" His mouth twisted briefly as he glanced in the direction of the servants' quarters. "There is no need for shame on either side." (*The Drums of Autumn*, ch. 59)

By contrast, in *Voyager,* Isobel's sister Lady Geneva, "a selfish, blackmailing little bitch" as Jamie thinks, rebels against her marriage to an elderly earl by seducing Jamie. When he refuses her advances, she threatens his family. While angry at being coerced, he feels sympathy for the young and foolish girl. He bears a confusing amount of responsibility as on the one hand she forced him into sex, but on the other he considers her a foolish child unclear what she wants while he is the responsible adult:

> He held her against his chest, not moving until her breathing slowed. He was conscious of an extraordinary mixture of feelings. He had never in his life taken a woman in his arms without some feeling of love, but there was nothing of love in this encounter, nor could there be, for her own sake. There was some tenderness for her youth, and pity at her situation. Rage at her manipulation of him, and fear at the magnitude of the crime he was about to commit. But overall there was a terrible lust, a need that clawed at his vitals and made him ashamed of his own manhood, even as he acknowledged its power. Hating himself, he lowered his head and cupped her face between his hands. (ch. 14)

Mostly the setup works to explain why Jamie would

sleep with a highborn virgin, or even be allowed to, though it seems an unlikely arrangement.

Lady Isobel, her sister, runs off with a rogue in *The Scottish Prisoner.* She and Wilberforce intend to rush to Gretna Green, just over the Scottish border where marriage laws are simpler. However, the man already has a wife. As Jamie thinks, "And she would indeed be stuffed, as Betty inelegantly put it, once Wilberforce had taken her maidenhead. Quite simply, her life would be ruined. And her family would be badly damaged - more damaged. They'd lost two of their three children already" (ch. 41). He rides after her and heroically brings her back, keeping her secret so her honor is preserved. Both sisters romantically wear their "wedding nightgowns" but appear quite unprepared for the reality of a wedding night and respond with shock and fear. Beforehand, both are naïve, with romantic infatuations more than sincere love or mutual understanding. Thus they seem a sad commentary on the naiveté of the English aristocracy, in contrast to the forthright Scottish characters.

Jenny Fraser strides up to Ian and announces plainly that she intends to wed him. As Ian tells it:

> "She came up to me out in the field one day, while I was tryin' to mend a wagon that sprang its wheel. I crawled out, all covered wi' muck, and found her standin' there looking like a bush covered wi' butterflies. She looks me up and down and she says—" He paused and scratched his head. "Weel, I don't know exactly what she said, but it ended with her kissing me, muck notwithstanding, and saying, 'Fine, then, we'll be married on St. Martin's Day.' " He spread his hands in comic resignation. "I was still explaining why we couldna do any such thing, when I found myself in front of a priest, saying, 'I take thee, Janet'...and swearing to a lot of verra improbable statements." (*Outlander,* ch, 29)

Similarly, Joan McKimmie tells Michael Murray, "In the Highlands, if a man's widowed, he takes another wife as soon as he can get one; he's got to have someone to mend his shirt and rear his bairns" ("The Space Between," 242). Nonetheless, the pair decide to go slowly and decide how they feel about each other before committing. While the series focuses on Claire and Jamie, other significant young women each choose their own defiant marriages, influencing what is to come.

Women's Issue Fiction

While the show and American book are called *Outlander,* the original manuscript published in England is *Cross Stitch,* a more blatantly feminine title. As Gabaldon explains:

> It's a weak play on "a stitch in time," with an (even weaker) reference to Claire's occupation as a healer (doctor-wound-stitch... that sort of thing), but it was my first book, after all....If she had returned in the first book, though, that would have made the "cross" – crossing back to the past and then forth to the future, which gave me the mental shape of an "X" – which is, of course, the shape of a cross-stitch. (*Outlandish Companion* 323)

She notes that the American publisher asked, "Well, we can't call it that, or people will think it's about embroidery. Can you think of something else, maybe a little more... adventurous?" Of course, calling it *Outlander* left it confusingly linked with the Sean Connery movies *Outland* (1981) and *Highlander* (1986).

Outlander, book and show, is a series for women, but what does that mean? "One of the defining generic features of the woman's picture as a textual system is its construction of narratives motivated by female desire and processes of spectator identification governed by female point-of-view" (Kuhn 146). Kristin Ramsdell, author of *Romance Fiction: A Guide to the Genre,* describes romances enticing readers with character stories of interpersonal relationships, and the moral values and dilemmas that accompany these. In addition, the romance offers love and optimism that all will turn out well. "It celebrates life and love with abandon and reaffirms one of the most basic of all fantasies, the triumph of true love against all odds" (20). As she adds:

> Closely linked to this moral advocacy is the fact that romances are increasingly dealing with serious social issues such as spousal or child abuse, alcoholism, racism, and mental and physical illness. While this aspect might not seem to be appealing on the surface, it speaks to the needs of many readers as it allows them not only to confront real-life problems through fiction, but also to envision healthy, hopeful, and successful solutions to them. (Ramsdell 20)

Certainly, relationships are central in the narrative. The love story drives the plot, especially in the first book. After their wedding, Jamie shyly asks Claire, "Is this...usual? What it is between us, when I touch you, when you ...lie with me? Is it always so between a man and a woman?" Claire must tell him that what they have is particularly special (*Outlander,* ch. 17).

While there is death, loss, and trauma, the good experiences outweigh these, and somehow, the heroes fight their way back from even the worst situations. Female desire is also central and Jamie spends their marriage pleasing Claire in a variety of ways, the camera centering on her blissful face. "Her sexuality is part of who she is," Balfe adds. "She is a very passionate woman, with such a zest for life, and her sexuality is very integral to that. She controls that; she has desires. *Quelle horreur,* women have desires, oh my god!" (Petersen).

Researching shows that cater to female audiences, Avis Lewallen describes the show *Lace* as "almost a mini-encyclopaedia of female sexuality" thanks to the topics it presents: "from loss of virginity, sexual desire, sexual satisfaction and frigidity, to prostitution, rape, adultery, lesbianism and transvestism. It also deals with pornography, alcoholism, plastic surgery, childbirth, miscarriage and abortion, and ... more than passing reference to women's lib" (89).

Outlander shares many of these: not plastic surgery, perhaps, but certainly most of the others. There's a touching moment in book one when a grandmother prevails on Jamie to save her grandson from an abusive father. He does so, but there are consequences when Jamie strong-arms the father who turns Jamie over to the British, only to in turn be attacked by the men of Lallybroch in a self-perpetuating cycle of violence. Claire's loss of virginity and chastity before and during marriage to Frank are left compellingly vague, but Brianna's experiences are fully documented for the reader, as are those of the later heroines Rachel and Dottie.

When asked whether *Outlander* is a feminist text, Gabaldon notes that it depends on one's definition of feminism: "[*Outlander*] is about a woman, who is quite confident in who she is as a woman, and that's one definition of feminist — you take yourself at your own worth, and you demand that others take you at your own estimation" (Petersen).

Prostitution, rape, and adultery are addressed from the women's point of view, from William's prostitute friend Jane to Claire's delightful adoption by a brothel's inhabitants in Edinburgh - a far cry from Littlefinger's callous exploitation of them in *Game of Thrones.* Jenny not only gives birth but discusses breastfeeding with Claire and expels excess milk. Struggling for inner peace in her own relationships, Claire of course must come to terms with her two husbands in two times, something she finally masters at the end of the first book after a long talk with Brother Anselm.

> "Now, from the standpoint of canon law," he said frowning, "there is no difficulty regarding your marriages. Both were valid marriages, consecrated by the church. And strictly speaking, your marriage to the young chevalier in there antedates your marriage to Monsieur Randall...considered from a strictly legal standpoint, you have committed neither sin nor crime in what you have done regarding these two men." (ch. 40)
>
> ...
>
> "You have been gone from your place for nearly a year. Your first husband will have begun to reconcile himself to your loss. Much as he may have loved you, loss is common to all men, and we are given means of overcoming it for our good. He will have started, perhaps, to build a new life. Would it do good for you to desert the man who needs you so deeply, and whom you love, to whom you are united in the bonds of holy matrimony, to return and disrupt this new life? And in particular, if you were to go back from a sense of duty, but feeling that your heart is given elsewhere – no." He shook his head decisively.
>
> "No man can serve two masters, and no more can a woman. Now, if that were your only valid marriage, and this" – he nodded again toward the guest wing – "merely an irregular attachment, then your duty might lie elsewhere. But you were bound by God, and I think you may honor your duty to the chevalier. (*Outlander,* ch. 40)

There's also legalities and customs of the time – Claire, as a married woman, cannot testify in court, though a widow can. Everywhere she goes, male doctors assume they're more qualified than she is. Wendigo tells Claire she's anachronistic because she doesn't act afraid of men, emphasizing the difference between the centuries. "Claire rails against the gender politics of 18th-century Scotland the same way that she would've railed against the gender politics of 1950s Western culture. She's a woman attempting to negotiate patriarchy and her own sexual and emotional desires" (Petersen).

Brianna cross-dresses in the past, and blithely faces shock and condemnation around her, in exchange for the freedom of trousers. Seeing her, Roger thinks: "In her own time, the clothes would have been so baggy as to be sexless. After months of seeing women in long skirts and arisaids, though, the blatant division of her legs, the sheer bloody length of thigh and curve of calf, seemed so outrageous that he wanted to wrap a sheet around her" (*The Drums of Autumn,* ch. 40).

When she falls pregnant, Jamie tries to have Young Ian marry Brianna. He makes logical points – that everyone will sneer at Brianna and her baby, that the child needs a father. At her aunt's house, Brianna finds herself "being put on show like a piece of bloodstock with doubtful lines. Being held up by the scruff of the neck like an orphaned kitten, in hopes somebody will take me in!" (*The Drums of Autumn,* ch. 58). Society's judgment is strong here, as Brianna fights her way through it with sheer stubbornness. She faces a great deal of misogyny in the past, including from her own family:

> His feathers ruffled from the argument, Young Jamie made one last attempt.
>
> "It's verra unseemly for a woman to be givin' her opinions sae free, and her with menfolk to look after her," he said stiffly.
>
> "You don't think women ought to have opinions?" Brianna asked sweetly.
>
> "No, I don't!"
>
> Ian gave his son a long look.
>
> "And you'll have been marrit what, eight years?" He shook his head. "Aye, well, your Joan's a tactful woman." (*The Drums of Autumn,* ch 35)

Brianna tells Roger she was studying sex in the book The *Sensuous Man,* to his dismay. "Roger rubbed a hand over his face, at a loss for words. If asked an hour before, he would have stoutly claimed to be in favor of sexual equality. Under the veneer of modernity, though, there was apparently enough of the Presbyterian minister's son left to feel that a nice young woman really ought to be an ignoramus on her wedding night" (*The Drums of Autumn*, ch 40). While both these moments are quickly subverted, as Roger appreciates Brianna's learning, and Ian smirks at his son's naïve superiority, the cloud of misogyny follows both heroines on their journeys.

Jamie is the first to be raped, emphasizing he has vulnerabilities he shares with the women, but Brianna then Claire endure it as well. Brianna's occurs when she chooses to wear a dress, emphasizing the dangers of women traveling alone in such times. As Jamie thinks after, her falling pregnant puts her at another risk: "If this MacKenzie wished it, he might claim Brianna as his wife by right of common law, with the coming bairn as evidence of his claim. A court of law would not necessarily force a woman to wed a rapist, but any magistrate would uphold the right of a man to his wife and child – regardless of the wife's feelings in the matter" (*The Drums of Autumn,* ch. 44).

Claire offers an abortion to Brianna, over Jamie's horror. She notes to herself that her Hippocratic Oath forbids it, but that Hippocrates wasn't a woman or a mother (*The Drums of Autumn,* ch. 49). Pregnancy and childbirth are described in detail along with the effort of breast feeding and childcare. As Brianna and Claire run the big house on Frasier's Ridge, they discover how much work housework can be. Brianna cries:

> "I've spent the last month here, up to my eyeballs in laundry and baby shit and screeching women and horrible children while you're out doing 'important things' and you come marching in here covered in mud and tromp all over the clean floors without even noticing they were clean in the first place! Do you have any idea what a pain it is to scrub pine floors on your hands and knees? With lye soap!" (*Fiery Cross*, ch. 33).

Male-centric war stories are unlikely to mention the household chores. Brianna is even more horrified when she discovers that a new wife is expected to sew her own shroud, in case she dies in childbirth. The grim realities of eighteenth-century life provide a number of threats she's forced to deal with. Matt Zoller Seitz, author of "*Outlander* Is No *Game of Thrones*, But That's a Good Thing" explains:

> There's also a sense in which *Outlander* can be watched not just as an involving fish-out-of-water adventure, but also as a commentary on female audience's often thorny relationship to mainstream genre fiction, which tends to be centered on issues of pride, honor, and goal-oriented journeys that end with the hero winning glory and a woman.

Claire's journey is one of personal discovery and ultimate risk, along with time spent in female occupations and moments of female friendship. There is also female-specific danger. In "The Search" (114), Claire sells herself in marriage to rescue Jamie, offering herself to Dougal if she cannot save Jamie. "If I fail, or he's already dead, I will marry you," she tells him solemnly. This emphasizes her precarious position –she has nothing else to offer that Dougal will accept. Claire and Brianna gradually encounter many different women in danger. Claire performs abortions for women with no other options in Paris, and meets Hugh Munro's wife and children, who have no support but his poaching.

Joseph Wemyss begs Brianna to take his fourteen-year-old daughter Lizzie as a servant, or the young girl will become indentured to a man who wants her as a concubine. Her father reveals that another man has bought his daughter's contract and can sell it to anyone he wishes. Lizzie's father is loving though conservative in his attitudes – he would rather he never see her again than she fall prey to such a fate, so he's willing for Brianna to take her to the colonies. "Better she should be gone from me forever to a wild place than to meet dishonor before my eyes" he insists (*The Drums of Autumn,* ch. 35). He also resolves to never speak to her again after her scandalous marriage.

Her unorthodox relationship is one of many disreputable moments of the sixth book. In *A Breath of Snow and Ashes,* as Gabaldon notes:

> There's rape, whores, several cases of the pox, threesomes, Indian women offered as gifts in pairs, incest, both true and false accusations of married men sleeping around, situations involving white slave owners and black slaves, and women who might turn to other women for "comfort" in jail (it's not just the fellas in Ardsmuir, evidently). It almost made me miss the days when it was just every homosexual man lusting after Jamie. Sex certainly complicates life, but it seemed like it turned up some very complicated situations in this particular novel, often involving babies and questions of parentage. ("A Breath of Snow and Ashes")

Nonetheless, Claire thinks, "So much love in one small place....Did it matter, really, how unorthodox the marriage at the center of this odd family was?" (*An Echo in the Bone,* ch. 11).

All these scandalous and unconventional scenes are related through the woman's perspective, emphasizing their role in history. They also function as a study of gender dynamics. As Claire concludes, "I saw just the same kinds of behavior between men and women in 1743 that you see now. some differences, of course, in how they each behave, but not so much in how they behave to each other" (*Voyager,* ch. 17).

In the eighties, a male writer surveyed large groups a thousand different people to determine how they defined femininity. Men of middle age and older defined femininity as related to men – women were most womanly while being attractive to men or having sex with them. While masculinity is often defined as working with other men, or sharing moments of camaraderie, the men surveyed didn't consider women as feminine while giving birth or nurturing children, only in relation to themselves. (Walker 35-36).

In a similar example of patriarchal bias, men are easier to track through history than women. Prince Charles, King Louis, Simon Fraser, Lord Lovat, and the American revolutionaries (Washington, Franklin, Lafayette, Benedict Arnold) are the historical characters incorporated into Gabaldon's works – famous women only get brief cameos. This is likely because far more is known of the men's stories.

Searching, Brianna finds Jamie not Claire when she goes looking. Back in the future, she and her husband trace both Frasers through the battles of the Revolutionary War. Claire's greatest visible mark on history is the medical book she writes – and for that she masquerades as a man.

Genre

> The genre romance novel appeals both generally and specifically. Its general appeal is that of all genre fiction – an escape fantasy that is predictable, enjoyable, and safe. Romance's specific appeal is more complex. It attracts readers for diverse reasons that include emotional involvement, female empowerment, the promotion of moral values, the celebration of life, the ultimate triumph of love, and a sense of unflagging optimism. (Ramsdell 18)

Gabaldon insists over and over her series isn't a romance – possibly because many readers approach it as one. In fact it has all the conventions of a romance, but also other genres – it has the research of historical fiction, the innovation of science fiction and the action and narrative of adventure fiction – some romance novels have these, while others touch on them exceptionally lightly, only offering enough token plot to carry readers to the next sex scene.

"One of the primary attractions of the romance is that it is emotionally engaging. Romances are books about relationships, and they appeal directly to readers' feelings and emotions. They are compelling, and they make the reader care about the characters and what happens to them" (Ramsdell 19-20). *Outlander* certainly offers this – Claire's personal journey, told intimately to the reader, is at the forefront, with her emotions and sensations all shared with the audience. It also offers other conventions – the slow falling in love, the sex scenes (of course) and florid prose in sensual metaphors: "And I voyaged into him, as he into me, so that when the last small storms of love began to shake me, he cried out, and we rose the waves together as one flesh, and saw ourselves in each other's eyes" (ch. 29).

"Romance narrative can constitute one of women's few entries to the public articulation and social exploration of psychic life" (Kaplan 165). This story offers all the steps of the heroine's journey as Claire travels through a magical world of the past, encountering enemies and loves that offer opportunities for soul growth. Further, the reader can experience these as well. Romantic epics invite "the female reader to identify across sexual difference and to engage with narrative fantasy from a variety of subject positions and at various levels" (Kaplan 145). By book three, Jamie and Lord John are viewpoint characters, and both continue the narrative that follows.

One critic notes that with too-perfect Jamie and rationalizations for the spanking and other violence, the work is too much fantasy to be taken on a straightforward level.

> The pleasures and problems of Starz's freshman series "Outlander" are precisely the same. Intoxicating though it may be, the series, like the book its adapted from, is at

> constant war with itself. "Outlander" wants to be an escapist, feminist romance novel, and while that's not an impossible goal to attain, it means that more often than not the series finds itself working at cross-purposes, not unlike its protagonist, Claire Randall. The problem is not that "Outlander" wants to have its cake and eat it, too; it's that it wants the entire blessed bakery. (Hill)

Similarly, historical feminists such as Mary Wollstonecraft and Jane Austen argued that romance novels stirred up the erotic at the expense of the rational, moral and maternal (Kaplan 145). They worried that such light reading would lead women down frivolous paths. *Outlander* of course blends the two sides, along with worthwhile historical teachings.

"Romance fiction has been described as a form of sexual foreplay that can function simultaneously as an expression and a containment of sexual desire (Lewallen 86). These stories return the reader to a premarital space of serious yet sexual desire, expressed in every chaste touch. Reading, or now watching, *Outlander* is all about more than titillation, but also the process of falling in love as Claire falls for Jamie. "The feeling it creates is interpreted by the women themselves as a general sense of emotional well-being and visceral contentment. Such a feeling is brought on by the opportunity to participate vicariously in a relationship characterized by *mutual* love" as the hero slowly charms and seduces heroine and reader together (Radway 70).

The heroine wants sex, but in many stories, only seeks it within the confines of demure marriage. This promotes women's social reality rather than freeing them from it. Today of course, she need not remain chaste before marriage, especially in fiction. Avis Lewallen, writing about romance as "Pornography for Women" notes that in modern women's fiction, the heroine seeks a career as well as love:

> The heroines not only willfully indulge in pre- and extra-marital sex, they sometimes eschew marriage altogether in favor of a career, and certainly do not view It as an end to their ambitions. They do seek the transcendental orgasm that will indicate they have found 'true love', but fulfilment is defined as the ultimate goal (88)

Claire grew up freely exploring the world and then nursing in the moral confusion of the war, but lives before the sexual revolution. She and Brianna both defy standards of the time and choose their romantic partners.

Several nods to romances appear, as Gabaldon addresses her books' possible labeling. All of these are humorous and playful in a self-aware manner as they toy with and critique the conventions: Hal, Lord John's brother, considers reading novels as "a form of moral weakness, forgivable, and in fact, quite understandable in their mother, who was, after all, a woman. That his younger brother should share in this vice was somewhat less acceptable" (*Brotherhood of the Blade*, ch. 1). Certainly, Gabaldon's books are novels, often dismissed as "women's fiction" as Lord John's favorites are.

Claire thinks skeptically that Black Jack is "A common name for rogues and scoundrels in the eighteenth century. A staple of romantic fiction, the name conjured up charming highwaymen, dashing blades in plumed hats" (ch. 35). As Jamie tells a tall tale, though one less strange than Gabaldon's own saga, he remarks that if his other occupations fail, he's such a creative storyteller that he might "find useful Employment as a scribbler of Romances" (*An Echo in the Bone,* ch. 89). He and Claire each read steamy books during a *Voyager* scene and mentally critique the sex scenes.

There are several homages to Sir Walter Scott. Though he is an anachronism for the time, "it is generally considered that the [historical romance] genre achieved both definition and popularity with the novels of Sir Walter Scott. Already an acknowledged narrative poet, Scott turned to the newer and somewhat suspect form, the novel, and in 1814 *Waverly* was published anonymously" (Ramsdell 117). In *Voyager,* Claire quotes from "Marmion," with "Oh, what a tangled web we weave/ When first we practice to deceive!" These two phrases are also chapter titles in *Lord John and the Private Matter.* Jamie later quotes Claire's own "Marmion" phrase back to her, saying of her: "When pain and anguish wring the brow, A ministering angel thou!"

Finally Brianna and Claire each fantasize about being trapped in romance novels or subvert the actions romantic heroines would take in their situation – these strong, opinionated women are more self-reliant than many damsels of fiction. In *Outlander,* Claire thinks, "One never stops to think what underlies romance. Tragedy and terror, transmuted by time. Add a little art in the telling, and voila! a stirring romance, to make the blood run fast and maidens sigh. My blood was running fast, all right, and never maiden sighed like Jamie" (ch. 35). She adds in the second book, "Lying on the floor, with the carved panels of the ceiling flickering dimly above, I found myself thinking that I had always heretofore assumed that the tendency of eighteenth-century ladies to swoon was due to tight stays; now I rather thought it might be due to the idiocy of eighteenth-century men" (*Dragonfly in Amber,* ch. 24). As the book ends, Claire complains about all the fiction and history that has romanticized Bonnie Prince Charlie and treated him as perfect, unlike Gabaldon's book: "The fault lies with the artists," Claire says. "The writers, the singers, the tellers of tales. It's them that take the past and re-create it to their liking. Them that could take a fool and give you back a hero, take a sot and make him a king" (*Dragonfly in Amber,* ch. 47).

Describing a sexual experience in her dream journal, Brianna crosses it out and writes, "Well, none of the books I've ever read could describe it, either!" (*Fiery Cross,* ch. 38). In *A Breath of Snow and Ashes,* she imagines her true love will ride up on a stallion to rescue her. Then, defying her romantic fantasy as well as the convention, she knocks a hole in the ceiling and escapes on her own.

Despite all this, this series might certainly be labeled historical as much as romance. In these stories

> the protagonist (most often male, but occasionally female) usually has a cause of some kind, which, in combination with the events of the period, motivates the story (e.g., the quest for political, social, or material success; revenge; the righting of an old family wrong; the settling of old debts; the clearing of a family name; and the regaining of a rightful heritage). In addition, there is usually some kind of romance plotline, which, though interesting, does not dominate the plot. (Ramsdell 121).

Claire begins by struggling to return home, but her driving force quickly widens, first to saving Jamie, then to working with him to stop the clans' slaughter at Culloden. Book two might be said to be more political intrigue than romance, though Jamie and Claire have their relationship ups and downs. Likewise, the later books are most obviously adventure, as Claire, Jamie, and their friends get shipwrecked, kidnapped, accused of murder, and everything else possible. At last, both march off to the Revolutionary War, turning it into a historical military saga. It's no wonder this is filed under general fiction.

> Like all romances, Historicals are not totally realistic. For example, while it is true that eighteenth-century London stank, medieval castles were cold and drafty, and the

> personal hygiene of most people prior to the twentieth century was appalling by today's standards, these aspects may be mentioned but are rarely dwelt upon. Most authors and readers prefer to consider the jewel-encrusted ballgowns and the well-cut Weston coats rather than the unwashed bodies they covered. (Ramsdell 116)

If this is part of the criteria, then Gabaldon's fiction is more realistic than romantic. Claire changes oozy diapers, describes toilet paper, digs privies, and meets countless unwashed people with rotting teeth. She treats her own family for crushed limbs and snakebite with maggots, leeches, and other revolting treatments. War's brutality fills more pages than its glory. Diseases and conditions of the time don't just appear but provide major subplots for Claire the physician.

One compromise here is the romantic historical, a genre in which "accurate historical settings, information, atmosphere, and characters ... are essential to the story," though "the actual romantic interest is typically centered around an invented, or real but lesser known, hero and heroine" (Ramsdell 112).

> In novels of this type, the love relationship is, to a large extent, shaped by the actual historical events of the period. Lovers are generally kept apart by wars or political circumstances rather than simple misunderstandings or romantic entanglements. In addition, if the heroine is an actual historical figure, the story will not usually contradict known facts about her, although considerable liberty is usually taken with those areas of her life that have not been documented. For example, while it may be fact that a certain earl married a certain lady, the details of the courtship may be wholly at the discretion of the author. Even if the important characters are not actual historical figures, they must behave in accordance with and must be subject to the events of the time. In general, romances of this type are well researched and exhibit a relatively high quality of writing, although there are the inevitable exceptions. (Ramsdell 112-113)

Balancing the two genres means an emphasis on the woman's side of history. While Jamie and Roger become viewpoint characters, Claire remains central, with an emphasis on her struggles. As such, this parallels another beloved historical, *Downton Abbey*. "Much of the stuff that makes *Downton* compulsively watchable is what makes *Outlander* irresistible. Both focus on the perils of womanhood – even in the most privileged classes – and both are equal parts feminine fantasy and feminist critique" (Saraiya). As Catriona Balfe adds:

> In the beginning – I wouldn't say she's enjoying learning and experiencing this – there's a moment of fascination like, "Wow, this is what life was actually like at this point." We get asked a lot, "If you could go back, what time would you go back to?" There is that sense of that for certain moments in history: "I wonder what life was really like. I wonder what people were like. Were they the same as us? Did they experience the same trials and tribulations that we did?" (Ng, "Caitriona Balfe on Claire")

Historical fiction is of course escapist, as it's set in far-off times like the Regency or Revolutionary War. "Not just any historical setting will do. In order to qualify, the historical period must be properly romantic, i.e., it must be far enough removed in time and place that it is surrounded by an aura of unfamiliarity and mystery," Ramsdell explains (111). Characters behave with gallantry or occasionally brutality not seen in modern times as much can be dialed to maximum emotional heights. Menzies explains:

> We watch drama and we watch stories to live vicariously and see people do the things we're not allowed to do and Jack is definitely in that honorable tradition. He says the things we wouldn't dare to say. Obviously he goes a lot further into much darker waters [this half], but I think we've always had the tradition of dark fairytales, from childhood

> onward, and I think humans are always drawn to dark stories. It's sort of a parable really, isn't it? It's a way of dealing with this sort of thing without having to experience it in our own lives. (Lutes)

The Lord John books are mysteries that the hero solves while moving through society London or adventuring in exotic locales, from Canada to the West Indies. They also have a trace of fantasy, as all appear in science fiction and fantasy anthologies with story titles like "Lord John and the Succubus" or "Lord John and the Plague of Zombies." Nonetheless, there is a prosaic explanation for everything, leaving the stories even less magical than the Claire and Jamie novels, once all is explained. Though the only point of view character is male, there is a strong gender component – the stories emphasize his status as Other as he encounters pitfalls of homosexuality.

Even more escapist than the Lord John novels are the Jamie and Claire books with their time travel elements. This could help to label the series as alternate reality or even science fiction/fantasy. Having Gabaldon's short stories in so many speculative fiction anthologies certainly reinforces this label.

> One of the more popular of the Alternative Reality Subgenres, the Time Travel romance features protagonists who are transported from one time period to another. The exchange is usually between the present and some time in the past, but other options are acceptable. Conflicts usually result because of time-based cultural differences (e.g., when a modem heroine ends up in the male-dominated past) or the fact that the hero and heroine are from different time periods and must make sacrifices to stay together. (Ramsdell 230)

Obviously, *Outlander* is a prime example of this small subgenre. It appeals to many fantasy readers, as between the elseworld nature of the historical setting and the magical elements it fulfils all the criteria of epic fantasy, though the magic is mostly subtle and rare.

> The essential appeal of the Alternative Reality Romance is to our imagination and inborn sense of wonder. As children most of us were fascinated by stories of fairies, elves, dragons, and other tales of myth and magic. As we grew older, ghosts, witches, vampires, and creatures both macabre and gruesome joined the list. By the time we had reached our teens, stories of aliens, space travel, interplanetary exploration, and intergalactic wars had caught our interest and fired our imaginations. And although we grew up and became more practical and realistic, most of us are still fascinated with the magical, the mystical, the supernatural, and the futuristic. It is to this basic interest that both the Fantastic Fiction genres and the Alternative Reality Romance directly appeal. (Ramsdell 212)

The show, however, downplays the fantasy connection, likely because its largest competitor uses it. "I think *Game of Thrones* certainly helped open the door for us but our worlds are really very different," says Balfe. "It exists in a fantasy world while *Outlander* is more of a historical drama" (Virtue). Though the show is repeatedly compared to *Game of Thrones,* it avoids fantasy elements besides the stone circle itself. For instance, Ron Moore specifically cut the appearance of the Loch Ness Monster to emphasize the show's realism. Claire explains away Geillis's witchcraft, presenting it as poisons and coincidence only.

The story turns spy thriller in book eight as Frank warns Brianna by letter of private parties in "the most shadowed realm of government" who will be interested in her time travel abilities or possibly the Fraser Prophecy (*Written in My Own Heart's Blood,* ch. 43). If her heirs will indeed rule Scotland, she's tied to politics with an ancient history link reminiscent of *The DaVinci Code.* And it's still not clear who knows about her. Did one of Frank's fellow spooks investigate his wife in the 1940s? Back in the American Revolution, Percy Wainwright is playing spy for French interests, perusing his own murky agenda, while Benedict Arnold is playing a more famous game. Meanwhile, Captain Richardson and Denys Randall-Isaacs are involved as well. Is Fergus truly a descendent of St. Germain and Master Raymond? What lies and secrets remain to uncover? Many fans are eager to see the resolution of all these plots in the final volume.

Women's Gender Roles

Strong Woman

Claire is a strong woman from the first line of dialogue Gabaldon wrote. She explains:

> The time-travel came in later, when I thought it would be interesting to have an Englishwoman to play off all these kilted Scotsmen, and she refused to shut up and talk like an 18th century person. She just kept making smart-ass modern remarks about everything she saw – and she also took over and started telling the story.

"It helps too that Claire is no passive plaything, but a frank, funny woman with a keen sense of survival and a sharp mind" (Hughes). She is the force behind the story – competent and commanding, no matter her surroundings. As Gabaldon adds:

> People commonly say to me, in tones of admiration, "But you write such *strong* women!" This is gratifying, but the simple fact of the matter is that I really don't like weak ones. In other words, Claire is not a competent person because I thought it was my social duty to provide a politically correct role model for young women – I just don't like ninnies and would find it a terrible chore to have to write about one. (*Outlandish Companion* 191)

Granted, strong women can be a difficulty in fiction, as they're often one-sided clichés. A warrior like Lady Sif in *Thor* or a woman seeking revenge for abuse like Lisbeth Salinger in *The Girl with the*

Dragon Tattoo often has nothing else to her personality than this aspect.

Carina Chocano comments in her essay on the subject that "strong woman" refers to the old-fashioned "strong, silent type," rather than a character with "blubbering, dithering, neuroticism, anxiety, melancholy or any other character flaw or weakness that makes a character unpredictable and human" (2). These last, of course, appear in the world's most beloved characters, giving them flaws readers can adore. Chocano adds:

> "Strong female character" is one of those shorthand memes that has leached into the cultural groundwater and spawned all kinds of cinematic clichés: alpha professionals whose laserlike focus on career advancement has turned them into grim, celibate automatons; robotic, lone-wolf, ascetic action heroines whose monomaniacal devotion to their crime-fighting makes them lean and cranky and very impatient; murderous 20-something comic-book salesgirls who dream of one day sidekicking for a superhero; avenging brides; poker-faced assassins; and gloomy ninjas with commitment issues. It has resulted in characters like Natalie Portman's in "No Strings Attached," who does everything in her power to avoid commitment, even with a guy she's actually in love with; or Lisbeth Salander in Stieg Larsson's *Millennium* trilogy; or pretty much every character Jodie Foster has played since "Nell" or, possibly, "Freaky Friday." (1)

Claire, certainly, is strong from her first line but has a vivid personality as well. She's clever and resourceful, but also makes serious mistakes. Her mouth runs away with her at the worst possible times and she acknowledges this, subverting her famous strength. In an even deeper subversion, she needs rescuing on many occasions, about as often as she saves Jamie. Her great strength that most humanizes her is her love for him, which outweighs practical concerns, from the doomed Jacobite rebellion to the lack of hot water and hygiene in the past.

As a strong woman, her mouth gets her in trouble time and again, to the audience's delight, as she's their contemporary representative and judge of the harsh culture. "*Outlander* is never more engrossing than when a scene emphasizes Claire's reactions as she's forced to decide whether to say what she really thinks of a man's behavior or assertion or recitation of policy, or err on the side of silence" (Seitz). In "The Garrison Commander" (106), Lord Thomas and the English offer her an escort to Inverness and thus the standing stones, before she opens her mouth and asserts: "The Scots just want the same freedoms we enjoy. Freedoms we take for granted. They are not the aggressors, Captain, we are. It is their land, and we are occupying it." They immediately assume life among the Scots has corrupted her.

She's more effective when she pushes the Duke of Sandringham on the show. When she tells him, "I need you as my friend, and I trust my friendship, no matter how lowly obtained, is preferable to a date with the gallows as a traitor to your king," he takes her seriously and considers Jamie's petition ("By the Pricking of my Thumbs," 110).

She and her companions make other equally strong decisions on their adventures. In "The Search" (114), Jenny and Claire both agree they must kill a Redcoat courier – only Murtagh's own knife stroke stops them before they carry it out. He admiringly calls them "natural outlaws." Meanwhile, Jenny tortures the soldier with chilly certainty, telling Claire that life in the Highlands is rough and uncompromising and "love forces you to choose." To save her family, especially on the show, she's willing to do whatever violent acts are necessary.

Describing Jenny's battle with Jack Randall, Jamie paints her as a hellion:

> Jamie stopped for a moment, jaw working. "He was holdin' Jenny's arm behind her back, but he let go then, to

> bring his hand round and put it down her dress, round her breast, like." Remembering the scene, he smiled unexpectedly. "So," he resumed, "Jenny stamped down on his foot and gave him her elbow deep in the belly. And as he was bent over choking, she whirled round and gave him a good root in the stones wi' her knee." He snorted briefly with amusement.
>
> "Weel, at that he dropped the pistol, and she went for it, but one of the dragoons holding me got to it first." (*Outlander* ch. 4)

She only submits to save Jamie – over his objections. Later she stands by her decision, adding: "And if your life is a suitable exchange for my honor, tell me why my honor is not a suitable exchange for your life ... Or are you telling me that I may not love you as much as you love me? Because if ye are, Jamie Fraser, I'll tell ye right now, it's not true!" (ch. 26).

In the podcast, Ron Moore discusses having Jenny and Claire go after Jamie in "The Search" (114), "riding out to the rescue with pistols and so on to go rescue the man" in a gender reversal of the classic tropes.

In "Both Sides Now" (108), Dougal's entire rent collecting party unites to teach Claire to defend herself – not one makes a comment about it being unsuitable for a woman. She carries a dagger or sock knife after, and uses it at need. Riding with Claire in "The Search," Jenny brings pistols and daggers for both of them and uses hers with competence.

Claire rarely has to fight for her life with Jamie, Murtagh, and others to defend her. Nonetheless, she has one striking moment all alone in the snow when she confronts a lone wolf. Sensing its wild instinct, she finds herself connecting with it, looking into its "wicked yellow" eyes and judging the moment it will jump. Fighting it, she transforms into a savage animal herself.

> I drove a knee viciously into its chest, eliciting a strangled yelp. Only then did I realize that the odd, growling whimpers were coming from me and not the wolf.
>
> Strangely enough, I was not at all frightened now, though I had been terrified watching the wolf stalk me. There was room in my mind for only one thought: I would kill this animal, or it would kill me. Therefore, I was going to kill it.
>
> There comes a turning point in intense physical struggle where one abandons oneself to a profligate usage of strength and bodily resource, ignoring the costs until the struggle is over. Women find this point in childbirth; men in battle.
>
> Past that certain point, you lose all fear of pain or injury. Life becomes very simple at that point; you will do what you are trying to do, or die in the attempt, and it does not really matter much which.
>
> I had seen this sort of struggle during my training on the wards, but never had I experienced it before. Now all my concentration was focused on the jaws locked around my forearm and the writhing demon tearing at my body. (*Outlander,* ch. 35)

She defeats the creature and faces its pack with "black rage" as her inner savagery bursts forth to save her.

With Prince Charles's Rising in *Dragonfly in Amber,* Claire leads the men of Lallybroch herself for a time, thinking, "If Jenny Cameron could lead her brother's men to Glenfinnan, I could take my husband's troops to Stirling" (ch. 42). At the climax, Claire plans to charge into battle at Culloden beside Jamie, dressed as a boy so she can die with him. Feeling "calm, with no trace of doubt," she tells him, "I can make a kilt of my arisaid; there are enough young boys with the army that I can pass for one. You've said yourself it will all be confusion. No one will notice" (*Dragonfly in Amber,* ch. 46).

At the Battle of Saratoga, she takes to the field to find Jamie. Though she discovers his sword is too heavy for her to wield, she swings it at the looters and rescues Jamie quite dramatically. These two attempts to take the field emphasize her role as support, while Jamie is acknowledged many times as a warrior. She and Jamie also muse over the nature of battle:

> "Why is it that women don't make war, I wonder?"
>
> "Ye're no made for it, Sassenach." His hand cupped my cheek, hard and rough. "And it wouldna be right. Women take so much more with ye, when ye go."
>
> "What do you mean by that?"
>
> He made the small shrugging movement that meant he was looking for a word or a notion, an unconscious movement, as though his coat was too tight, though he wasn't wearing one at the moment.
>
> "When a man dies, it's only him," he said. "And one is much like another. Aye, a family needs a man, to feed them, protect them. But any decent man can do it. A woman..." His lips moved against my fingertips, a faint smile. "A woman takes life with her when she goes. A woman is...infinite possibility."
>
> "Idiot," I said, very softly. "If you think one man is just like any other." (*An Echo in the Bone,* ch. 57)

Claire is symbolically the giver of life – it is her job to heal, not to kill. Nonetheless, this is an equal kind of strength.

Lord John, on meeting Claire in an epidemic, notes, "I had thought your distress due only to a woman's natural compassion, but I see it is something quite different ... I have been a soldier, an officer ... I know what it is to hold men's lives in your hand ... and to lose them" (*Voyager,* ch. 48). In the same story, Claire is accepted as ship's surgeon with little fuss, as "It was commonly the gunner's wife – if he had one – who dealt with the small injuries and illnesses of the crew" (*Voyager,* ch. 42).

Certainly, Claire is a World War II nurse, used to the brutality and horrors of surgery, amputation, and all the rest. Each time Jamie goes to war, at Culloden and in the New World, he never dreams of leaving Claire behind. He recognizes her battlefield skills and welcomes her healing all the men in need, not only himself. She's fierce and competent in the sickroom, even with reluctant patients:

> "There," I said, fastidiously rinsing my hands in the basin. "Now, I will take this precious packet of dispatches across to Mr. Cameron. You will both rest, drink hot tea, rest, blow your nose, and rest, in that order. Got it, troops?"
>
> The tip of a long, reddened nose was barely visible above the bedclothes. It oscillated slowly back and forth as Jamie shook his head.
>
> "Drunk wi' power," he remarked disapprovingly to the ceiling. "Verra unwomanly attitude, that."
>
> I dropped a kiss on his hot forehead and swung my cloak down from its hook.
>
> "How little you know of women, my love," I said. (*Dragonfly in Amber,* ch. 38)

"Women did not perform masculine roles such as soldiering. For if women participated in such roles, it would challenge the myth that men are naturally warlike whilst women are peace-makers" (Goodman 75). Nonetheless, women, especially British ones, took many jobs in the war. It was their war on many levels, as aerial bombardment put women's lives in Britain at risk as much as the men's.

As the show begins, Claire, drenched in a young man's blood, operates on his horribly maimed leg. Suddenly, the war is over, and she swigs champagne straight from the bottle. Her character has been established. Not only does the war prepare her for battle dressings and violence, but it hardens her. Her sailor-like language comes from the army, to the horror of Frank and the Scots alike.

In flashback, Frank and Claire say goodbye as she goes off to war, and Claire offers the traditional comment, "What I want is my husband at home with me. But I can't have that right now," as he fusses that she shouldn't be the one going to war in France:

> Frank: This is backwards. I should be the one leaving for the front lines.
> Claire: Welcome to the 20th century. ("The Way Out," 103).

Gabaldon calls herself a "defacto feminist" but "not agenda-driven" (Loughlin). The word "feminism" means a belief that women should have equal rights with men. Of course, this word has certainly changed in meaning over the decades as women's needs and rights have transformed. First wave feminists sought the vote, along with the right to own property and be treated as more than dependents. "With the coming of World War I, the existing social structure began to crumble as women, forced from the home into the workplace in unprecedented numbers, learned to become self-sufficient and gradually gave up their total dependence upon men" (Ramsdell 112). They got the vote in England in 1928 (1920 in the US), shortly after Claire's birth. In World War II, women's roles changed and women were asked to take men's jobs in factories. Claire, a war nurse, is very much a product of her time. Balfe adds:

> I think so many women of that time, it was a real emancipation of women. During the war, women went to work. They worked in the factories. They were doing the jobs that the men were doing before. And they were in ownership of their lives at that point. It was a time when women felt useful outside of the home, not to detract from anyone who does that. I think it's important to show that at that time, that's kind of where women were at. (Vineyard, "Caitriona Balfe")

After the war, nurses were still needed in England. "There were 7198 women doctors and 549 women dentists at the end of the war, compared with 2580 and 82 respectively in 1928" (Braybon and Summerfield 261). Nonetheless, Claire leaves that part of her life behind.

Frank encourages Claire to fill up her time

collecting plants now that she's no longer a nurse, but this of course appears more of a hobby, as he and Claire plan to move to Oxford for his career. There she, once a trained nurse, will be simply a "don's wife," managing the house and having his children.

> Gazing in the shop window, she longs for the vase she sees there since she's never had a real house or chance to practice domesticity. "I sometimes wonder what would have happened if I'd bought that vase and made a home for it," she adds. By this she seems to mean, what if she had resolved to settle down permanently instead of continue wandering. A vase was the token of Mother Rhea in Greek myth, suggesting the beneficent mother doling out enormous gifts to the people. Thus it symbolizes heavenly beneficence but also the maternal world. Blue is a color of striving and celestial enlightenment, as it's the color of the sky. "It is also the infinite and the void from which all life develops" (Bruce-Mitford 107). As such, it suggests striving for spirituality and self-improvement rather than settling.
>
> While Claire's time travel is an accident, she makes several decisions, including seeking the flower in the first place – which she might not have made if she'd chosen to settle. There's a disturbing hint here that if Claire had been satisfied with domesticity – buying vases and homemaking instead of herbalism and combing the countryside for plants, she wouldn't have left. The book mentions that Frank "suggested" Claire take up botany "to occupy [her] mind" once she was finished with nursing (ch. 1). After the war, she is restless and seeking occupation. Gathering forget-me-nots is the best she can do, before she must settle down to the life of an Oxford don. Instead, of course, she travels to a place where her medical skills are needed and finds her destiny. (Frankel, *Symbolism and Sources of Outlander* 47)

It may be something of a Freudian slip that Claire, seeking her plants, stumbles through the standing stones and into a world where her skills are valued by everyone, especially her new husband. Claire gets everything in the past with the fantasy new man, "the handsome man who supported both the liberated workplace woman's ambitions and her sexuality off the job" (Kutulas 223).

Jamie indeed supports Claire as a professional woman, thinking quite early on that having a woman who can patch him up will be an asset. Yet he doesn't insist she confine her skills to the home. Each time he rides to battle, it's understood that she'll go beside him. She puts up her shingle in Philadelphia and barters her skill to the neighbors in North Carolina.

In book two, Jamie objects strenuously to Claire's having a career while married and pregnant – especially a medical career tending "beggars and prostitutes." He calls her "the kind who would abandon her husband to go and play with scum in the gutter" and insists she should be taking care of her household. Claire must point out that the housekeeper manages the household and Jamie has an outside life. "Is being married to me sufficient occupation for *you*? I don't notice you hanging round the house all day, adoring me" (ch. 11). When Jamie discovers the sort of primping bored housewives attempt in Paris, he finally gives in.

Mary Prior writes: "Under common law *femme sole,* that is single woman or widow, suffered no legal constraints which would handicap her in her trade. Things were very different for the married woman. Under common law, the legal identity of the married woman was merged with that of her husband. The wife was described as *femme couverte.* Her husband, her baron, was both her "sovereign" and her "guardian" (102-103). Jenny (who manages Lallybroch) and Claire (keeper of the physician's studio in Castle Leoch) are both married, though they have these jobs before marriage and keep them after. Ian in fact leaves his own family farm to aid Jenny with hers (presumably his married sister's family has inherited back home). In the new world,

Claire and Brianna both offer their skills on the barter system in their rural world – Claire as doctor and Brianna as artist. These are more specialized skills than their husbands' general labor.

Throughout her adventures, medicine remains Claire's touchstone, something she can rely on and trade to others. As she prepares Jamie's shoulder dressing early on, she uses familiar herbs and thinks, "The preparations had steadied me a bit. If I didn't know for certain where I was, or why I was there, at least I knew what to do for the next quarter of an hour" (*Outlander*, ch. 4). Balfe explains:

> I think all of that is her finding confidence within herself – "I know things about this time. I know certain things these people don't know." That's what allows her to believe she can survive and perhaps maneuver her way or figure out a way to be useful. She could use her information to get by. The [medical condition] with Colum is great because, knowing what she knows about his medical condition, she gains empathy toward him and it makes him more human to her, so he's not this completely intimidating figure. Being able to figure out the balance of power between Dougal and Colum, that comes into play as well.
>
> She believes, at this point, she won't be here very long. There's a nice moment where she enjoys taking in this time and learning about it, kind of watching it with a fascination of somebody who has the ability to have a window into another time and place and see what life was really like. She's an interested person in history and in people. This really allows her to feed into that. (Ng, "Caitriona Balfe on Claire")

Claire also learns from the wisewomen of the past – she discovers the doctors of the new world are often flat wrong, but the women like Mrs. Fitz dispensing household remedies know what's needed.

> "Still bleedin' under the skin. Leeches will help, then." She lifted the cover from the bowl, revealing several small dark sluglike objects, an inch or two long, covered with a disagreeable-looking liquid. Scooping out two of them, she

> pressed one to the flesh just under the brow-bone and the other just below the eye.
>
> "See," she explained to me," once a bruise is set, like, leeches do ye no good. But where ye ha' a swellin' like this, as is still comin' up, that means the blood is flowin' under the skin, and leeches can pull it out." (*Outlander*, ch. 6)

Medieval female physicians were rare but a few stand out in the history books – Trotula of Salermo studied at Italy's medical college during the eleventh century and then wrote the groundbreaking medical book *The Diseases of Women.* Marie Colinet of Berne, a German traveling doctor and surgeon around 1580, actually invented a technique of removing shrapnel safely with a magnet, though her husband was given the credit. Certainly beyond this were numerous midwives and healers of their local communities. Gabaldon explains:

> Aside from the fact that it would be helpful to know how to dress wounds and treat minor problems like scurvy, I'd noticed in the course of research that there were in fact almost no "official" physicians at all in the Highlands. ... In most times and places, there has been no medical assistance save for the wisdom and experience of family and neighbors – and among family and neighbors, those who are most likely to have any knowledge or skill in medical matters are the women because (owing to the undeniable fact that women bear and nourish children) they are the members of the community who are stuck at home, growing plants, feeding all and sundry, and generally keeping things going while the menfolk are out killing mammoths or each other (*Outlandish Companion* 191-192)

Only in the third book does Claire become a doctor, with Frank looking after their child during the day. He offers support and encouragement for finding her true calling in life, adding, "I haven't got that absolute conviction that there's something in life I'm meant to do – and you have" (*Voyager,* ch. 7). Meanwhile, Jamie notes that healing through use of a knife is "a nice contradiction" that suits Claire

(*Voyager,* ch. 27). It's likely Claire's adventures in the past that gave her the strength to chart a new path for herself.

Of course, this too has pitfalls, at a time when female doctors were rare. She raises Brianna through the fifties and sixties – post-war years when women were pushed back into the home. As such, Claire stands out for her profession. Telling Jamie a story of young Brianna, Claire explains:

> "It was what they called Career Day ... Anyway, they'd always ask me to come, because it wasn't at all common for a woman to be a doctor then."
>
> "Ye think it's common now?" He laughed, and I kicked him lightly in the shin.
>
> And when I'd got done speaking and asked if there were any questions, an obnoxious little boy piped up and said that his mother said women who worked were no better than prostitutes, and they ought to be home minding their families, instead of taking jobs away from men."
>
> "I shouldna think his mother can have met many prostitutes."
>
> "No, I don't imagine. Nor all that many women with jobs, either. But when he said that, Brianna stood up and said in a very loud voice, 'Well, you'd better be glad my mama's a doctor, because you're going to need one!' Then she hit him on the head with her arithmetic book, and when he lost his balance and fell down, she jumped on his stomach and punched him in the mouth."
>
> I could feel his chest and stomach quivering against my back.
>
> "Oh, braw lassie! Did the schoolmaster not tawse her for it, though?"
>
> "They don't beat children in school. She had to write a letter of apology to the little beast, but then, he had to write one to me, and she thought that was a fair exchange. The more embarrassing part was that it turned out his father was a doctor too; one of my colleagues at the hospital."
>
> "I wouldna suppose you'd taken a job he'd wanted?"
>
> "How did you guess?" (*The Drums of Autumn,* ch. 21).

Brianna is warrior, hunter, and engineer – more blatantly taking on men's roles than Claire. She always has a knife. Roger thinks admiringly about the "buffalo-hunting, turkey-shooting, goddess – huntress, pirate-killing side of her" (*Echo in the Bone* cg. 16). As a child, she learns to shoot as well as ride. He also thinks, "The girl that stood on the hearthrug, hissing and spitting in defense of her paternity, flamed with the wild strength that had brought the Highland warriors down on their enemies like shrieking banshees" (*Dragonfly in Amber,* ch. 47). When kidnapped, she immediately fashions a weapon:

> They'd taken away the fouled dress, and left her in shift and stays. Well, that was something. She pulled off the stays, and by picking at the ends of the stitching, extracted the busk – a flat, twelve-inch strip of ivory that ran from sternum to navel. A better weapon than a hairbrush, she thought. She took it over to the chimney, and began to rasp the end against the brick, sharpening its point.
>
> Could she stab someone with it? Oh, yes, she thought fiercely. And please let it be Emmanuel. (*A Breath of Snow and Ashes*, ch. 107)

It's in the 1980s, however, that Brianna encounters the most prejudice, as she applies for a job as hydroelectric plant inspector and the hiring manager only offers her a job as secretary. She gets herself the better job, but is subjected to acts of brutal hazing as her crew lock her in the dark tunnels and giggle outside "like little boys" (*An Echo in the Bone* ch. 27). She notes that it was her time as a mother that alerted her that something was wrong, thanks to the men's "looks of secretive delight or prenatural innocence" (ch. 27). Rob Cameron subjects her to slight sexual harassment, looking her up and down on meeting her and calling her "hen," as Roger does on occasion. However, he reveals his dangerous side when he assaults her, luring her husband away then attempting to rape her. As he notes, she's been sticking it to him professionally so he may as well return the favor. She fights him off with war cries and her son's cricket bat.

She wears jeans to work, echoing the buckskin trousers she wore in the eighteenth century. Both allow her to claim a masculine identity and role in the traditionally male workplace.

> The transvestite wears clothes which signify a different sexuality, a sexuality which, for the woman, allows a mastery over the image and the very possibility of attaching the gaze to desire. Clothes make the man, as they say. Perhaps this explains the ease with which women can slip into male clothing. As both Freud and Cixous point out, the woman seems to be more bisexual than the man. ...
>
> While the male is locked into sexual identity, the female can at least pretend that she is other – in fact, sexual mobility would seem to be a distinguishing feature of femininity in its cultural construction. Hence, transvestism would be fully recuperable. The idea seems to be this: it is understandable that women would want to be men, for everyone wants to be elsewhere than in the feminine position. (Silverman 139).

Trousers protect Brianna while traveling, giving her male authority. To give her medical book a similar authority, Claire writes it as C.E.B Fraser, M.D., with a masculinized portrait of herself. Thus she changes identity for her contribution to history.

Jamie refuses to teach Claire to use a pistol and she assumes he thinks "women aren't bright enough to understand the workings of a gun" (*Outlander* ch 18). He's forced to tell her that the recoil could literally knock her teeth out – this is a dense weapon from centuries before what she's used to. She reluctantly accepts his judgment.

Nonetheless, Brianna and occasionally Claire claim male power in trousers while going on long expeditions. Jamie is nonplussed but indulgent of this behavior:

> He did laugh then, and bending, kissed me thoroughly, his hands carefully exploring the outlines of my rear, snugly

> confined in buckskin. He squeezed gently, making me squirm against him.
> "Take them off," he said, pausing for air.
> "But, I –"
> "Take them off," he repeated firmly. He stepped back and tugged loose the lacing of his flies. "Ye can put them back on again after, Sassenach, but if there's flinging and ravishing to be done, it'll be me that does it, aye?" (*The Drums of Autumn,* ch. 13)

Roger too admires his strong career woman, requesting Brianna wear her hard hat to bed. Both women can "wear the pants" in their relationships as well as in public.

Promiscuous Heroines

Of course, Claire also worries over her lack of femininity. In France, she sighs that while Jamie describes a woman he once admired as "graceful as the wind," he's unlikely to describe her that way. He retorts that while she's not, "I talk to you as I talk to my own soul" and "your face is my heart" (*Dragonfly in Amber,* ch. 11).

Her story appears within something many readers and viewers label "women's fiction" or even "romance." Nonetheless, this does not stop Claire's story from being inspirational:

> Another important, and perhaps most controversial, of the attractions of romance is the theme of female empowerment. Contrary to popular misconceptions, romances are not about submissive heroines who give up everything for the hero. In fact, they are not about women giving up at all. They are stories of women who win, who get what they want, and who tame the hero in the process. As Krentz says, "With courage, intelligence, and gentleness she brings the most dangerous creature on earth, the human male, to his knees. More than that, she forces him to acknowledge her power as a woman." This aspect of the romance makes the genre one of the most subversive genres of all literatures, because in affirming the

> empowerment of women, romances invert the traditional patriarchal, male-dominated order and allow women to be "heroes" in their own right.
>
> Even though it is not always acknowledged openly, romances also appeal because they are sensual, sexual fantasies for women. Written primarily by women for women, these novels describe relationships, romance, and sex in ways with which women can identify; and while this is rarely the primary reason a woman reads a romance or enjoys a particular author, it is a factor that needs to be recognized. (Ramsdell 20)

In a world that has too long insisted that men should brag about sex while the chaste, proper women refuse it, it's a triumph to see Claire deciding what she wants sexually and finding two men who will give it to her at her direction.

"*Outlander* exerts a mysterious pull, both in book and television form. In part that's because it's so unapologetic about the nature of lust" (Hughes). The book begins with Claire going on an outing with Frank without her underwear as she intends to have sex. The first episode of the show has her doing the same, plus pushing Frank down so he can give her oral sex. Balfe notes:

> What was really important for us, and this was something we talked about with Ron from the beginning, is that we want to show that Claire owns her own sexuality. I think that's why we liked that scene, and we liked that she was the one sort of asking for it, and she was the one directing Frank what to do, and I think it shows quite an important side of her character. Like we're so used to seeing women being objectified, and as objects of desire of men, but it is very rare when you see a woman owning her own sexuality, and directing it, or orchestrating the sequence of events! I think that's one of the very cool things about Claire, and it's not a big issue or a big deal to her. It's just a part of who she is. She's just a very passionate person, and that manifests sexually and in every other aspect of her life. Claire is asking for pleasure, and that's the modern thing about her. (Vineyard, "Caitriona Balfe")

Significantly, Claire has had sex before, with Frank, and thus becomes Jamie's sexual tutor. She even had her first kiss much younger than Jamie's fifteen.

> "And what of you, my bonny Sassenach?" he asked, grinning. "Did ye have the wee laddies panting at your heels, or were ye shy and maidenly?"
> "A bit less than you," I said circumspectly. "I was eight."
> "Jezebel. Who was the lucky lad?"
> "The dragoman's son. That was in Egypt. He was nine."
> "Och, well, you're no to blame then. Led astray by an older man. And a bloody heathen, no less." (*Outlander,* ch. 28)

Jamie in turn is thrilled that Claire finds pleasure in going to bed with him, telling her, "I will tell you this: it is a gift and a wonder to me, to know that I can please you—that your body can rouse to mine. I hadna thought of such a thing—beforehand" (ch. 16). He's perfectly happy being her student and relying on her experience.

It's unclear whether Claire has slept with other men, especially during the war. She notes: "I had not slept with many men other than my husband, but I had noticed before that to sleep, actually sleep with someone did give this sense of intimacy, as though your dreams had flowed out of you to mingle with his and fold you both in a blanket of unconscious knowing" (*Outlander,* ch. 4). Later she adds: "I had kissed my share of men, particularly during the war years, when flirtation and instant romance were the light-minded companions of death and uncertainty" (ch. 16). In *An Echo in the Bone,* Claire more specifically suggests aloud that she's slept with men other than Frank and Jamie. When asked if this matters to Jamie, he responds that he's not sure (ch. 79). Claire deliberately doesn't confirm or deny the idea.

In all these moments, Claire emphasizes her

sexual autonomy – she can sleep with men outside of marriage as a liberated woman. It's the more reserved and emotional Jamie who chooses not to, for the most part. (In *Voyager,* he tells Claire that he hasn't precisely been a monk when desperate enough, though he appears to have had very few encounters with Mary McNab, Geneva Dunsany, and Laoghire, all of which were the women's idea.) Claire also uses her experience as a tool. She and Jamie are both comfortable with a relationship in which she can teach him, and she passes her knowledge on to the next generation later.

Claire is framed as able to take care of herself, but the wartime climate also saw relaxed sexual rules– anyone might die at any time, so indiscretion could be excused. One young woman wrote, "It was more permissive during the war. It was wartime and you didn't know if you were going to die" (Goodman 95). At the same time, servicemen often felt that any woman in uniform was a legitimate target for sexual harassment, seduction, and worse, and the double standard still existed. "The presence of women in previously constructed masculine spaces and/or working in mixed gender occupations made them targets for the label of amateur prostitute" (Goodman 92).

Meanwhile, separation from their wives for years at a time made men's having girlfriends or sleeping with prostitutes more socially acceptable. Frank does not admit clearly whether he has done so, but Claire suspects. Of course, such moments were common during the war, for both genders: "There was a four-fold increase in the number of divorce petitions filed for adultery between 1939 and 1945, and whereas before the was over half the petition had been filed by wives, in 1945, 58% came from husbands" (Braybon and Summerfield 214).

A probation officer of World War II commented,

"Many excellent young mothers have been unable to stand the loneliness at home...Hasty war marriages on embarkation leave, sometimes between comparative strangers, with a few days or weeks of married life, have left both parties with little sense of responsibility towards one another" (Braybon and Summerfield 214). While Claire and Frank wed before the war, they suffer from this condition after, as "strangers to each other" who haven't had much married life together. Thus Claire begins the first book seeking to sexually and emotionally reconnect with her husband, then finds a more mutual relationship soon after.

Brianna grows up in the sixties and takes advantage of the sexual revolution. She tells Roger straightforwardly that she wants to have sex with him, but when he discovers she's unsure about marrying him, he withdraws at once. He is the one to say they can only have sex if it means permanent commitment. Brianna makes choices as she wishes, though her family in the Enlightenment Age are less certain:

> "He said ye wanted him; that ye'd asked him to take your maidenheid," Ian said. He spoke coolly, his eyes on Brianna.
>
> She drew in breath with a ragged sound, like paper being torn.
>
> "I did."
>
> I glanced involuntarily at Jamie. His eyes were closed, his teeth fixed in his lip.
>
> Ian made a shocked sound, and Brianna drew back a hand like lightning and slapped him across the face.
>
> He jerked back, lost his balance, and half fell off the bench. He grabbed the edge of the table and staggered to his feet.
>
> "How?" he shouted, his face contorted in sudden anger. "How could ye do such a thing? I told Uncle Jamie that ye'd never play the whore, never! But it's true, isn't it?"
>
> She was on her feet like a leopard, her cheeks gone from white to blazing fury in a second.

> "Well, damn you for a self-righteous prig, Ian! Who gave you the right to call me a whore?"
>
> "Right?" He sputtered for a moment, at a loss for words. "I – you – he –"
>
> Before I could intervene, she drew back a fist and punched him hard in the pit of the stomach. With a look of intense surprise, he sat down hard on the floor, mouth open like a suckling pig. (*The Drums of Autumn* ch. 50).

She makes her own choices and won't be judged by the men around her.

Mothers

Claire's story is intertwined heavily with motherhood from the third book on as her story offers many snapshots of changing diapers, telling Brianna *A Christmas Carol* when they're stranded in the snow, giving her class a lecture about hygiene, and so on. When Claire leaves Brianna, she gives her a touching letter of love that calls Brianna "perfect and wonderful" and adds, "You are worth everything - and more" (*Voyager,* ch. 42).

When Frank announces he's moving to England and taking Bree, Claire's anger is for what Bree wants, while Frank is only concerned with himself and his relationship with Claire – to say nothing of possessiveness. Claire trusts their daughter's choices, Frank does not:

> "Not one I expect she wants," I said. "She won't want to leave her friends, especially not just before graduation. And certainly not to go to an English boarding school!" I shuddered at the thought. I had come within inches of being immured in just such a school as a child; the scent of the hospital cafeteria sometimes evoked memories of it, complete with the waves of terrified helplessness I had felt when Uncle Lamb had taken me to visit the place.
>
> "A little discipline never hurt anyone," Frank said. He had recovered his temper, but the lines of his face were still tight. "Might have done you some good." He waved a hand, dismissing the topic. "Let that be. Still, I've decided to go back to England permanently. I've a good position offered

> at Cambridge, and I mean to take it up. You won't leave the hospital, of course. But I don't mean to leave my daughter behind."
>
> "Your daughter?" I felt momentarily incapable of speech. So he had a new job all set, and a new mistress to go along. He'd been planning this for some time, then. A whole new life – but not with Brianna.
>
> "My daughter," he said calmly. "You can come to visit whenever you like, of course…"
>
> "You…bloody…bastard!" I said.
>
> "Do be reasonable, Claire." He looked down his nose, giving me Treatment A, long-suffering patience, reserved for students appealing failing grades. "You're scarcely ever home. If I'm gone, there will be no one to look after Bree properly."
>
> "You talk as though she's eight, not almost eighteen! For heaven's sake, she's nearly grown."
>
> "All the more reason she needs care and supervision," he snapped. "If you'd seen what I'd seen at the university – the drinking, the drugging, the…"
>
> "I do see it," I said through my teeth. "At fairly close range in the emergency room. Bree is not likely to –"
>
> "She damn well is! Girls have no sense at that age – she'll be off with the first fellow who –"
>
> "Don't be idiotic! Bree's very sensible. Besides, all young people experiment, that's how they learn. You can't keep her swaddled in cotton wool all her life." (*Voyager* ch 19)

Book three climaxes with Claire killing to protect her daughter, emphasizing a mother's ferocity. In later books, Brianna shoots her assailant in the crotch and even sweet, sheltered Marsali shoots to defend herself and her babies. Book eight describes "Marsali wi' a horse pistol in her hand, and her two wee lasses behind her, fierce as archangels, each with a billet of wood, ready to crack a thief across his shins" (ch 3). Both women are mothers, but far from passive.

Jenny rules Lallybroch as the perfect settled mother and finally grandmother, in contrast with wandering, restless Claire. She herds children, visitors, and tenants with perfect calm, a steady voice in the midst of chaos at Lallybroch. When Claire quips that Jenny is an expert dressmaker or perhaps brothel madam while dressing her for a seduction, Jenny responds, "I've got three daughters, nine granddaughters, and there's sixteen nieces and great-nieces on Ian's sister's side. It's often much the same sort o' thing" (*Written in My Own Heart's Blood,* ch. 6). After giving birth to one child, Jenny rides out to save Jamie, and moments after birthing another, she lies to invading Redcoats and protects her family as a tower of strength.

The series has heavy musings on motherhood, shared philosophy between Gabaldon (herself a mother) and her readers:

> But from the very start, there is that small streak of steel within each child. That thing that says "I am," and forms the core of personality.
>
> In the second year, the bone hardens and the child stands upright, skull wide and solid, a helmet protecting the softness within. And "I am" grows, too. Looking at them, you can almost see it, sturdy as heartwood, glowing through the translucent flesh.
>
> The bones of the face emerge at six, and the soul within is fixed at seven. The process of encapsulation goes on, to reach its peak in the glossy shell of adolescence, when all softness then is hidden under the nacreous layers of the multiple new personalities that teenagers try on to guard themselves.
>
> In the next years, the hardening spreads from the center, as one finds and fixes the facets of the soul, until "I am" is set, delicate and detailed as an insect in amber." (*Dragonfly in Amber,* ch. 4)

> "I've thought that perhaps that's why women are so often sad, once the child's born," she said meditatively, as though thinking aloud. "Ye think of them while ye talk, and you have a knowledge of them as they are inside ye, the way you think they are. And then they're born, and they're different - not the way ye thought of them inside, at all. And ye love them, o' course, and get to know them they way they are...but still, there's the thought of the child ye once talked to in your heart, and that child is gone. So I think it's

> the grievin' for the child unborn that ye feel, even as ye hold the born one in your arms." (*Dragonfly in Amber,* ch. 35)

> "Love for a child cannot be free; from the first signs of movement in the womb, a devotion springs up as powerful as it is mindless, irresistible as the process of birth itself. But powerful as it is, it is a love always of control; one is in charge, the protector, the watcher, the guardian – there is great passion in it, to be sure, but never abandon." (*Voyager,* ch. 35)

> "I have noticed," she said slowly, "that time does not really exist for mothers, with regard to their children. It does not matter greatly how old the child is – in the blink of an eye, the mother can see the child again as it was when it was born, when it learned to walk, as it was at any age – at any time, even when the child is fully grown and a parent itself." (*Voyager,* ch. 40)

> "A child was a temptation of the flesh, as well as of the spirit; I knew the bliss of that unbounded oneness, as I knew the bittersweet joy of seeing that oneness fade as the child learned itself and stood alone.
>
> But I had crossed some subtle line. Whether it was that I was born myself with some secret quota embodied in my flesh, or only that I knew my sole allegiance must be given elsewhere now...I knew. As a mother, I had the lightness now of effort completed, honor satisfied. Mission accomplished." (*The Fiery Cross,* ch. 32)

The dangers of motherhood also appear. In the eighteenth century "childbirth was one of the most dangerous thing a woman could do...Infection, ruptured placenta, abnormal presentation, miscarriage, hemorrhage, puerperal fever – in most places, surviving birth was roughly a fifty-fifty proposition" (*The Drums of Autumn,* ch. 48). Statistically, in the 1740s, roughly ten percent of women died in childbirth (though the starvation conditions of the time likely aided in this). By the 1750s and 60s it dropped to about 2% thanks to advancements in forceps and medical knowledge (Marshall 227). From 1739-69 childbirth accounted for 3.7% of women's deaths in the Edinburgh parishes of Greyfriars and St. Cuthberts, 557 out of 15,306. Childbirth was gaining medical knowledge. Only in the 1770s did Charles White of Manchester, followed by Alexander Gordon of Scotland a full twenty years later, insist that Puerperal fever, which carried off many newly delivered mothers, was infectious. Their insistence on fumigation and cleanliness finally managed to halt the frequent deaths.

Brianna's story follows her pregnancy, with years of tending to her small child amid the chores of daily farm life. She hesitates to have a second child then struggles with the difficulty of conception that follows:

> It had taken a true leap of faith, across the vertiginous abyss of knowledge, for her to put aside her dauco seeds, those fragile pellets of protection. But she'd done it. And nothing. Lately, she'd been thinking uneasily of what Ian had told her about his wife and their struggles to conceive. True, she had suffered no miscarriage, and was profoundly grateful for that. But the part he had told her, where their lovemaking became more mechanical and desperate – that was beginning to loom like a specter in the distance. It hadn't gotten that bad yet – but more often than not, she turned into Roger's arms, thinking, Now? Will it be this time? But it never was. (*A Breath of Snow and Ashes*, ch. 77)

Her day to day life as mother, carried on through the later books, draws readers into this world, celebrating all the tasks of motherhood.

Jamie loses his own mother at age eight. Nonetheless, she's quite significant to the story for her effect on Jamie and his family. He tells Claire: "My mother was verra learned – she was educated at Leoch, ye ken, along with Colum and Dougal, and could read Greek and Latin, and a bit of the Hebrew as well as French and German. She didna have so much opportunity for reading at Lallybroch, of course, but my father would take pains to have books fetched for her, from Edinburgh and Paris" (*The Fiery Cross,* ch. 18). After her death, she remains a presence, with her pearls and portraits to say nothing of the home she made at Lallybroch. At his wedding of the show, Jamie notes:

> Jamie: I plan to be wed but one time, Murtagh. So I'll do so in a way that would make my mother proud. What do you make of her?
> Murtagh: Mistress Beauchamp. She'll do.
> Jamie: I think my mother would have approved.
> Murtagh: Do I look like a gypsy to you, huh? Able to commune with the spirits? Have you still got your brooch? [laughs] Your mother had the sweetest smile. Would warm a man to the backbone just to see it. Claire's smile is just as sweet. Here.

He wears her brooch to the ceremony and gives Claire her pearls after. Nearly drowning in the third book, Jamie fancies he hears his mother calling to him on the isle of the Selkies. "I could hear her plain as day but I couldna see anything... I thought perhaps she was callin' me from Heaven" (*Voyager,* ch. 33).

William has a similar encounter, as he thinks the ghost of his mother appears to him in the fog at Helwater when he's little:

> He'd heard his mother – his real mother – whisper to him, too. That was why he'd gone into the fog. They'd been picnicking on the fells, his grandparents and Mama Isobel and some friends, with a few servants. When the fog came down, sudden as it sometimes did, there was a general scurry to pack up the luncheon things, and he had been left by himself, watching the inexorable white wall roll silently toward him.
>
> And he'd swear he'd heard a woman's whisper, too low to make out words but holding somehow a sense of longing, and he had known she spoke to him.

> And he'd walked into the fog. For a few moments, he was fascinated by the movement of the water vapor near the ground, the way it flickered and shimmered and seemed alive. But then the fog grew thicker, and in moments he'd known he was lost.
>
> He'd called out. First to the woman he thought must be his mother. *The dead come down in the fog.* That was nearly all he knew about his mother – that she was dead. She'd been no older than he was now when she died. He'd seen three paintings of her. They said he had her hair and her hand with a horse.
>
> She'd answered him, he'd swear she'd answered him – but in a voice with no words. He'd felt the caress of cool fingers on his face, and he'd wandered on, entranced. (*An Echo in the Bone*, ch. 36)

Majorie (Dolly) Roger's mother, is a point of view character for part of "A Leaf on the Wind of All Hallows." She is a stay-at-home war wife, tending their baby while her husband goes on clandestine missions in his fragile spitfire. Jerry's lucky ritual involves holding the lucky stone from their honeymoon and imagining her. Thus she's his talisman. The story follows Frank Randall visiting with the message of her husband's loss, a nod to the women of World War II and all they endured. She flies into a rage and rejects the medal, with a fully human response instead of the self-possession the British expected in wartime. The story ends with her death when in an act of blinding courage and faith, she flings her tiny son at her husband - shockingly returned to life and there before her. Husband and wife die together, but Roger survives.

When Lord John points out that women are famously changeable, even his mother Benedicta, her jilted fiancé Lord Stanley replies that "She is the most logical woman I have ever met. To a point that some would consider unwomanly" (*Lord John and the Brotherhood of the Blade,* ch. 16). When her husband is killed, she makes it look like suicide to protect her grown son from tracking down the murderer. She then runs off to France making herself a target to hopefully catch the killer. Through the series she speaks frankly of matters that horrify her sons and remains the steady matriarch of her family.

The intricacies of family life become a strong part of the story on Fraser's Ridge, with Jamie and Claire settled as they watch new families grow, along with many kinds of love and interconnection. When her engagement is broken, Lizzie is most devastated at losing her in-laws:

> Lizzie, beyond a certain initial mortification, seemed not terribly upset at the rupture of her engagement. Bewildered, confused, and sorry – she said – for Manfred, but not desolated by his loss. And since she seldom left the Ridge anymore, she didn't hear what people said about her. What did trouble her was the loss of the McGillivrays – particularly Ute.
>
> "D'ye see, ma'am," she told me wistfully, "I'd never had a mother, for my own died when I was born. And then Mutti – she asked me to call her so when I said I'd marry Manfred – she said I was her daughter, just like Hilda and Inga and Senga. She'd fuss over me, and bully me and laugh at me, just as she did them. And it was ... just so nice, to have all that family. And now I've lost them." (*A Breath of Snow and Ashes,* ch. 46)

Playing the Housewife

The capable housekeeper, Mrs. Fitz is a significant force. Murtagh mentions that when Claire is accused of witchcraft "Mrs. Fitz turned the castle upside-down, then, and made Colum send a down a man to the village" (ch. 31). She also nags Colum to intervene until Ned Gowan volunteers to go in a compromise.

Colum's lady Letitia is most remembered for obediently sleeping with her husband's brother to conceive a child. Nonetheless, she's a force herself. Jamie says on the show:

> Jamie: I'm laird, and you are my lady. We should both conduct ourselves as such.
> Claire: I'm not the meek and obedient type.
> Jamie: Don't think anyone would ever make that mistake, Sassenach, but then I don't think anyone would ever say the same of Colum's wife, either.
> Claire: Letitia?
> Jamie: Aye. Strong woman, respected, feared even, but she never crossed her husband's word in public. Now behind closed doors, let's just say my uncle dodged his share of crockery in his time.
> Claire: Be careful, my laird. I have a much better throwing arm than the fair Letitia. ("Lallybroch," 112)

The chatelaine or lady of the household was a powerful adjunct to the lord throughout Europe. She managed acres of land, crops and animals, along with often hundreds of dependents. The lady would defend the castle or even lead the army when her husband was away. She would supervise the preparation of huge amounts of food and other household goods, much like managing a small hotel and restaurant.

Balfe notes: "There's a misconception that women were much weaker in those times but when you get down to it, even if they weren't out fighting on the battlefield, they were definitely running the show behind the scenes – and I think that's true to this day. Women provide the strength at the core of family units, and in most endeavours you'll find a strong woman in there somewhere" (Virtue).

Book one sees Claire attempting to be Lady of Lallybroch. Ron Moore adds:

> I think it's a show that I've never seen before. It's a different kind of story. There's not a home base – it's not like there's the police station or the hospital or even the starship. The show evolves and continues and it's a journey. So even though Claire goes back in time and she ends up at Castle Leoch right after the first episode, she's not there that long. She's only there for a little while. Then she leaves and she's

> pretty much on the road and going to different places. So it's not like each show is similar to the one before. (Prudom)

Lallybroch is more romanticized as a place on the show, as Jamie has Claire's ring made from the key to Lallybroch so Claire will always know she's mistress there. About to send her back through the stones, he tells her stories of the place in a spun-out fantasy, and she agrees to go "home" with him, only to discover he means the twentieth century. When she returns from him, she offers the new line of "Take me to Lallybroch," emphasizing that she won't just stay with Jamie but will integrate herself into his "place."

This promise of a home means much to Claire: Claire has not yet had a home, thanks to her nomadic childhood. She and Frank had yet to build a life together, and she and Jamie camp as they travel, or stay at a room assigned to them at Castle Leoch, home of Jamie's uncle. In all this time, only their short visits to Lallybroch truly feel like a home. It bears strong traces of the feminine, with Jamie's mother's paintings on the walls, especially the self-portrait, and all her belongings about, from trinkets to garden.

> I had never actually had a home. Orphaned at five, I had lived the life of an academic vagabond with my uncle Lamb for the next thirteen years. In tents on a dusty plain, in caves in the hills, in the swept and garnished chambers of an empty pyramid, Quentin Lambert Beauchamp, M.S., Ph.D., F.R.A.S., etc., had set up the series of temporary camps in which he did the archaeological work that would make him famous long before a car crash ended his brother's life and threw me into his. ...
>
> The roving life had continued with Frank, though with a shift from field to universities, as the digging of a historian is usually conducted within walls. So, when the war came in 1939, it was less a disruption to me than to most.
>
> I had moved from our latest hired flat into the junior nurses' quarters at Pembroke Hospital, and from there to a

> field station in France, and back again to Pembroke before war's end. And then, those few brief months with Frank, before we came to Scotland, seeking to find each other again. Only to lose each other once and for all, when I had walked into a stone circle, through madness, and out the other side, into the past that was my present. (*Dragonfly in Amber,* ch. 31)

Claire's independence and social qualities reflect the new women of the Enlightenment. "At one time, their wives had remained safely at home, tied down by the cares of the household. Now, with long hours of leisure, the lady in town was apt to go her own way, spending her days in a round of pleasure which took her out to theatres and balls and friends' houses and gave her ideas about doing as she pleased and flouting her husband's wishes" (Marshall 189).

"Women's integration into polite society was dependent, at the most basic level, on their ability to travel" (Glover 164). Claire and Jamie usually travel rough, but Claire's entry into society appears most clearly at Versailles. "Access to travel signaled wealth and leisure, and more subtly, a familial culture that was open to the notion of expanding mental and physical horizons" (Glover 164). At the French court, Lord and Lady Broch Turach are exoticized from their far-off origins. The king admires Claire and Jamie plays politics with the men. Meanwhile, Prince Charlie's mistress Louise comes to confide in Claire, though she gives Claire a leg waxing and perfuming that revolts Jamie.

The French ladies are terribly modern, with piercings, waxing, and sophistication unseen in rural Scotland of the time. Thus Claire and Jamie find themselves at a new level of culture. Instantly, Claire must gossip with aristocrats and preside over perfect dinner parties as Lady Broch Turach, not just Jamie's wife. In one memorable moment, she holds a dinner party after being assaulted and nearly raped on the streets of Paris. As she adds, "What I wanted at the moment was peace, quiet, and total privacy in which to shake like a rabbit" (ch. 18). Nonetheless, she entertains and charms their guests, while teasing them for vital information.

Jenny of course has been lady of Lallybroch from a very young age. Jamie tells Brianna:

> "She was ten when our mother died, Jenny was," he said at last. "It was the day after the funeral when I came into the kitchen and found her kneeling on a stool, to be tall enough to stir the bowl on the table.
>
> "She was wearing my mother's apron," he said softly, "folded up under the arms, and the strings wrapped twice about her waist. I could see she'd been weepin', like I had, for her face was all stained and her eyes red. But she just went on stirring, staring down into the bowl, and she said to me, 'Go and wash, Jamie; I'll have supper for you and Da directly.'"
>
> His eyes closed altogether, and he swallowed once. Then he opened them, and looked down at her again.
>
> "Aye, I ken fine how strong women are," he said quietly. (*The Drums of Autumn,* ch. 48).

As Jenny points out in the book, obeying Captain Randall was the only thing she could do when he attacked her at Lallybroch. Nonetheless, she is a more practical keeper of Lallybroch than her brother:

> "Oh, disobey your orders, is it? That's what eats at ye, Jamie, isn't it? You know best, and we'll all do as ye say, or we'll come to rack and ruin, nae doubt." She flounced angrily. "And if I'd done as you said, that day, you'd ha' been dead in the dooryard, Faither hanged or in prison for killing Randall, and the lands gone forfeit to the Crown. To say nothing of me, wi' my home and family gone, needing to beg in the byroads to live."

While the book has them mend fences in their first conversation, the show has them quarreling for an entire episode as Jamie takes his role as laird but ignores all Jenny and Ian have been doing in his absence. Jenny insults Claire repeatedly, from calling her a trollop to quipping to Jamie, "Never thought you'd be so trusting of the English." In the book by contrast she tests Claire cautiously but is tentatively friendly.

Ian plays peacemaker, but Jamie continues to be a bad listener. Claire must finally shout sense into him:

> [Shoves him out of bed] Good. Now I have your attention. And you're going to listen to me. I did not marry the laird of Lallybroch. I married Jamie, but I haven't seen much of him since we walked through the gates of this place. ... I am speaking, and you can talk when I'm finished. Your father's dead, Jamie, but if he were here, I wager he'd give you a thrashing for the way you've been acting. You're trying to be someone you're not, and in the process you're wrecking the family that you do have left. And if you're not careful, you're going to lose them, too. ("Lallybroch," 112)

Jenny is the one to maintain Lallybroch while her untethered brother goes off on adventures. Jamie considers Ian the part of him that never left Lallybroch. Similarly, Jenny is like the side of Claire that stayed home and had babies instead of venturing into the world.

She's unworldly, never leaving her home, but keeping a practical competence about all matters of Lallybroch and also her family. The show has her running to warn Jamie of a Redcoat patrol, even while heavily pregnant. Despite her new baby, she goes with Claire seeking Jamie and only leaves when Murtagh comes to take her place. She prepares to hurry home in the middle of the night, over Murtagh's protests, telling him, "You see as far as the end o' your nose, duine, and that's short enough ... And if ye've lived so long without knowing better than to stand between a nursing mother and a hungry child, ye've not sense enough to hunt hogs, let alone find a man in the heather" (ch. 33).

In the eighteenth century boarding schools in

Edinburgh gained popularity. Jenny, however, does not go to the big city for increased culture. She remains within ten miles of Lallybroch for most of her life, only departing in the eighth book. She does however maintain education in small ways, with the well-stocked library of books her mother and brother have supplied. Reading varied wildly from household to household, but at the time it was one of the women's greatest means of participating in Enlightenment Culture. In addition, reading was a social activity, as men and women would discuss what they had enjoyed. Claire thinks to herself, "Alone among the Highland farms, I was sure, the women of Lallybroch waulked their wool not only to the old traditional chants but also to the rhythms of Molière and Piron" (*Dragonfly in Amber,* ch. 34). Of course, Jenny's ties to home can also be a threat, as she urges Jamie to remarry a local woman so he'll always return to the Highlands.

In book four, Claire and Jamie settle down permanently, after three books of traveling and field doctoring. Upon doing so, Claire suddenly becomes housewife as well as doctor, and is seen doing the house's cooking while Jamie and Ian build and hunt. She sews everyone's clothes though "sewing was not my favorite occupation" (*The Drums of Autumn,* ch. 21).

> Jamie had been simultaneously shocked and amused to find that I didn't know how to knit. The question had never arisen at Lallybroch, where Jenny and the female servants kept everyone in knitted goods. I had taken on the chores of stillroom and garden, and never dealt with needlework beyond the simplest mending.
>
> "Ye canna clickit at all?" he said incredulously. "And what did ye do for your winter stockings in Boston, then?"
>
> "Bought them," I said.
>
> He had looked elaborately around the clearing where we had been sitting, admiring the half-finished cabin.

> "Since I dinna see any shops about, I suppose ye'd best learn, aye?"

To her embarrassment and surprise, Jamie and Young Ian teach her, as both have done so all their lives:

> And so he and Ian – who, it turned out, could also knit and was prostrated by mirth at my lack of knowledge – had taught me the simple basics of knit and purl, explaining, between snorts of derision over my efforts, that in the Highlands all boys were routinely taught to knit, that being a useful occupation well suited to the long idle hours of herding sheep or cattle on the shielings.
>
> "Once a man's grown and has a wife to do for him, and a lad of his own to mind the sheep, he maybe doesna make his own stockings anymore," Ian had said, deftly executing the turn of a heel before handing me back the stocking, "but even wee laddies ken how, Auntie." (*The Drums of Autumn,* ch. 28)

Claire also gathers berries, nuts, and plants for their dinner and makes cake out of nut flour. "Ye should *see* what Uncle Jamie and I have been eaten' while ye've been gone," Young Ian tells her (*The Drums of Autumn,* ch. 23).

One might make the case that Claire is less experienced with hunting deer or building a cabin from scratch, so cooking porridge and shelling peas is the logical task for her, but being in the wilderness catapults her into a traditional gender role – the one with the dirty work. As she thinks after Jamie and Young Ian build a smoking shed:

> My only doubts were regarding the smoking. I'd seen it done in Scotland, and knew that smoking meat required a certain amount of attention; someone had to be at hand to keep the fire from burning too high or going out altogether, had to turn the meat regularly, and baste it with fat to avoid scorching and drying.
>
> I had no difficulty in seeing who was going to be nominated for this task. The only trouble was that if I didn't

> manage to do it right, we'd all die of ptomaine poisoning. (*The Drums of Autumn,* ch. 19)

Caring for an ill Lord John and Ian, she's stuck emptying chamber pots and cooking dinner as well as making medical infusions, but she is hostess and the only well person in the house as well as the woman, so it's arguable which capacity she's acting in.

Marsali takes a similar role as traditional woman by the next book. In addition, she's given the tedious paid job of watching the mash for Jamie's whiskey. Her household has gender difficulties, as one-handed Fergus is unsuited for "man's work" like farming. As Claire thinks to herself, "Fergus could have been making supper... Not that he would think of such a thing, the little French layabout. Milking the goat was as far as he was likely to go in the direction of 'women's work'" (*A Breath of Snow and Ashes*, ch. 27). Thus Marsali, generally pregnant and balancing small children, must work out of the home with the mash as well to support the family.

In the fifth book, the Bugs come to join the household as factor and chef. Claire describes Mrs. Bug's excellent cooking and management skills as she "was sweeping children and debris out of the back door with ruthless efficiency, while issuing a stream of orders" (ch. 22). While Mrs. Bug hates Claire's mold experiments, she respects Claire and Jamie and runs their household perfectly. At the same time of course, she conceals enough strength to commit murder to protect her secrets.

With a motherly cook/housekeeper, Claire is freed from "women's work" to concentrate on her surgery and the production of penicillin and other medicines. She acts now like the lady of a grand household, busy as healer but also assigning orders to her cook/housekeeper.

On further adventures, she often combines her

household with Marsali's – she does some of the laundry and cooking but also puts out a shingle advertising her medical practice.

> It was the work of a few moments to acquire a small shingle with TEETH EXTRACTED on it. And within twenty-four hours of hanging out my shingle, I was proudly depositing my earnings on the kitchen table—which was also my herbal-preparations counter and Jamie's desk, as it occupied the center of our single room.
>
> "Well done, Sassenach!" Jamie picked up a small jar of honey, taken in payment for a nastily impacted wisdom tooth. He loved honey. I'd also acquired two large speckled turkey eggs (one of them filled the entire palm of my hand), a loaf of reasonably fresh sourdough bread, six pennies, and a small silver Spanish coin.
>
> "I think ye could support the family all on your own, a nighean," he said, dipping a finger in the honey and licking it before I could stop him. "Ian and Fergus and I can all retire and become gentlemen of leisure."
>
> "Good. You can start by making supper," I said, stretching my back. Stays did keep you upright through a long day's work, but I was looking forward to taking them off, eating supper, and lying down, in quick succession.
>
> "Of course, Sassenach." With a small flourish, he drew the knife from his belt, cut a slice off the loaf, drizzled honey on it, and gave it to me. "There ye are." (*An Echo in the Bone,* ch. 126)

Femme Fatales

Gabaldon's short story "Virgins" appears in the collection *Dangerous Women,* and it's soon evident why. The story follows Jamie and Ian, young French mercenaries in 1740. The pair are hired to escort a young Jewish woman to her wedding, though they're beset by bandit attacks. While staying at an inn, Rebekah bat-Leah Hauberger drugs Jamie and seduces Ian, only to escape out her window with her maid and dowry. By the time the pair track her down, they're too late to do more than attend her wedding to her childhood sweetheart.

Nonetheless, Jamie confronts the bride and tells

her he realizes she has orchestrated the bandits' attacks, in order to steal back her dowry bit by bit. Jamie confronts her "with a terse brutality" (522) of how one man she hired was tortured and killed for her scheme, then demands she at least return the precious Torah from her dowry to her aging grandfather whom she's robbed and betrayed. If she does not, he will tell her new husband "what a ruthless, grasping wee besom ye really are" (522). On his way out with Ian, Jamie compares her to a praying mantis, who kills her mate even while seducing him.

While Rebekah is the femme fatale, it's amusing how easily she dupes two hormone-crazed young men along with her grandfather and the story's other men. Her grandfather describes her as a possession, but she takes her circumstances into her own hands, writing letters in her grandfather's name and choosing herself a husband of her own liking. She wins in all ways that matter, though she parts with the Torah, as she fears her husband will learn of her callous cruelty enough.

In another Gabaldon short story, "The Space Between," Michael Murray has lost his beloved wife Lillie, and her sister Léonie climbs into his bed to seduce him, as she's pregnant with another man's child. She tells Michael candidly, "You were Lillie's husband...It couldn't be like that between you and me, and I didn't like betraying her" (218). However, as an unwed mother she would disgrace her family, so she feels she has little choice. Sadly, she aborts her child to free herself from the difficulty.

Back in Castle Leoch, Laoghire has likely never left her home parish and Jamie is attractive with his university education and adventures in France. He however, falls for Claire who's from a far more exotic time and place. The show exacerbates their conflict as she doesn't just betray Claire as a witch, but undoes her dress and begs Jamie to seduce her. Claire confronts her, adding to the show's catfighting just before Claire meets Jenny:

> Claire: Look, I know you have deep feelings for Jamie, and that when tender regard is denied, it can be very hurtful, especially in one so young as yourself. I even understand why your jealousy would be directed at me, even though I never conspired to take Jamie from you. The truth is he was never yours to begin with.
> Laoghire: That's a lie. Jamie Fraser was and is mine, and ye did us both a wrong past bearing when ye stole him away.
> Claire: You're mistaken, child.
> Laoghire: My poor Jamie, trapped in a loveless marriage, forced to share his bed with a cold, English bitch. He must have to get himself swine drunk of a night before he can stand to plow yer field.
> Claire slaps her.
> Claire: I shouldn't have done that. Sorry.
> Laoghire: Aye. I did put that ill wish 'neath yer bed in the hope it would make Jamie hate ye as much as I do. He belongs with me, and one day it will be so.
> Claire: I hope the price you paid wasn't too dear, because that will never happen. ("By the Pricking of my Thumbs, 110)

In book one, Geillis and Laoghire are foils for Claire – the bad wives or lovers as she is the good one. Her honest love and lack of guile contrasts with their schemes over and over.

Geillis is obviously the worst femme fatale as she weds her husband the fiscal for his wealth, sends it to Prince Charles to further her political goals, falls pregnant by another man, and murders her husband when he discovers it. She deliberately uses men, seducing Dougal so she can control him through his child. She adds that "Colum would have been better" but is "the one man in the world I couldn't touch with the weapon I had" (*Outlander* ch. 25). She writes in her journal, "Shall I kiss you, child, shall I kiss you, man? Feel the teeth behind my lips when I do. I could kill you, as easily as I embrace you" (*Drums* ch. 32). In the West Indies, "Mrs. Abernathy" repels Lord John as she shrugs off her husband's recent death. She swims in a pool without "banks of concealing reeds or other vegetation," body clearly visible in another offer of seduction ("Lord John and the Plague of Zombies," 340).

"It's great to watch these two women. There's so much tension and animosity between them in the beginning and then they slowly have to learn [to understand each other]," Balfe says of her growing relationship with Geillis. "Claire can be very judgmental and very 'this is black and white,' and I think she has to learn with Geillis that no, it's not black and white. There are reasons behind her actions and there are reasons bigger than herself, and she really has to learn to empathize with her" (Prudom, "Devil's Mark"). Though Claire understands her friend's goals, she cannot share her methods – she refuses to charm Dougal or anyone else, treating her new husband Jamie with forthrightness and trust.

Jocasta Cameron from the fourth and fifth books is a less literal seductress, but she charms her nephew Jamie and offers him status as her heir and manager, in an act Jamie sees through:

> "I suppose it would be a great chance," I said, my voice sounding strained and unnatural to my ears. "You'd be in charge of everything..."
>
> "My aunt is not a fool," he interrupted, with a slight edge to his voice. "She would make me heir, but not owner in her place. She would use me to do those things she cannot – but I would be no more than her cat's-paw. True, she would ask my opinion, listen to my advice; but nothing would be done, and she didna wish it so."
>
> He shook his head.
>
> "Her husband is dead. Whether she was fond of him or no, she is mistress here now, with none to answer to. And she enjoys the taste of power too well to spit it out."

> He was plainly correct in this assessment of Jocasta Cameron's character, and therein lay the key to her plan. She needed a man; someone to go into those places she could not go, to deal with the Navy, to handle the chores of a large estate that she could not manage because of her blindness.
>
> At the same time, she patently did not want a husband; someone who would usurp her power and dictate to her. Had he not been a slave, Ulysses could have acted for her – but while he could be her eyes and ears, he could not be her hands.
>
> No, Jamie was the perfect choice; a strong, competent man, able to command respect among peers, compel obedience in subordinates. One knowledgeable in the management of land and men. Furthermore, a man bound to her by kinship and obligation, there to do her bidding – but essentially powerless. He would be held in thrall by dependence upon her bounty, and by the rich bribe of River Run itself; a debt that need not be paid until the matter was no longer of any earthly concern to Jocasta Cameron. (*The Drums of Autumn,* ch. 13)

Prostitutes

Prostitutes fare badly in the novels sometimes, beginning with the one killed by accident when Jamie gets in a brawl in France. Another is burned alive in *An Echo in the Bone,* for having pox. One madam notes that no one has money anymore and the men have turned savage. "When times are fair, so are men, mostly. But pinch them a bit, and they stop seeing just why they need to pay for their pleasure – after all, what does it cost me? And I cannot refuse, or they will simply take what they want and then burn my house or hurt us for my temerity" (*An Echo in the Bone,* ch. 17).

Gabaldon mostly regards them as people like any others, with honor, humor, and friendship. The prostitutes of Edinburgh are Jamie's friends and customers, who welcome Claire among them. Fergus of course is raised in a brothel and learns many practical matters of soothing women, fastening their garments, and even inducing labor.

Sexual healing is also emphasized: after his first killing, Young Ian loses his virginity with a prostitute. Jamie explains to Claire, "What a man most often does, when he's soul-sick wi' killing, is to find a woman ...His own, if he can; another if he must. For she can do what he cannot - and heal him" (*Voyager,* ch. 28).

Similarly, Rakoczy, the Comte de Saint-Germain, pays a Madame for exclusive rights to one of her prostitutes. He intends to impregnate the girl solely to give himself a child to anchor to - an act of unsentimental selfishness. However, after they sleep together, he feels "the rudiments of sexual magic" are taking place even without intention ("The Space Between" 206). Lying beside her, he revels in the mystery of her body as her egg and his seed combine and glow with power. He's tempted to stay and watch the miracle of life, but settles for treating her tenderly and promising her a house when she becomes pregnant.

John Grey's special friend Agnes, or Nessie, is a spy. He meets her while visiting a house of prostitution solving a mystery in *Lord John and the Private Matter* and is charmed by her Scottish accent. Nessie, at first a whore then a madam, respectably married, provides Grey with a safe haven in London when he needs one, as well as valuable gossip from her young ladies.

The eighth book features William's relationship with Jane Pocock. A prostitute who calls herself Arabella, she meets William just after he discovers who he is, when he throws wine at her and leaves in a fury. After, when the brutal Captain Harkness wants to terrorize her, William trades his gorget for an entire night with her and gallantly refuses to sleep with her. However, she seduces him and tells him whores have debts of honor as well. When she follows him to the army, she corners him while he's bathing and asks protection. While she does her best "to look winsomely earnest and doing it damned well," even charming William's horse with apples, she truly wants safety for herself and her sister Fanny (ch. 53). In a world where she and her sister have no protection from men, she humanizes the prostitutes' desperation. William continues to fight as her champion, even as he discovers dire truths about her. As he tells Jamie, she's not his love, but he's taken her under his protection. Their mostly nonsexual friendship echoes through the book, as Jane's courage and willfulness stand out even in the Revolutionary War.

Women and Politics

As Terry Dresbach notes in her blog (August 2014):

> [At the Gathering] Geillis is wearing an Arisaid, a Scottish woman's plaid. It is purely an ornamental garment, obviously, as it is made of sheer fabric, and clasped at the shoulder with a Lovers Eye brooch.
>
> I used a man's leather belt, with a jeweled buckle, at her waist, as both a nod to Highland men, and as a way to provide contrast to her delicate, translucent costume. Feminine, but dangerous.

Dancing for the Pagan gods, Geillis wears the same Arisaid, though without her hefty Scottish gown under it. The painted eye of the brooch comes from a portrait of Charles Stuart. This allows Geillis to show her loyalty subtly – most people would have no idea whose eye is painted on her shoulder. While the lover's eye jewelry was popular at the time, it too has an occult association, especially for modern viewers. At the witch trial, she reveals at last that she time-traveled to change history and make Prince Charles's campaign for the throne succeed.

Many women were involved in the Jacobite cause. According to Duncan Forbes of Culloden, "all the fine ladies, except one or two, became passionately fond of the Young Pretender and used all their arts and industry for him in the most intemperate manner" (qtd. in Glover 129). In the manhunt for Charles after, the man in charge, General Campbell, noted that "The Women in most parts of the Country are under a sort of possession, they depart altogether from their Character & really Forfeit the regards which are due to them" – by playing politics, he insists they had turned quite unfeminine" (qtd. in Glover 129).

Enemies of the rebellion emphasized how it made women intemperate and manipulative to the point of possession. They also trivialized the women's political fervor by insisting they were only attracted to the romanticized prince and his handsome face.

Claire meets few women in the first two books who play politics – even Charles's mistress is more concerned with her child than her lover's throne. However, on the eve of the Battle of Culloden, Claire discovers the legendary Jenny Cameron of Glendessary has arrived.

> It was she who had led three hundred Cameron clansmen across the mountains to join Prince Charles, when he had raised his banner at Glenfinnan on the coast. Her brother Hugh, arriving home belatedly and hearing what had happened, had ridden posthaste to Glenfinnan to take the chieftain's place at the head of his men, but Jenny had declined to go home and miss the fun. She had thoroughly enjoyed the brief stop in Edinburgh, where Charles received the plaudits of his loyal subjects, but she had been equally willing to accompany her Prince on his way to battle. (*Dragonfly in Amber,* ch. 36)

Historically, she is a romanticized figure, a famed warrior woman riding to battle with sword aloft. In *Dragonfly in Amber,* she is practical as well and efficiently organizes medical facilities for Claire.

Minerva "Minnie" Wattiswade is a delightful

character. She begins as "the seventeen-year-old daughter of a bookseller in Paris who dealt in information and more than once had carried messages between her father and Jamie, during his days of intrigue there before the Rising" (*The Scottish Prisoner,* ch 8). Minnie was busy spying when Hal, Lord John's brother, caught her one night, breaking into his desk. Instead of reporting her to the magistrates, he "had her on the hearth rug" instead. She disappeared the next day and Hal searched for her for six months. He at last found her in Amsterdam, heavily pregnant to his shock, picked her up and married her straightaway. She thus becomes Duchess of Pardloe and they have four children who are adults by the events of the later books. Through the Lord John books, she continues to be a resourceful information gatherer, even while a respectable wife, mother, and duchess. By *An Echo in the Bone,* Hal reports that if he doesn't take the recommended health cures, "Minnie says she will divorce me by petition in the House of Lords on the grounds of insanity caused by immoral acts" and he does as ordered (ch. 32).

When discussing the heroines of Culloden, the most famous must be Flora MacDonald, who smuggled the prince to safety. He dressed as her Irish maidservant "Betty Burke" in "a flowered linen gown, a light-coloured quilted petticoat, a white apron, and a mantle of dun camlet made after the Irish fashion, with a hood" (Bell, ch. 84) and sailed with her to the Isle of Skye on June 27, 1746. As Charles's secretary retells the story:

> Miss Macdonald was about twenty-four years of age, of the middle size, and to the attractions of a handsome figure and great vivacity, she added the more estimable mental qualities of good sense, blandness of temper, and humanity. ...As O'Neil recollected that Miss Macdonald had expressed, in his presence, an earnest desire to see the

> prince, and had offered to do any thing in her power to protect him, it occurred to O'Neil that, on the present occasion, she might render an essential service to the prince if, after dressing him in female attire, she would pass him off as he maid-servant, and carry him to Skye. O'Neil at once proposed his plan to the young lady; but she thought it fantastical and dangerous, and at first positively refused to engage in it. As parties of the Macdonald, Macleod, and Campbell militia were roaming over the island of South Uist in quest of Charles, as no person could leave the island without a passport, and as there was a guard posted at every ferry, and the channel between Uist and Skye covered with ships of war, the utter hopelessness of such an attempt appeared evident. Bent, however, upon his plan, O'Neil was resolved to try what effect Charles's own presence would have upon the young lady in inducing her to yield, and he accordingly introduced her to the prince. Miss Macdonald was so strongly impressed with his critical and forlorn state, that, on seeing Charles, she almost instantly consented to conduct him to Skye. She describes the prince at this time as in a bad state of health; and though of a thin and weak habit of body, and greatly worn out by fatigue, yet exhibiting a cheerfulness, magnanimity, and fortitude, which those only who saw him could have credited. (Bell, ch. 84)

Flora was arrested and imprisoned in the Tower of London but was released in 1747 under a general amnesty. She was even celebrated in London as having "still the Character of a Woman, possessed of all that amiable Softness of Temper and Constitution that adorn the Fair" but carrying "these social and endearing Virtues of Mercy and Compassion to an unreasonable Height" (Glover 132). Claire, however, is absent from this part of the story and only meets the heroine when she emigrates much later to North Carolina.

Older Women

Claire learns from several wisemen and -women who help to direct her toward her calling. Mother Hildegarde in *Dragonfly in Amber* welcomes her to the hospital and describes how she chose her life's path, one Claire admires:

> "There was something about that that appealed most strongly to me. 'An eminently useful life.'"
> She smiled at me. "I could think of many worse epitaphs than that milady." (ch. 15)

Mother Hildegarde runs the Couvent des Anges – the Convent of the Angels in Paris, where she insists on building L'Hopital des Anges, where she and her nuns minister to the poor. The church was another haven where women could gain power, even in medieval times. Mother Hildegarde thrives there, a virtuoso of medicine and music, living a life of service with no man to command her. Claire views her as a mentor in the second book. Gabaldon notes:

> Mother Hildegarde was another who named herself. Having decided upon her profession and avocation, I set out to write her, and found the name "Hildegarde" being insistently shoved under my nose. Nonsense, I said, I don't think Hildegarde is even a French name. Surely she ought to be Berthe or Matilde or something. But no, it was "Hildegarde" and nothing else. Fine, I said, already used to argumentative characters. Have it your way, Hildegarde. We can always change it later, if the copy editor tells me it isn't French. A year or two later, I found myself in London, in a store called Past Times, which specializes in the reproduction of art and artifacts from ... er ... past times. They had a rack of musical recordings, compositions dating from the tenth century to the twentieth, performed on period instruments and according to the performance conditions appropriate to the time of the composition. Finding this interesting, I thumbed through the rack, only to find a tape of songs composed by ... one Mother Hildegarde. Hildegarde von Bingen, to be exact (as I recall, my actual exclamation at the time was, "Ha! So it *isn't* French!"). A mystic, a composer – and an abbess – from the twelfth century. But Mother Hildegarde, nonetheless. (*Outlandish Companion* 137)

Later, Joan McKimmie joins the convent seeking

peace from her visions and vocation in God's service. Michael notes that her clothes are "like a soldier's uniform, no? Ye're doing your job when ye wear it and everybody as sees it kens what ye are and knows what ye do" ("The Space Between," 220). To him, women that work for the church are part of God's army, especially under the formidable mother.

There's also Master Raymond, who teaches Claire about herbs and French politics. Not only does she find a kindred spirit in him, but he seems to inspire her ambition. Claire says to Master Raymond, "I'm not a real physician. Not yet." As she adds to herself, "I couldn't have said what made me add that last sentence" (*Dragonfly in Amber,* ch. 20)

While both train her in medicine and herbs, their greatest lessons come from perceiving illness with senses beyond the physical – Mother Hildegarde has actually trained her dogs in this skill. Master Raymond of course can sense auras, and as he works on her body, she sees the traces of blue that indicate her own magic for the first time.

In *The Drums of Autumn,* the wisewoman Nayawenne of the Tuscarora tribe brings Claire a charm that she treasures and teaches her deep secrets of healing magic. Gabaldon explains why she incorporated this into the story:

> Since it *is* unknown, there exists an area of mystery in the realm of healing, which in some cultures is called "magic" or "shamanism" – but which is nonetheless an important component of the art of healing, regardless of the forms involved. For example, a modern doctor may under some circumstances dispense treatment that he or she knows has relatively little therapeutic value, but that nonetheless makes the patient feel better or recover more quickly, owing to the placebo effect....In other words, there is a magical aspect to the practice of medicine, and always has been, though this aspect was decried and ignored for some time. (*Outlandish Companion* 194)

Nayawenne teaches Claire about the plants and spiritual beliefs of the New World. The Tuscarora believe everything around them is part of an infinite web. Nayawenne also has dreams of the future, paralleling Claire. Her tribe calls Claire White Raven, after Nayawenne's vision.

> "My husband's grandmother says that when she dreamed of you, it was here." Gabrielle gestured over the pool, and looked back at me with great seriousness.
>
> "She met you here, at night. The moon was in the water. You became a white raven; you flew over the water and swallowed the moon."
>
> "Oh?" I hoped this wasn't a sinister thing for me to have done.
>
> "The white raven flew back, and laid an egg in the palm of her hand. The egg split open, and there was a shining stone inside. My husband's grandmother knew this was great magic, that the stone could heal sickness." (*The Drums of Autumn,* ch. 20)

Showing Claire a sapphire and giving her a special amulet, Nayawenne tells Claire that she will gain her greatest power when her hair is white. In fact, in the seventh book, when Claire heals Henry Grey, "He looked up at her, a great white bird" and she sees the blue aura. Gabaldon explains:

> It is quite possibly not coincidental that Ishmael (*Voyager*) asks Claire whether she "still bleeds," explaining that only old women can work real magic – nor is it coincidental that the Tuscaroran seer, Nayawenne, told Claire that she would achieve her full power "when your hair is white" (*Drums*). On the other hand, it was purely coincidental that Geillis Duncan's hair should have been a blonde so pale as to be "almost white, the color of heavy cream." Or at least I think it was. (*Outlandish Companion* 196)

Among many cultures, wielding magic was reserved for the elders of the community –women who could no longer menstruate were believed to hoard their personal magic rather than spending it on procreation. "Many cultures believed that by retaining menstrual blood within, the crone claimed power over her magical energy and became an awesome figure....The crones are mentors or soothsayers, prophesying the triumphs of kings and the downfall of kingdoms" (Frankel, From Girl to Goddess 275). Claire, in her fifties and sixties in the late books, has become a crone and wisewoman as well as a grandmother.

When Jamie is troubled, Calls-in-the-Forest, an elder of the local tribe comforts him:

> "Come and lie down, Bear-Killer," she said. Her voice was kind and gruff. "I've come to comb the snakes from your hair."
>
> She drew him unresisting to the couch, and made him lie down with his head in her lap. Sure enough; she unplaited his hair and spread it out across her knees, her touch soothing to his throbbing head and the painful knot on his brow.
>
> He had no idea how old she might be, but her fingers were muscular and tireless, making small, rhythmic circles in his scalp, on his temples, behind his ears, near to the bone at the base of his skull. She had thrown sweet grass and some other herb on the fire; the chimney hole was drawing well and he could see white smoke rising upward in a wavering pillar, very calm, but a sense of constant movement in it.
>
> She was humming to herself, or rather whispering some song, the words too indistinct to make out. He watched the silent shapes stream upward in the smoke, and felt his body growing heavy, limbs filled with wet sand, his body a sandbag placed in the path of a flood.
>
> "Talk, Bear-Killer," she said very softly, breaking off her chant. She had a wooden comb in her hand; he felt the teeth of it caress his scalp, rounded with wear.
>
> "I cannot call your words to me," he said, searching for each word in Tsalagi, and thus speaking very slowly. She made a small snorting noise in reply.
>
> "The words don't matter, nor the tongue in which you speak," she said. "Only talk. I will understand."
>
> And so he began haltingly to speak – in Gaelic, as it was the only tongue that didn't seem to require any effort. He understood that he was to speak of what filled his heart,

> and so began with Scotland – and Culloden. Of grief. Of loss. Of fear. (*A Breath of Snow and Ashes,* ch. 44)

Women among the Cherokee were equal to men. War Women sat on the Council, while kinship and living arrangements followed the mother's side of the family. Women also had the responsibility of torturing and executing prisoners, as they were the community mothers. They could take prisoners as slaves, adopt them, or condemn them as they pleased.

Young Ian finds a home for a time among the Cherokee. With them, Ian learns to cook succotash and strives to become a father, a responsibility he can't achieve. When his romance falls apart, he wants to fight for his love, but the women of her community and his tell him that once his lover has chosen to end it, he can do nothing. Brianna reminds him it's "All the mothers. The grandmothers. The women" who are against his union (*A Breath of Snow and Ashes,* ch. 70). As Ian tells the story, his wife's grandmother, Tewaktenyonh, appeared to him in the forest.

> "Grandmother," he said, and nodded in wry acknowledgment of her skill. Ancient she might be, but no one moved more softly. Hence her reputation; the children of the village lived in respectful dread of her, having heard that she could vanish into air, only to rematerialize in some distant spot, right before the guilty eyes of evil-doers. (ch. 70)

She doesn't tell him that his wife has found another or that he no longer belongs among them. "She had led him away from the village, through the forest, to the head of a deer trail. There she had given him a bag of salt and an armlet of wampum and bade him go" (ch. 70). Having no choice, Ian does.

The prologue of *Written In My Own Heart's Blood*

emphasizes aging, with allusions to the Bible and its emphasis on only telling the men's side of the story:

> IN THE LIGHT OF eternity, time casts no shadow.
>
> Your old men shall dream dreams, your young men shall see visions. But what is it that the old women see?
>
> We see necessity, and we do the things that must be done.
>
> Young women don't see – they are, and the spring of life runs through them.
>
> Ours is the guarding of the spring, ours the shielding of the light we have lit, the flame that we are.
>
> What have I seen? You are the vision of my youth, the constant dream of all my ages.
>
> Here I stand on the brink of war again, a citizen of no place, no time, no country but my own ... and that a land lapped by no sea but blood, bordered only by the outlines of a face long-loved.

By this point, Jamie and Claire have indeed become grandparents, the oldest generation in contrast to the young revolutionaries around them.

When she returns to the past, Jamie surprises Claire with the knowledge that she's a great aunt, though he adds, "I've never seen a great-auntie wi' a lovely plump arse like that" (*Voyager,* ch. 29). Aging together becomes a gift for them, especially Jamie, who has had so many close calls. "To see the years touch ye gives me joy, Sassenach," he explains, "for it means that ye live" (*The Fiery Cross,* ch. 85). By the later books, Claire herself is a granny and mentor to the next generations.

Jamie notes that age has made him fear death less:

> "I shouldna like dying, of course–but there'd maybe be less regret in it. On the other hand–" One side of his mouth turned up as he looked at me. "While I'm maybe less afraid for myself, I'm that wee bit more reluctant to kill young men who've not yet lived their lives."

> "Going to assess the age of the people shooting at you, are you?" I asked, sitting up and beginning to brush hay out of my hair.
>
> "Difficult," he admitted.
>
> "And I sincerely hope that you don't propose to let some whippersnapper kill you, merely because they haven't had such a full life as yours yet."
>
> He sat up, too, and faced me, serious, ends of hay bristling from hair and clothes.
>
> "No," he said. "I'll kill them. I'll just mind it more." (*An Echo in the Bone,* ch. 57)

He and Claire both outlive their parents and discover themselves trying to learn how to grow up without a model. Claire tells him, "You invent yourself ...You look at other women – or men; you try on their lives for size. You take what you can used, and you look inside yourself for what you can't find elsewhere" (*The Fiery Cross,* ch. 58). She and Jamie do well without mentors, often too busy with the concerns of the next generation to assess how well they still operate as a pair.

At the same time, Claire has anxiety over aging, especially when a younger woman covets her husband and insults her cuttingly.

> You're an old woman.
>
> See how the veins stand out on your hands.
>
> The flesh has fallen away from your bones; your breasts sag.
>
> If he were desperate, needing comfort . . .
>
> He might reject her, but could never turn away from a child of his blood.
>
> I closed my eyes and fought a rising sense of nausea. The hail had passed, succeeded by heavy rain, and cold steam began to rise from the ground, vapor drifting upward, disappearing like ghosts into the downpour.
>
> "No," I said aloud. "No!"
>
> I felt as though I had swallowed several large rocks, jagged and dirt-covered. It wasn't just the thought that Jamie might – but that Malva had most certainly betrayed me. Had betrayed me if it were true – and still more, if it were not.

> My apprentice. My daughter of the heart. (*A Breath of Snow and Ashes,* ch 80)

Both she and Jamie quest to come to terms with their aging even as they continue to shape history.

Goddesses

Many characters swear by "Jesus, Mary and Bride," emphasizing the female aspects of God in the Highlanders' belief system. Bride is explained as Jesus' midwife, but is probably derived from the Celtic goddess Brigid, incorporated later into the pantheon, as her religion was too strong to stamp out. She was "a Triple Goddess, a Virgin Mother, a Lawmaker, a Virgin Saint, and finally a folk image whose shadows still move over Ireland" (Condren 55). Unlike smaller gods and goddesses of places, Brigid-Bride was a large scale goddess of smithcraft and poetry as well as the maternal realm. Her popular worship spread through the Celtic world and out to Rome.

> There were several Brides, Christian and pre-Christian, leading to a confusion of legends as many tales and characters merged. The culmination of these was a Bride who presided over fire, art, and all beauty, *fo cheabhar agus fo chuan,* beneath the sky and beneath the sea. As Christ's midwife, she presided over the birth of man and dedicates each newborn to the trinity. When a woman is in labor, the midwife goes to the door, and standing on the *fad-buinn,* doorstep, with her hands on the jambs, softly beseeches Bride to come:
>
> Bride! Bride! come in,
> Thy welcome is truly made,
> Give thou relief to the woman,
> And give the conception to the Trinity.
> (Frankel, *Symbolism and Sources of Outlander* 125)

St. Ninian's spring, in the first book and the sixth episode, is a place of water magic and truth, revered as a refuge and source of blessing. All these of course are feminine symbols. Dougal takes Claire here to drink from the water as he asks whether she's a spy. As he tells her, "The water smells o' the fumes of hell. Anyone who drinks the water and then tells untruth will ha' the gizzard burned out of him" (*Outlander*, ch. 13). Later, Joan, who has the Second Sight, meets a young woman here and, using her gift of the sight, tells her she'll have a healthy child ("The Space Between" 221).

Standing stones, too, are a goddess symbol. The circle dancers twirl in spirals among the circle of stones – both shapes are feminine, in contrast with masculine straight lines and corners. Passing through an opening suggests birth as well as sex magic, as Claire uses the power to travel to another place and discover another self. Ancient people would visit the stone circles and walk through them seeking a similar regeneration, a practice that continues today. "Passing through large, pierced stones is a ritual commonly seen throughout the world's folk medicine traditions. In Greece and Scotland, women desiring children would wade into the sea and then pass through large waterworn holes in nearby rocks" (Varner 14). Lover's vows were considered permanent when the pair clasped hands through a stone's opening. In Saintongue, France, women "passed their newborn infants through holes in dolmens to guard them against evil, present and future" (Varner 15).

Jamie also encounters the Wild Hunt, a group of fairy travelers led by their queen in a moment of otherworldly sight. He hears "Horns. Like the blowing of trumpets, but trumpets such as he had never heard, and the hair rippled on his body."

> *They're coming.* He didn't pause to ask himself who it was that was coming but hastily put on his breeks and coat. It didn't occur to him to flee, and for an instant he wondered

> why not, for the very air around him quivered with strangeness.
>
> Because they're not coming for you, the calm voice within his mind replied. Stand still.
>
> ...
>
> They were closer now, close enough to make out faces and the details of their clothing. They were dressed plain, for the most part, dressed in drab and homespun, save for one woman dressed in white – *why is her skirt no spattered wi' the mud?* And he saw with a little thrill of horror that her feet did not touch the ground; none of them did – who carried in one hand a knife with a long, curved blade and a glinting hilt. (*The Scottish Prisoner,* ch. 37)

Fairies, while not precisely figures of worship, were always accorded great respect. They were originally visions of the dead who lived "under the hills" and might come out to steal or toy with the living. The fairies and Wild Hunt alike were often led by an unearthly queen, distant and powerful.

In *The Drums of Autumn,* the wisewoman Nayawenne of the nearby Tuscarora tribe trains Claire. The tribes of the area told creation myths of Sky Woman, whose body fashioned the earth:

> They tell a creation story popular on the East Coast of the Woman Who Fell From the Sky, or Ataensic. Sky Woman lived far above the Earth. However, one day she grew curious and pulled up a large plant that grew there, creating a hole. She fell far to the vast ocean below. Floating there, she watched as Turtle, Muskrat, and other animals brought earth for her to lie on. Soon after, Sky Woman gave birth to twins, one evil and the other good. The evil one burst through her side and killed her. While the good one created the sun, moon, stars, mountains, and many animals and plants, the evil one created darkness, monsters, and storms. This story parallels Claire, as she too, gave in to curiosity and tumbled through to a new land. More importantly, it establishes woman as the source of all life and knowledge in the world. (Frankel, *Symbolism and Sources of Outlander* 193)

Nayawenne, a leader of her community, parallels Sky

Woman as her own tribe's genocide and despair destroys her. She and then Claire must heal their two peoples, as much as possible.

In the Caribbean, Geillis smirks that the slaves worship the female form, displaying many small goddess statues and comparing them to pornography. While she's simplifying and being condescending about their religion, certainly many African traditions have a powerful goddess. Among the slaves, Claire and Jamie encounter their female seer, while Lord John has a mystical encounter with a snake loa, itself a symbol of Brigit and many other goddesses. As the snake was an ancient goddess symbol, patriarchal religion attacked the iconography – thus the Bible shows Eden as a paradise destroyed when Adam and Eve listen to the snake not the father-god. Likewise, St. George, St. Patrick, and other Christian heroes destroy snakes and their cousins the dragons. Along with this symbolic destruction came a more literal tearing apart of women's communities and status (Condren 24).

> As Merlin Stone notes in her groundbreaking *When God Was a Woman*, "Despite the insistent, perhaps hopeful, assumption that the serpent must have been regarded as a phallic symbol, it appears to have been primarily revered as a female in the Near and Middle East and generally linked to wisdom and prophetic counsel." Sumerians worshipped the great Mother Serpent of Heaven, and the snake was found coiled around many Great Goddesses such as Asherah, Ishtar, Athena, and Hathor. The Minoan snake goddess likewise dominated Crete, leaving behind figures of woman and snake entwined. The snake tempted Eve, offered prophecies, allowed Cleopatra's triumph. "The symbol of the Serpent was the one most widely used to represent or adorn the Goddess of the Ancient Near East or to depict, or mediate, the relationship between goddesses and human culture," explains Mary Condren in *The Serpent and the Goddess.*
>
> The snake reflected the Great Goddess, changing from young to old and then cycling back to young as the world

> renewed in the spring. It contained the insight only known to priestesses of the time, and it shed its skin, like a woman birthing a new organism from itself. Depicted coiled in several successive rings, the serpent mimics cyclical evolution and reincarnation. It coils sinuously as the seasons and the fluidity of female cycles, devoid of straight lines. (Frankel, *From Girl to Goddess* 69-70)

Circle Dancers, Travelers, and Witches

Mrs. Graham, leader of the Circle Dancers, shares her feminine magic with Claire in the kitchen:

> Claire: Well? Am I going to meet a tall, dark stranger - and take a trip across the sea?
> Mrs. Graham: Could be. Or could not. Everything in it's contradictory. There's a curved leaf, which indicates a journey, but it's crossed by a broken one, - which means staying put. And there are strangers there, to be sure. Several of them. And one of them's your husband, if I read the leaves aright. Show me your hand, Dear. Odd. Most hands have a likeness to them. There are patterns, you know? But this is a pattern I've not seen before.
> Claire: Oh.
> Mrs. Graham: The large thumb, now, means that you're strong-minded and you've a will not easily crossed. And this is your mount of Venus. In a man, it means he likes the Lasses. But it is a bit different for a woman. To be polite about it, your husband isna likely to stray far from your bed. [Laughs] The lifeline's interrupted, all bits and pieces. The marriage line's divided. Means two marriages. But most divided lines are broken. Yours is forked. ("Sassenach," 101)

Obviously, her fortune-telling proves prescient, as everything she says takes place. After, Frank tells Claire, there's "a local group that still observes rituals on the old sun-feast days." When they sneak off to see it, the book describes the beautiful solemnity of the dance:

> They assembled outside the ring of stones, in a line from eldest to youngest, and stood in silence, waiting. The light in the east grew stronger.

> As the sun edged its way above the horizon, the line of women began to move, walking slowly between two of the stones. The leader took them directly to the center of the circle, and led them round and round, still moving slowly, stately as swans in a circular procession.
>
> The leader suddenly stopped, raised her arms, and stepped into the center of the circle. Raising her face toward the pair of easternmost stones, she called out in a high voice. Not loud, but clear enough to be heard throughout the circle. The still mist caught the words and made them echo, as though they came from all around, from the stones themselves.
>
> Whatever the call was, it was echoed again by the dancers. For dancers they now became. Not touching, but with arms outstretched toward each other, they bobbed and weaved, still moving in a circle. Suddenly the circle split in half. Seven of the dancers moved clockwise, still in a circular motion. The others moved in the opposite direction. The two semicircles passed each other at increasing speeds, sometimes forming a complete circle, sometimes a double line. And in the center, the leader stood stock-still, giving again and again that mournful high-pitched call, in a language long since dead.
>
> They should have been ridiculous, and perhaps they were. A collection of women in bedsheets, many of them stout and far from agile, parading in circles on top of a hill. But the hair prickled on the back of my neck at the sound of their call.
>
> They stopped as one, and turned to face the rising sun, standing in the form of two semicircles, with a path lying clear between the halves of the circle thus formed. As the sun rose above the horizon, its light flooded between the eastern stones, knifed between the halves of the circle, and struck the great split stone on the opposite side of the henge.
>
> The dancers stood for a moment, frozen in the shadows to either side of the beam of light. Then Mrs. Graham said something, in the same strange language, but this time in a speaking voice. She pivoted and walked, back straight, iron-grey waves glinting in the sun, along the path of light. Without a word, the dancers fell in step behind her. They passed one by one through the cleft in the main stone and disappeared in silence. (*Outlander,* ch. 2)

Claire first sees the standing stones with the

dancers weaving among them. Their ritual links the story to older times and emphasizes a pagan magic present still. Mrs. Graham is their leader, she who inherited palm and tea reading from an older time and offers the ancient magic of the women (notably no men perform the ritual). In the book, Frank notes that the dance words are ancient Norse but the dance is "very much older." He speculates it's from the Beaker Folk.

The vanished culture of the Picts was matrilineal, and the Beaker culture, 2800 – 1800 BC, stretches back even earlier, following the Neolithic culture that built the megalithic passage tombs. On the show, the scene is filmed to be eerie, beautiful, and magical. As Claire describes it: "They should have been ridiculous. And perhaps they were. Parading in circles on top of a hill. But the hairs on the back of my neck prickled at the sight. And some small voice inside warned me, I wasn't supposed to be here. That I was an unwelcome voyeur to something ancient and powerful" ("Outlander," 101). The dance is of course a women's ritual, presided over by the female elders of the community. It represents a women's-only space and links the standing stones themselves with women's magic. Claire and Frank trespass and both their lives are torn apart because of it.

With unearthly chanting and ghostly shapes of women, misty against their bright torches, the scene is dramatically mystical. Certainly, this culture is not a part of modern Scottish belief, but with the emphasis on fairies and ancient teachings, to say nothing of lost cultures like the Druids, it certainly feels believable. The gauzy tunics hint at a *Mists of Avalon* culture of women's mysteries from pre-Roman times. Composer Bear McCreary explains creating the music for this scene with a Celtic harp and twined female voices:

> No music from the Druids survives today, and much of the music people associate with Druids today is based on mythology built up from pop culture, about as historically accurate as Spinal Tap. With no true piece to draw upon, I decided instead to adapt the oldest lyric from the region that I could. Adam found a number of contenders and I chose the one I felt matched the scene the best, the first stanza of a poem called "Duan Na Muthairn," or "Rune of the Muthairn." These were drawn from a collection by Alexander Carmichael called *Carmina Galedica,* published in 1900, that was at the forefront of the Gaelic revival movement of that time period. Translated into English, the text reads:
>
> Thou King of the moon,
> Thou King of the sun,
> Thou King of the planets,
> Thou King of the stars,
> Thou King of the globe,
> Thou King of the sky,
> Oh! lovely Thy countenance,
> Thou beauteous Beam.
>
> For the music, I composed an original theme, setting this text. I wrote it in the Dorian Mode, a scale I employ frequently for this show for its "old world" flavor, and elegant implied harmonies. Underneath the melody, I composed a distinctly modern harmonic progression to give the theme an other-worldly quality. Listen for the interaction between the F# in the melody and F natural in the bass line. Historically speaking, these scale tones would rarely if ever both appear in a folk song in A minor. With that, I had composed the Stones Theme.

In book four, Mrs. Graham's granddaughter explains that her grandmother was a Caller, "The one who calls down the sun." As she adds, "It's one of the auld tongues, the sun-song; some of the words are a bit like the Gaelic, but not all of it. First we dance, in the circle, then the caller stops and faces the split stone" and chants until the sun peeps through (*The Drums of Autumn,* ch. 87).

In the books, Gwyllyn the bard tells two

significant tales, first of the Wee Folk who stole Ewan MacDonald's wife to be a wet-nurse to their own fairy children, a parallel for Claire, now stolen away to doctor the folk of the past.

> "It was a time, two hundred years ago..." He spoke in English, and I felt a sudden sense of déja vu. It was exactly the way our guide on Loch Ness had spoken, telling legends of the Great Glen.
>
> It was not a story of ghosts or heroes, though, but a tale of the Wee Folk he told.
>
> "There was a clan of the Wee Folk as lived near Dundreggan," he began. "And the hill there is named for the dragon that dwelt there, that Fionn slew and buried where he fell, so the dun is named as it is. And after the passing of Fionn and the Feinn, the Wee Folk that came to dwell in the dun came to want mothers of men to be wet nurses to their own fairy bairns, for a man has something that a fairy has not, and the Wee Folk thought that it might pass through the mother's milk to their own small ones.
>
> "Now, Ewan MacDonald of Dundreggan was out in the dark, tending his beasts, on the night when his wife bore her firstborn son. A gust of the night wind passed by him, and in the breath of the wind he heard his wife's sighing. She sighed as she sighed before the child was born, and hearing her there, Ewan MacDonald turned and flung his knife into the wind in the name of the Trinity. And his wife dropped safe to the ground beside him." (*Outlander,* ch. 8)

Following this comes the tale of the wife of the Laird of Balnain. A man wandering late at night hears a woman singing "sad and plaintive" from the rocks of a fairy hill. He hears the words: "I am the wife of the Laird of Balnain, The Folk have stolen me over again."

> So the listener hurried to the house of Balnain and found there the owner gone and his wife and baby son missing. The man hastily sought out a priest and brought him back to the fairy knoll. The priest blessed the rocks of the dun and sprinkled them with holy water. Suddenly the night grew darker and there was a loud noise as of thunder. Then the moon came out from behind a cloud and shone upon

> the woman, the wife of Balnain, who lay exhausted on the grass with her child in her arms. The woman was tired, as though she had traveled far, but could not tell where she had been, nor how she had come there. (*Outlander,* ch. 8)

The story of course parallels Claire's own situation and provides her with hope – after their travels, the women usually return home. The show's version, told by Gwyllyn the bard, is even more blatant, with the woman finding a lover in a different time, then returning to her man at home. As Jamie translates for Claire:

> Now this one is about a man out late on a fairy hill on the eve of Samhain who hears the sound of a woman singing sad and plaintive from the very rocks of the hill. "I am a woman of Balnain. The folk have stolen me over again," the stones seemed to say. "I stood upon the hill, and wind did rise, and the sound of thunder rolled across the land. I placed my hands upon the tallest stone and traveled to a far, distant land where I lived for a time among strangers who became lovers and friends. But one day, I saw the moon came out and the wind rose once more. So I touched the stones and traveled back to my own land and took up again with the man I had left behind." ("The Way Out,"103)

This is the first fellow traveler Claire learns of, anticipating Geillis's story. Returning through the stones, Brianna also quotes, "I am the wife of the laird of Balnain. The fairies have stolen me over again" (*A Breath of Snow and Ashes,* ch. 120). As Claire thinks after hearing the song:

> "It was a time, two hundred years ago..."
>
> It's always two hundred years in Highland stories, said the Reverend Wakefield's voice in memory. The same thing as "Once upon a time," you know.
>
> And women trapped in the rocks of fairy duns, traveling far and arriving exhausted, who knew not where they had been, nor how they had come there.
>
> I could feel the hair rising on my forearms, as though with cold, and rubbed them uneasily. Two hundred years. From 1945 to 1743; yes, near enough. And women who

> traveled through the rocks. Was it always women? I wondered suddenly. (*Outlander,* ch. 8)

In book one, Claire and Geillis are the only travelers, and stories like that of the Woman of Balnan likewise emphasize women being stolen away. Thus the magic of traveling seems a female power. "Maybe it's only women it works on" Claire speculates. "It's always women in the legends. Or maybe it's only me" (ch 25).

Jamie cannot hear the stones – Claire hears the stones singing and feels their power, but he does not. Only in book two is it suggested that Roger has the power to travel as well, while Claire accepts it as given that Brianna likely has the power. She meets Master Raymond and learns more about the stones' power, but only after the stones' introduction through the female community. While Raymond has amassed significant book lore, Claire is seen traveling only by faith and love, fixing on a person, wearing only her wedding rings for protection, and going. Those who are more learned are greatly impressed by her natural ability. Women's powers are traditionally more intuitive, based in emotion or connection, while men's gifts, traditionally, are the product of logic and study. Claire takes the former path, but proves this can be the most powerful of all.

Geillis studies travelling and goes for reasons of patriotism – to change the past and fully develop her own power. She's seen studying the magic of spells and gemstones, and finally using blood sacrifice to fuel her rituals. In the past, Claire finds her a puzzle.

> "So it isn't a rumor, then, is it?" I said, smiling. "You really are a witch." I wondered just how far it went, and whether she believed it herself, or whether these were merely the trappings of an elaborate make-believe that she used to alleviate the boredom of marriage to Arthur. I also wondered just what sort of magic she practiced – or thought she practiced.

> "Oh, white," she said, grinning. "Definitely white magic." (*Outlander* ch. 25)

She appears to truly be a witch, as she believes in the standing stones enough to experiment with them. "They say I'm a witch," she said, widening her brilliant eyes in feigned astonishment. She grinned. "But my husband's the procurator fiscal for the district, so they don't say it too loud" (ch. 9). On the show she greets Claire by noticing the mushrooms she's picking are poisonous and adds, "Who is it you're planning to do away with? Your husband, perhaps? Tell me if it works, and I'll try it on mine" ("Castle Leoch," 102). Lotte Verbeek (Geillis) adds:

> It is interesting how much of it is actually witchcraft. Geillis uses her knowledge of herbs in a different way than Claire does. I found myself to be quite the herbalist; I found myself knowing a lot about it and if you live in L.A. and everything is in organic, that definitely puts you in contact with nature. There are modern witches – I think it's wicca – but witchcraft has a negative [connotation] and back in the day you could get burned for being caught in witchcraft and for being too much of a lightweight, for not weighing enough. In Holland there are scales in marketplaces where you could be put on the scale and if you were too light or too odd or different, that was a way to prove one was a witch. (Ng, "Lotte Verbeek")

Roger eventually discovers her journal. She writes, "This is the grimoire of the witch, Geillis. It is a witch's name, and I take it for my own; what I was born does not matter, only what I will make of myself, only what I will become" (*The Drums of Autumn,* ch. 40). Gabaldon writes that there's a real female witch named Geilis Duncane in *Daemonologie*, King James the First's book on witchcraft. She adds:

> Geillis Duncan was a conscious choice.... I liked the name – and had also seen a passing reference in one of Dorothy Dunnett's novels (which I much admire) to Geillis as "a

> witch's name." Little did I realize that the woman who bore it in *Outlander* had also chosen it deliberately, and for the same reason! She so informed me, sometime later, when she chose to reveal her real name – or what I must presently assume to be her real name – Gillian Edgars. (*Outlandish Companion* 137)

Terry Dresbach garbs Geillis in gowns that make her look like a fairy or nature spirit. Her mourning gown (also worn for the witch trial) is raven-like with a heavily feathery texture. The lace at her throat suggests wings. Likewise, Geillis's gray dress for her first appearance seems made of feathers or fur. Her Gathering outerwear resembles a filmy Greek tunic. Meanwhile, her coat in the Changeling scene makes her appear a wizard or elf with its high peaked hood and motley of scraps.

Moore describes Geillis as Claire's "one female friend" in the early part of the series ("Inside the World," 103), who opens her mind to a deeper reality. On the show, she insists, "There are powers beyond our ken beyond what we can see and hear and touch. Demon, fairy, devil doesn't matter what name we put on them." When Claire looks skeptical, Geillis adds, "Have you never found yourself in a situation that has no earthly explanation?" ("The Way Out," 103). Thinking of the stone circle, Claire cannot reply.

Book and show leave it ambiguous how much of a witch Geillis is. On the show she dances naked by the full moon and prays to her goddesses to let her be with Dougal. Immediately his wife drops dead. While Geillis believes her prayer had a hand in this, skeptical Claire calls it coincidence and points out that Geillis's poisoning of her own husband had nothing occult about it.

In the sixties, Geillis is seen getting involved with a group of ancient believers. Centuries ago, wise women ruled their clans with ancient lore and valuable healing skills. Many believe these teachings vanished underground but weren't abandoned, kept alive through communities like the circle dancers before becoming accepted once more as Neo-Paganism. Roger uncovers this spell in Geillis's notes:

> I raise my athame to the North,
> where is the home of my power,
> To the West,
> where is the hearth of my soul,
> To the South,
> where is the seat of friendship and refuge,
> To the East,
> from whence rises the sun.
>
> Then lay I my blade on the altar
> I have made.
> I sit down amid three flames.
>
> Three points define a plane, and
> I am fixed.
> Four points box the earth and mine
> is the fullness thereof.
> Five is the number of protection;
> let no demon hinder me.
> My left hand is wreathed in gold,
> and holds the power of the sun.
> My right hand is sheathed in silver,
> and the moon reigns serene.
> I begin.
>
> Garnets rest in love about my neck.
> I will be faithful. (*The Drums of Autumn,* ch. 40)

Roger notes that the four directions are traditional Celtic. "As for the blade, the altar, and the flames, it's straight witchcraft" (*The Drums of Autumn*, ch. 40). Modern wiccans sometimes use gemstones. They certainly use the four cardinal points, five points of the pentagram, and threefold triple goddess.

The show frames her as something of a Neo-

Pagan, praying to the ancient gods for her desires as she dances naked in a manner like the Circle Dancers and prays to Mother Nature with the Stones theme playing and a flashback to the scene for Claire. Bear McCreary, the composer, explains:

> Raya's voice is familiar by now: she is the singer of our Main Title. But, her approach to the Stones Theme is more ethereal, almost like a different voice entirely. The summoning cue begins as Claire witnesses Geillis, with a solo Raya vocal introducing the theme against the same harp and celeste backdrop I used in the first episode. When Claire has flashbacks to the dancers at the stones, I introduce a second pass of Raya's voice, singing a harmony line. Raya sings the same melody and lyrics as she did before (the lyrics are posted in my first episode blog entry), but this arrangement feels much more intimate.

In the moonlight, Geillis wears the filmy arisaid with Prince Charles's painted eye as the brooch – Geiliss's actress calls her nudity "very freeing" (Nemiroff). As the two women are hauled away for witchcraft, Bear McCreary adds: "Raya Yarbrough's vocals return for the end credits, providing a funereal statement of the Stones Theme. Unlike previous versions, this rests above an ominous bed of strings and low pipe drones. The end credits reference to the Stones Theme is meant to imply that Geillis' summoning ceremony will come back to haunt them both."

In book and show. Geillis emphasizes how the witch trials work – the primitive villagers, driven by mob rule torture and kill those who appear different from themselves. As Ned Gowan explains, "the worst of these trials take place in a climate of hysteria, when the soundness of evidence may be disregarded for the sake of satisfyin' blood-hunger" (ch. 25).

"Ye still dinna understand, do ye?" Geillis tells Claire. "They mean to kill us. And it doesna matter much what the charge is, or what the evidence shows. We'll burn, all the same" (ch. 25). The evidence presented is flimsy and inflammatory, based only on superstition:

> She and her husband had an ailing child, born healthy but then turned puny and unthrifty. Finally deciding that the child was a fairy changeling, they had placed it in the Fairy's Seat on the hill of Croich Gorm. Keeping watch so as to recover their own child when the fairies should return it, they had seen the two ladies standing here go to the Fairy's Seat, pick up the child and speak strange spells over it.
>
> The woman twisted her thin hands together, working them under her apron.
>
> "We watched through the nicht, sirs. And when the dark came, soon after there cam' a great demon, a huge black shape comin' through the shadows wi' no sound, to lean ower the spot where we'd laid the babe."
>
> There was an awed murmur from the crowd, and I felt the hair on the back of my neck stir slightly, even knowing as I did that the "great demon" had been Jamie, gone to see whether the child still lived. I braced myself, knowing what was coming next.
>
> "And when the sun rose, my man and I went to see. And there we found the changeling babe, dead on the hill, and no sign of our own wee bairn." At this, she broke, and threw her apron over her face to hide her weeping.
>
> As though the mother of the changeling had been a signal of some sort, the crowd parted and the figure of Peter the drover came out. I groaned inwardly when I saw him. I had felt the emotions of the crowd turn against me as the woman spoke; all I needed now was for this man to tell the court about the waterhorse.
>
> Enjoying his moment of celebrity, the drover drew himself up and pointed dramatically at me.
>
> "'Tis right ye are to call her witch, my lords! Wi' my own eyes I saw this woman call up a waterhorse from the waters of the Evil Loch, to do her bidding! A great fearsome creature, sirs, tall as a pine tree, wi' a neck like a great blue snake, an' eyes big as apples, wi' a look in them as would steal the soul from a man." (ch. 25)

Father Bain, the greatest misogynist of the community, arrives and publicly condemns Claire, twisting her offer of medical aid into one of seduction and curses. When Claire cries, "I am a healer" on the show, Ned tells her to stop incriminating herself. "I wondered, what made these good people so eager to watch us burn, regardless of the evidence?" she thinks.

By contrast, Geillis's claim that's she's slept with the Devil is only made to save Claire and cater to the superstitious of the town. Ron Moore notes that in this moment they establish that they're true friends as well as fellow time travelers – Claire refuses to sacrifice Geillis, but Geillis does so to save the other woman ("Inside the Episode 11 The Devil's Mark").

Geillis hypnotizes Claire with herbs and poisons her husband. In book three, she uses jewel magic for a variety of spells of control and seduction. Geillis also calls Claire another witch, insisting the ability to use the stones is a hereditary gift. Citing the infamous *Witch's Hammer,* she adds, "Some people can leave their bodies and travel miles away....Other people see them out wandering, and recognize them, and ye can bloody prove they were really tucked up safe in bed at the time...some people have stigmata ye can see and touch – I've seen one. But not everybody. Only certain people" (*Voyager,* ch. 60). It's unclear to what extent this is true.

Thanks to Geillis, Claire barely escapes with her life. However, by book's end, she's chosen to own the label and the power it brings her: "Witch I am. Witch, and I curse you. I curse you with knowledge, Jack Randall – I give you the hour of your death," she says (*Outlander,* ch. 35). When Colum asks, she flippantly tells him, "Better call me a witch...It's as close as you're likely to get" (*Dragonfly in Amber*, ch. 37). Later on, Claire calls herself a doctor or healer but admits she's more often called "wisewoman, or conjure woman. Or ban-lichtne" (Gaelic for female healer) (*A Breath of Snow and Ashes,* ch. 22). Dougal says, "Well, you're a healer. Surely ye believe in the powers of magic," linking the concepts (Episode 106).

Young Ian and his brothers debate whether Claire is a "ban-sidhe," a "conjure-woman" a "witch" or an "Auld One" (*An Echo in the Bone,* ch. 80). The people of Lallybroch all assume Claire is a supernatural wisewoman or fairy woman. Gabaldon notes that the Age of Enlightenment in the eighteenth century signaled a transition from magic to science:

> Consequently, there are echoes throughout all the *Outlander* books – superstition and magic resonating through the practice of rational medicine – that exemplify the unique attitudes of the second half of the eighteenth century. The Age of Enlightenment was a period of transformation, in terms of culture, society, and thought – magic, if you will, brought about by the power of reason. Claire, with her peculiar perspectives, personifies the practice of medicine, mingling the rational and the metaphysical, the traditional and the modern, in pursuit of the ancient goals of the healing arts: the preservation and restoration of health. (*Outlandish Companion* 194)

In episode eleven "The Witch's Mark," Ned Gowan insists that witchcraft trials ended in 1735 and the procedure is illegal. Claire comments in the book that she "had thought it a practice common to the seventeenth century, not this one. On the other hand, I thought wryly, Cranesmuir was not exactly a hotbed of civilization" (ch. 25). Witch trials were basically over by the time of Claire's arrival, though they took a terrible toll on Scotland. Between 1560 and 1707, over 3000 people were executed. Across the world, the numbers were far worse, as the church launched an attack on all wisewomen and women of power and status in their communities. "The story of the witches, or the genocide of women healers, is one of those epochs in human history so devastating and beyond comprehension that it has scarcely been touched by historians. Scholars are still not in agreement as to how many women were put to violent death; estimates range from one hundred thousand to nine million" (Condren 166).

> The Inquisition persecuted witches (literally wise women), who had always been bastions of advice and cures for the village. Many of their remedies had a psychic component, leaving them open to accusations of magic. These women were natural leaders of the encroaching economy, first feudal and then industrial, and thus Church and State combined to target them as obstacles. These witches were accused of casting spells, having intercourse with the devil, cursing men and animals, and (rather tellingly) causing impotence or painless childbirth. Women were meant to suffer, and men to be virile and rule the household; any attack on that status quo was deemed deviltry. Of course, those who claimed innocence were generally tortured to death, while only those who pled guilty were allowed to do appropriate "penance." The infamous water test in which women could only drown or affirm their guilt by floating was one in a series of grisly devices employed to rid the earth of wise women. (Frankel, *From Girl to Goddess* 289)

"I've yet to see the auld woman believes in witches, nor the young one, neither. It's men think there must be ill-wishes and magic in women, when it's only the natural way of the creatures," Murtagh notes (*Outlander,* ch. 31). This was gender war, conducted by the church's men.

In Scotland, a suspected witch was stripped naked and "cross-bound," that is, her right thumb to the left toe and her left thumb to the right toe, and then thrown in the water. If guilty, she would float, if innocent she would drown. When Claire protests this treatment, they whip her publically instead. As Gabaldon explains:

> I wanted to have a witch trial, but looking into it, I could see that the last witch trial in Scotland took place in 1722. So I was telling my husband that I'd really like a witch trial, but it doesn't fit. He looked at me and said, "You start right off with a book in which you expect people to believe that

> Stonehenge is a time machine, and you're worried that your witches are 20 years too late?" [Laughs] So I did stretch that point. I figured that possibly this witch trial was an ad hoc affair that didn't make it into the record. That's the only place where I can remember I deliberately moved something that I knew was not quite there. (DeLuca)

Thus as she tangles with Father Bain in the third episode, saves a changeling child, as the ignorant villagers think, and befriends the adulteress Geillis, Claire breaks the rules of society and is condemned by the ignorant, like so many before her.

Characters as Other

Nationality, Race and Religion

Queer reading emphasizes characters' deviation from the norms, as whatever their sexuality, they are subversive or defy traditional standards, thus serving as role models for those who wish to follow suit. Characters from Spock to Sherlock Holmes are "queered" in their portrayal, with their differences from the community emphasized, whether or not the characters are meant to be homosexual.

When a character teaches a different way to live or represents a different lifestyle as "Other," they promote a queer view. Lizzie with her alternate household counts, as do homosexual John Grey and the Duke of Sandringham. But Geillis, Claire, Roger, and Brianna are also "Other" for their unworldly knowledge and different way of living, especially as Claire and Brianna wear trousers in public and Geillis dances naked in the moonlight. Young Ian joins the Mohawk for a time and continues to dress and act far removed from his Scottish heritage. De Beauvoir observes that most cultures, and indeed, people, picture the Self and the Other – generally women take this second role.

Slave culture appears in the third, fourth, and fifth books. They of course are the most Othered of all, treated as property rather than people. They find their own ways of coping with the world. Several times this is sexual, as a male slave and his white mistress have a child together, or Lord John has a homosexual liaison among the slave cabins at night. Slave women seduce the white men around them to improve their position as Phaedre and Pollyanne, the midwife slave from book four, do. Claire thinks to herself, "Would I do differently? ... If I knew that my life depended on a man? Would I not do anything I could to ensure he would protect me, in the face of unknown danger?" (*The Drums of Autumn,* ch. 14). Fanny Beardsley, too, has a half-black child and abandons her to run off with her lover in the woods, leaving the child to collect her dead husband's property. Fanny and Pollyanne find safety and freedom in the forest, escaping society and its rules. The former lives with escaped slaves, the latter with the Cherokee.

Jamie, Claire and Brianna are horrified by the concept of owning slaves. While the women of course have African-American friends and colleagues in the future, Jamie's attitude is rooted in his own status as Other. Jamie has spent all his life as a Scot in an English-ruled country. After Culloden, he is branded a traitor, another black mark beyond his heritage. He has been chained and beaten like the slaves, dismissed as a savage like the Native Americans. When Jamie learns that all the slaves must watch a slave be executed to dissuade them from such attempts, he quips, "I believe that was the Crown's notion in executing my grandsire on Tower Hill after the Rising" (*The Drums of Autumn,* ch. 11). In his mind, African-Americans and Scots have faced similar hardships.

When he is a prisoner and convicted traitor, he labors all day and is whipped, as well as being subjected to acts of petty cruelty by the guards. He maintains what dignity he can, reminding Lord John several times that he will not be coerced to serve his captor beyond the bounds of the law. "I have lived as a slave, Claire," he says. "And I couldna live, knowing there was a man on earth who felt toward me as I have felt toward those who thought they owned me" (*The Drums of Autumn,* ch. 16). He is quick to free Lizzie and her father from indentured servitude, and compels no one's service on the Ridge.

Hal's son finds himself in an interracial love affair in the late books. "It was clear to me, as it was to John, that there was a serious - and deepening - affection between the free black woman and her aristocratic young lodger," Claire narrates (*Written in My Own Heart's Blood,* ch. 5). Claire notes that the woman's race is not an absolute barrier in Colonial America, though it is a problem, possibly less of one than her class: "I couldn't imagine that John's brother, the very firm-minded Duke of Pardloe, would be delighted at hearing that his youngest son meant to marry the widow of a carpenter, whatever her color" (*Written in My Own Heart's Blood,* ch. 5). Of course, the biggest hurdle is the uncertainly of war – the carpenter may still be alive.

In Jamie's time, Chinese, Blacks, and other races were treated extremely badly, as shown through the books. However, Jamie proves himself incredibly enlightened, defending Mr. Willoughby when no one else does and speaking to the escaped slaves of *Voyager* as equals. He learns to speak all their languages, reaching out to them symbolically as well as literally. Likewise, he welcomes the Native Americans as fellow warriors and allies. Other marginalized characters in multicultural America include the rare Polish and Russian immigrants who speak a little French but no English. Upon meeting both, Jamie sympathetically acts as translator.

As a university student, Jamie is acquainted with a few Jews in Paris, despite the stigma they bear. In the short story "Virgins," Jamie speaks with Jewish clients in polite Hebrew, and insists on returning a priceless Torah scroll to its owner rather than leaving it with the man's treacherous granddaughter.

William grows up in the ultimate state of privilege as one of the richest and most eligible men in England. However, like the red hair that grows where no one can see it, he has a shameful secret. Roger notes than learning the truth of his heritage, as he finally does "would force him to live in a state of deceit and denial, which would eat him alive" as he would publicly claim a title he knew he didn't deserve (*An Echo in the Bone,* ch. 85)

On the Ridge, Jamie's Catholicism makes him vulnerable to being thrown out by Governor Tryon if he doesn't obey the man's commands, even while Jamie is ultimate authority of his own people. The Protestant-Catholic split is prominent there, though Jamie and Roger attempt to bridge the gap through example of their cross-religious partnership. Brianna has a little public difficulty with her own mixed marriage, though she and Roger find a friendly compromise. By the final books Quakers are introduced – characters who reject wealth and status, speaking and dressing in a way that sets them apart as they turn their back on the Revolutionary War in favor of pacifism. Rachel and Denzell Hunter have further difficulties as they are radicals among their Quaker community and are forced out of Meeting for revolutionary sympathies. They too are inducted into the Frasers' community.

As America splits into Loyalists and Revolutionaries, British and Americans, where one community once existed, many characters find their status shifting as they decide whether to join the mainstream or reject it.

Disability

Several disabled (at least to some extent) male characters appear, as each finds a way to manage his condition. They too of course are Othered in a world of pioneers and hard labor. Jamie insists on providing for men who aren't "able-bodied" like Fergus and Duncan Innes and welcoming them into his community. He soon discovers another benefit to housing them:

> "Any man between sixteen and sixty must serve in the militia, Sassenach."
>
> ...
>
> "Hmm. So you're thinking that if you take the available men from the Ridge – can't you leave out a few?"
>
> "I havena got so many to start with, Sassenach," he pointed out. "I can leave Fergus, because of his hand, and Mr. Wemyss to look after our place. He's a bond servant, so far as anyone knows, and only freemen are obliged to join the militia."
>
> "And only able-bodied men. That lets out Joanna Grant's husband; he's got a wooden foot."
>
> He nodded.
>
> "Aye, and old Arch Bug, who's seventy if he's a day. That's four men – and maybe eight boys under sixteen – to look after thirty homesteads and more than a hundred and fifty people." (*The Fiery Cross,* ch. 12)

For this reason he recruits the Beardsleys – a fourteen-year-old hunter and his partially deaf twin, as they will be able to help provide for the settlement.

Back at Lallybroch, Ian of course is largely homebound with his amputated leg. He provides an excellent steward, but does not accompany Jamie on adventures anymore. When his wooden leg is stolen or broken, he's even more helpless, so much so that Jenny is the one to search the Highlands for her brother. Jenny comes to Jamie before the Rising and asks him to take Ian to war. She insists, "I'll have a whole man or none." She adds that she's a whole man to her "but if he thinks he's of no use to you, he wilna be whole to himself. and that's why I'll have ye take him" (*Dragonfly in Amber,* ch. 35). Nonetheless, Ian refuses Jamie's invitation and says he'll remain at Lallybroch, guarding Jamie where he's vulnerable. (This requires posturing and finally arm wrestling from both men to establish their male dominance.) In a later book, Jamie discovers that Ian switches Jenny, with her permission. Grannie MacNab helps him understand this, telling Jamie "that Jenny was only makin' it clear to Ian – and maybe to herself, as well – that she still thought he was a man, leg or no" (*A Breath of Snow and Ashes,* ch. 47)

Hugh Munro with his badly burnt feet and missing tongue helps Jamie and Claire several times. He tries to find Jamie a pardon through legal channels and finally saves Claire. Along with poaching, he apparently makes a good living begging at many different parishes, and has a wife and children he supports (*Outlander,* ch. 17)

Duncan Innes has lost an arm as, as he explains, "I tore a small hole in my hand wi' a nail one day and it festered" (*Voyager,* ch. 43). He is one of Jamie's men at Ardsmuir, set free to starve as with the arm lost he's deemed unworthy of transporting. Innes adds, "I should have been dead of starvation by now, had Mac Dubh [Jamie] not come to find me" (*Voyager,* ch. 43). In the New World, Jamie insists on keeping him as one of his men, while others call him unfit for labor. He even weds, though his revelation that he was kicked by a horse and is therefore impotent causes him to worry. The wedding takes place nonetheless.

Fergus is one of Jamie's top lieutenants, as close as family, though the English cut off his hand. In book six, however, he's rough with his wife, and Claire watches Marsali work in the whiskey shed all day with children to manage as well. At last, he despairs and tries to kill himself. Jamie explains to

Claire that Fergus knows he can't support his family as a farmer and wants his wife to remarry. Claire tells him "Don't *any* of you know? That it's *you.* Not what you can give or do or provide. Just you" (ch. 64). They finally find a useful occupation for Fergus as a printer and he begins a subversive rebel newspaper.

Lord John's friend and later lover Stephan von Namtzen has an arm amputated, and Lord John shows his lack of revulsion by kissing the stump, something Stephan truly appreciates. Arch Bug has lost two fingers, forced to choose between them and an eye when the Frasers of Glenhelm catch him poaching. "The man had come to terms with his crippled hand, turning from the bow he could no longer draw to the use of an ax, which he wielded and threw with a skill equal to any Mohawk's, despite his age" (*An Echo in the Bone,* ch. 2). Though too old to be conscripted, he's a strong worker and able factor for the estate.

Then there is Henri-Christian, a terribly sweet little boy who cuddles everyone. However, the adults whisper that he's a changeling or devil child and the children try to drown him, all because he's a dwarf. Nonetheless, the Frasers protect him as do his parents. Claire explains, "I'd seen parents who had given birth to children with defects; often their response was to withdraw, unable to deal with the situation. Marsali dealt with it in the other way, becoming fiercely protective of him" (*A Breath of Snow and Ashes,* ch. 36). In Philadelphia, he's welcomed among a Jewish family who "apparently felt some kinship with a person whose differences set him apart" (*Written in My Own Heart's Blood,* ch. 112). Claire and Jamie reassure Fergus that Henri-Christian can have a normal life outside a brothel and can do whatever taller people can.

Roger's throat and voice are damaged, perhaps

permanently, and Jamie finds him tasks that will make him feel useful. He tells Brianna she should still rely on him to protect her and treat him as a man. Claire muses, "More than anyone, [Jamie] knew what it meant, to have a life kicked out from under one – and what strength was required to rebuild it" (*The Fiery Cross,* ch. 75). She thinks at the end of the sixth book that Roger may keep his roughened voice, even with therapy, as "He'd fought for it, and earned it" (ch. 123).

Illness is also a factor for some characters. Colum MacKenzie has his Toulouse-Lautrec Syndrome, though his external weakness sharpens his mind, leaving all in fear of his schemes. Though Lizzie is Brianna's indentured servant, Brianna spends much time caring for her after she contracts malaria. Unfortunately, the disease goes into remission but cannot actually be cured. Lizzie' outbreaks make her dependent on expensive quinine, and prone to bouts of helplessness. Still, she remains a capable worker on the Ridge.

Homosexuality

Claire thinks, "No matter what Jamie's status as condemned prisoner, if he stood at the foot of the gallows come morning and claimed abuse at the hands of Randall, his claims would be investigated. And if physical examination proved them true, Randall's career was at an end, and possibly his life as well" (*Outlander,* ch. 35).

Several homosexual characters appear in the series, amid a great deal of controversy. First mentioned in this context is the Duke of Sandringham. In Castle Leoch, Jamie tells a humorous story about how the duke tried to seduce him as a fifteen-year-old and how he made his escape, finally by giving himself severe stomach problems. While the duke appears something of a predator, with his far greater status and Dougal's interest in appeasing him by any means, Jamie describes himself as able to fend off the advances, and he doesn't fear hunting with the duke later. The duke in fact is treated as more of a running joke. On this second encounter, Jamie apparently lets drop that he's married and the duke tries nothing further. Gabaldon explains of him:

> The Duke himself is not shown engaging in any really discreditable behavior *as a gay man.* He's a major-league political plotter, and thoroughly conscienceless in terms of his goals, but beyond Jamie's story in *Outlander* and the Duke's vague remarks about Jack Randall, we never see him in a sexual context. In other words, his homosexuality is incidental; simply one facet of his character, but not one that particularly affects our perception of him as good or evil. When he revealed himself (so to speak) as being gay in *Outlander,* I decided to keep him as a sort of grace note in counterpoint to Jack Randall – that is, making it clear that simple homosexuality was neither inherently evil nor regarded as such, whereas Jack Randall's particular perversion was Something Quite Different. Most readers fortunately observed the distinction. (*Outlandish Companion* 398)

In "By the Pricking of my Thumbs" (110), the MacDonald sons hurl insults at the homosexual Duke of Sandringham and his lover, as they think, Jamie. They say "Aye, I for one refuse to drink with mollies." "Go and couple together like the filthy dogs you are" and so forth, until Jamie fights back, with words then fists. The Duke rises above it all, preferring to ignore the insults than descend to brawling.

The much more significant predator is Jack Randall – when pressed, Jamie finally reveals that Black Jack offered to cancel the second whipping if Jamie would submit to him sexually. Gabaldon mentions that while a few readers object to any homosexual portrayal at all, more are concerned with

Black Jack as a negative stereotype. Gabaldon retorts:

> One pervert scarcely condemns an entire segment of the sexual populace. Black Jack Randall is who he is – an individual – and he fulfills his fictional purpose in *Outlander* and *Dragonfly in Amber* without in any way implying a reprehensible view of gay men as a group.
>
> Also, as I point out to the occasional reader who writes me with this concern – the fact is that Jack Randall isn't gay; he's a pervert (and no, those really aren't the same thing). Jack Randall is a sadist; he derives sexual pleasure from hurting people. In *Outlander,* four separate sexual attacks by Randall are described – two on men, two on women (men: Alexander MacGregor and Jamie Fraser; women: Jenny Murray and Claire Fraser). Clearly, he's not all that particular about the gender of the person he's hurting; it's the pain and the act of domination that turns him on. (*Outlandish Companion* 396)

Nonetheless, Black Jack demonstrates rue obsession with Jamie. He tells Claire, "I have had him as you could never have him. You are a woman; you cannot understand, even witch as you are. I have held the soul of his manhood, have taken from him what he has taken from me. I know him as he now knows me" (*Dragonfly in Amber,* ch. 38). Of course, she's revolted by the entire concept, but he appears to devoutly believe this. Meanwhile, Black Jack's honest yet incestuous romantic love for his heterosexual brother is a possible source of his anger and savagery. This brother in turn serves to humanize Black Jack as Alexander loves and trusts his brother despite all his darkness.

A far more significant gay character comes along in the person of Lord John (who has a minor appearance in book two and significant appearances in the following books, along with a spinoff series of his own). He is known for his perfect honor in every situation, and thus as a protagonist he provides a contrast with Black Jack and Sandringham. He's also in love with Jamie, the one man he can never have, leaving him in a tragic romance.

> "Do you know," he said again, softly, addressing his hands, "what it is to love someone, and never- never!-be able to give them peace, or joy, or happiness." He looked up then, eyes filled with pain. "To know that you cannot give them happiness, not through any fault of yours or theirs, but only because you were not born the right person for them?" (*Voyager*, ch. 59)

His life reveals much about the difficulties of being homosexual at the time. After losing his lover at the Battle of Culloden, Lord John spends a year around London's shadier molly-walks and discovers the infamous Lavender House, which offers many untrustworthy partners. He's eventually sent to an unattractive post in Scotland when one of his "indiscretions" is discovered. On several other occasions, John is "outed" and must fight duels to retain his good name.

Lord John and the Brotherhood of the Blade features several men being condemned to death for sodomy, as well as public panic over "a sodomite conspiracy to undermine the government by assassination of selected ministers" (ch. 2). Lord John notes to himself that sodomite conspirators seem to appear whenever the news is slow. He operates carefully, perpetually aware that he is just as guilty as those condemned, but doesn't think much about the unfairness of the world that persecutes homosexual relationships with death. Gabaldon explains in her comments afterward that the quotes heard on the streets are taken from actual newspaper clippings of the time, reproduced in *Homophobia: A History* by Byrne Fone.

He also has a problematic relationship with his new step-brother, Perseverance Wainwright – when Percy is discovered in the army having sex with another man. Grey must have him arrested. When

Percy asks Lord John if he wishes he were different, adding, "You must admit – it would make things less difficult." Lord John does not. Lord John adds later that "Men are made in God's image ... Is it reasonable than to create men whose very nature – clearly constructed and defined by yourself – is inimical to your own laws and must lead inevitably to destruction?" It seems God intends people to like men or women as they are born to do, even ones of the same sex (*Lord John and the Brotherhood of the Blade,* ch 19).

Percy reappears in *An Echo in the Bone*, having recently married.

> "My congratulations on your marriage," Grey said, not bothering to keep the irony out of his voice. "Which one are you sleeping with, the baron or his sister?"
>
> Percy looked amused.
>
> "Both, on occasion."
>
> "Together?"
>
> The smile widened. His teeth were still good, Grey saw, though somewhat stained by wine.
>
> "Occasionally. Though Cecile – my wife – really prefers the attentions of her cousin Lucianne, and I myself prefer the attentions of the sub-gardener. Lovely man named Emile; he reminds me of you ... in your younger years. Slender, blond, muscular, and brutal."
>
> To his dismay, Grey found that he wanted to laugh.
>
> "It sounds extremely French," he said dryly, instead. "I'm sure it suits you. (ch. 1)

Thus the French aristocracy, or a few of them, value Percy's flexibility as they share it.

Lord John and Stephan von Namtzen of Germany become increasingly closer, and after years of acquaintance become lovers. Their relationship is treated as one of real respect and affection. Nonetheless, the object of John's true love is Jamie.

While Jamie calls him a "wee sodomite" on occasion, Jamie comes to trust Lord John and values his friendship greatly, calling on his connections several times in the series. Their prickly, defensive, guarded friendship reveals much about the nature of love and trust:

> Could you call a man who would never touch you – would recoil from the very thought of touching you- your lover? No. But at the same time, what would you call a man whose mind touched yours, whose prickly friendship was a gift, whose character, whose very existence, helped to define your own? ("Lord John and the Plague of Zombies" 318)

Of course the Lord John novels, from John's own perspective, reveal him as an honorable, loving man and sympathetic figure. Gabaldon describes needing a character to fulfill a debt of honor to Jamie in the third book, and finally she settled on Lord John's older brother.

> But then, it was obviously necessary for Lord John to meet Jamie in person somewhere else, later – and the situation with the prison popped into my head immediately. What better sort of conflict? A man with a profound hatred of another man, put in a position where he holds complete power over his enemy – but is prevented by honor from using that power. What better sort of conflict? Well, what if the man in the position of power finds his hatred being gradually… changed to something else? And then, what if the man to whom he tentatively offered his budding affection could not under any circumstances accept even the thought of it – owing to the secrets of his own traumatic past?
>
> Well, heck, I couldn't pass up an opportunity to make things difficult. So we – and Jamie – discover that Lord John is gay, with concomitant complications. However, Lord John revealed himself as a gay man because he was; i.e., that facet of his personality was key to the part of the story in which he appears – rather than because I felt any need to include a "good" gay character as an antidote to Jack Randall. (*Outlandish Companion* 399-400)

With such a prominent gay character, other characters' homophobia appears on occasion. John propositions Jamie a few times and each one, Jamie threatens seriously to kill him. Jamie reveals in *Lord John and the Brotherhood of the Blade* that he believes men can't love each other romantically. He tells John, "Only men who lack the ability to possess a woman – or cowards who fear them – must resort to such feeble indecencies to relieve their lust" (ch. 32).

John retorts that he doesn't speak of rape – which men do to women more than they do to men – but to actual love.

Rejecting this concept, Jamie calls him "a pervert who minces about and preys upon helpless boys." Obviously, Jamie's experience with Jack Randall has had a profound effect. Either Jamie is speaking from anger here, or his further adventures with John teach him to trust the man: in fact, about six years later, when Jamie learns John will be his child's stepfather, Jamie offers his body in return for this generous act. John refuses him, pointing out that accepting would be dishonorable and adding, "You cannot give me what you do not have." Jamie offers him friendship and a kiss as a token of true esteem. As Jamie tells Claire later:

> "He loved me, he said. And if I couldn't give him that in return – and he kent I couldn't – then he'd not take counterfeit for true coin."
>
> He shook himself, hard, like a dog coming out of the water.
>
> "No. A man who would say such a thing is not one who'd bugger a child." (*A Breath of Snow and Ashes,* ch. 9)

Of course, John only has relationships with consenting adults in the series – and is hurt much more than he finds any sort of mutual relationship.

He tells Brianna that he does "like women" and marries Lady Isobel Dunsany, deciding that it's a good arrangement, though without sexual passion. "Our families have known each other for decades. It is entirely suitable match. ... There is more to a marriage than carnal love. A great deal more" (*Voyager,* ch. 59). Later he protects Brianna and Claire through love of Jamie, though he grows to care for the women themselves. Nonetheless, he warns Brianna that she shouldn't play with fire because he'd love nothing better than to have a child that mingled Jamie's blood with his own. With William, of course, he does.

Men's Gender Roles

New Men

> "Ah lass, are ye widowed, then?" His voice was so full of sympathetic concern that I lost control entirely.
>
> "No...yes...I mean, I don't...yes, I suppose I am!" Overcome with emotion and tiredness, I collapsed against him, sobbing hysterically.
>
> The lad had nice feelings. Instead of calling for help or retreating in confusion, he sat down, gathered me firmly onto his lap with his good arm and sat rocking me gently, muttering soft Gaelic in my ear and smoothing my hair with one hand. I wept bitterly, surrendering momentarily to my fear and heartbroken confusion, but slowly I began to quiet a bit, as Jamie stroked my neck and back, offering me the comfort of his broad, warm chest. My sobs lessened and I began to calm myself, leaning tiredly into the curve of his shoulder. No wonder he was so good with horses, I thought blearily, feeling his fingers rubbing gently behind my ears, listening to the soothing, incomprehensible speech. If I were a horse, I'd let him ride me anywhere. (*Outlander* ch. 4)

With women's liberation came a new staple character to the screen. "The new sensitive man stood between the liberated woman and what television suggested were two unattractive extremes, spinsterhood and feminism," explains Judy Kutulas in "Liberated Women and New Sensitive Men" (223). While the heroine couldn't wed the chauvinist, she could wed the man who put her needs and even her career before her own. While Frank doesn't offer this to Claire in the 1940s, Jamie does, two hundred years before. As such he offers viewers a familiar touchpoint.

> The new sensitive men added the final critical touch to the portrait of the liberated woman. He provided the legitimacy that equated her from the feminist. He modeled sensitivity for male viewers, reassuring them that there was still a place for then. in liberated women's lives and teaching them how to treat female coworkers as friends and equals. Perhaps more importantly, off the job, the new sensitive man found his sensitivity rewarded in sexual ways not available to earlier television working singles. More than the cute apartment. new job, and stylish clothes, he promised that being liberated had its own set of payoffs; payoffs that could cycle a working woman into traditional domesticity or, like Mary Richards, keep her proudly careerist.
>
> Together. the liberated woman and the new sensitive man carefully separated the most palatable aspects of feminism and packaged them into a neat consumer-friendly ideal. From the start, television's notion of liberation was fraught with contradictions, but a lot of its appeal was its complexity, which signified its realism. That complexity eased the frustrations and pleasures of real women's lived experiences – their uncertainty, their sense of being trapped between ideologies, their objectification, and their new consumer identities. (Kutulas 224)

"The 'sensitive guy' increasingly became a cultural ideal during the late twentieth century, and the term became a buzzword," notes John Ibson in the "Sensitive Male" entry of *American Masculinities: A Historical Encyclopedia.* Jamie is the clichéd sensitive guy of television, one who eagerly changes his behavior to please Claire. He vows fealty to her and allows her to dictate the terms of her marriage, even to leaving him for Frank if she wishes. He cries on occasion, including when her hair is cut off. Gabaldon notes on the CompuServe forums: "Jamie is more like a modern man. His unconventional acceptance of Claire, and support of her is one of the things that separates him from his peers (in Claire's eyes). He wants Claire to be strong."

Jamie comes from a barbaric time, not only of wife beatings but of lashings, primitive medicine, infant death, and poor hygiene. Yet he's also a blank slate romantically, eager to be taught. On the show, he acts like a pompous, high-handed idiot when he takes over Lallybroch, and Claire must give him a verbal spanking, emphasizing his need to be educated by his smarter spouse. From Claire he learns marriage equality, hygiene (as in book three he washes the food utensils), and compromise. His laying down a paternal strictness with Brianna fails and once more he explores compromise. One critic echoes the comments many male watchers are saying:

> As the show stands, Jamie is simply too good to be believed. Even things like beating his wife come from a place of true concern and loyalty to how his world works. He's beautiful and strong, smart and kind. He has flaws, but they're like the flaws you list in a job interview when asked what your weaknesses are: "I have a tendency to care too much and be too passionate," "I often make decisions without thinking about the risk to myself," "The whole of my previous sexual history came from watching barnyard animals fornicate, but luckily, I seem to be a prodigy." As unwaveringly nice as this makes the character, it also makes him slightly dull. (Hill)

The "New Man" of course is common in sitcoms as the emotional, gentle "nice guy" who often gets the girl. As Kutulas notes, "He was a media creation, a man himself liberated from gender stereotypes and open to his feelings, genuinely interested in women as people, nurturing and warm, a man not afraid to cry" (223). He's Ross or Chandler from *Friends,* Frasier from *Cheers* then his own show, Ted from *How I Met Your Mother,* Raj or Leonard from *The Big Bang Theory.*

Of course, the opposite trend appears as well, with other characters on *How I Met Your Mother,* Raj or *The Big Bang Theory* performing the roles of endearingly sexist pig. "Traditional masculinity is thought to be in crisis. This perceived taste of crisis, and the development of the 'new man,' have resulted in a small programming backlash in which the aim is to reclaim traditional masculinity," notes Buck Clifford Rosenberg, author of "Masculine Makeovers: Lifestyle Television, Metrosexuals and Real Blokes" (145). Thus men on *The Tudors* or *Game of Thrones* heroically rape and abuse women, in shows appealing to the male demographic. Rosenberg sees traditional masculinity "based on physical strength, resourcefulness, stoicism, and pragmatism, and frequently, physical labor" in crisis thanks to second wave feminism, which triggered many social changes, and a de-industrialization of jobs in favor of "an increasingly feminized service sector" (146). The male audience in some cases empathizes with this plight and wants to see men dominate women in a fantasy of simpler times.

"Jamie might be a respected warrior but he is also solicitous, largely ego-free and in touch with his emotional side. It's a neat switch in which the hero is a virgin, often in danger, while the more experienced leading lady hitches up her skirts and rides to the rescue" (Hughes). Both women appreciate his old-fashioned loyalty and determination to protect his women with his life out of love as well as responsibility. He hunts for them, fights for them, builds cabins for them, and they are grateful for his efforts. Balfe notes:

> I think there was an immediate recognition of a kindred soul there. For whatever reason there is a chemistry between them, and he doesn't seem like the rest of the men there. There's something different about him. He becomes a friend and an ally at this time. Dougal and Angus are very

> suspicious of her. They're weary of her, and they don't treat her very well. Jamie has this gentleness and kindness. He's just got that wit and that humor. Very quickly, what you see is the developing of their friendship. (Ng, "Caitriona Balfe on Claire")

His sensitivity comes from farm life, among other things. Claire first comes to know him as a humble stable-worker, one who soothes and comforts horses all day. Claire notes several times that Jamie's training with the animals has taught him a great deal of gentleness and describes him as "horse-gentling" with his touch on their wedding night. In the second episode, Jamie trains a white horse until it gets spooked and hurts his injured shoulder. However, Jamie explains, "She's just a girl with spirit is all. That's always a good thing." He certainly seems to be referencing Claire as well. Years later, he walks a pregnant Brianna around her room "like a horse with colic" (*The Drums of Autumn,* ch. 64).

He's very aware of Claire's menstrual cycles, in what seems to be more farm influence:

> I was always a trifle taken aback to realize how acutely he observed such things-but he was a farmer and a husbandman, after all. He was intimately acquainted with the gynecological history and estrus cycle of every female animal he owned; I supposed there was no reason to think he'd make an exception simply because I was not likely either to farrow or come in heat. (*The Fiery Cross*, ch. 12)

When Claire tells Jamie on the show that she can't have children, Jamie only pauses a moment before responding with sympathy. In the book, Geillis tells him (in what seems a betrayal of Claire), giving Jamie time to come to terms with the knowledge in advance. In both versions he points out that he wouldn't want her to suffer through childbirth, an attitude once again sympathetic with a woman's side.

Indeed, Jamie may not be such as anachronism as he appears. As Ibson adds:

> American culture commonly discourages males from expressing emotions associated with tenderness and vulnerability. The "sensitive male" is often thought a weakling, a sissy, or perhaps gay. Yet this stigmatizing of men's sensitivity developed only in the late nineteenth century, when middle-class men's fear of overcivilized softness and homosexuality prompted a new cultural emphasis on male toughness. ...
>
> Before the late nineteenth century, men were free to express tender feelings – to women and to each other – with politicians as uninhibited as poets. "Accept all the tenderness I have; wrote Massachusetts senator Daniel Webster in a letter to college friend lames Hervey Bingham, while the salutations "Lovely Boy" and "Dearly Beloved" opened their letters to each other. Early photographs often show men holding hands, one sitting on the other's lap, or casually reclining against each other. Pictured alone, men often struck poses of gentle reflection. The mainstream masculine ideal was apparently one that would later seem an androgynous combination of male and female qualities.

Lord John is sensitive, not only in his diplomacy but his depth of feeling. In "Lord John and the Haunted Soldier," Lord John writes in an unsent letter to Jamie, "I am afraid of death, of mutilation, incapacity – but any soldier fears these things, and fights regardless ... I am afraid I might find myself unable. Not only unable to fight, but to command." Even while trained to war, he worries over whether he can manage. There's also the expectations of a gentleman. Lord John tells his new stepbrother, who wasn't brought up in society, that "Dancing is most necessary for any man of good education, and the more so for an officer" (*Lord John and the Brotherhood of the Blade,* ch. 12). He and Jamie both take refuge in excessive politeness when threatened, reflecting the dictates of British society.

Jamie of course is also incredibly gallant, a trait that wins Claire's affection. In courtly fashion, Jamie sleeps outside Claire's door to protect her and refuses an invitation to sleep on her floor with rather prudish horror. He insists that it would be wrong to seduce her without marriage, and for the wedding, one of his conditions is a fine gown for her, to make her feel better.

All of this behavior seems straight from a play, and Jamie to some extent treats it as a script her should follow. "There appears to have been a level of awareness among men of the eighteenth-century Scottish elite that the refined masculinity they performed was constructed" (Carr 57). As such, Jamie must be the chief to the men of Lallybroch, Ardsmuir and Fraser's Ridge, but can be far more vulnerable around his family, especially Claire.

Only as men became disconcerted by their shifting world, with women entering the factories of the Industrial Revolution and men finding indoor jobs instead of backbreaking farm labor did men seek to reassert their manhood. "Sports became more popular as well as more violent, and much more directly linked to definitions of masculinity. As physical power became increasingly unnecessary in everyday life, many men overcompensated, prizing strength as never the province of women or effeminate men" (Ibson).

Jamie is caught in the clash of attitudes. In an era in which masculinity is thought to be in crisis, Jamie's many male friends offer him advice. Murtagh, memorably, tells Jamie with the best intentions that women don't take pleasure from sex so it's best to wrap it all up quickly. The other men are the ones to insist Jamie spank Claire, and he does it on their behalf, insisting Claire endangered the others, and this is the crime that deserves punishment. Though his father and Ian are "new men," happy to obey their wives' orders and do anything to please them, Dougal, Colum, and the

MacKenzie clan are traditionalists. As such, sensitive Jamie gets more than a little heckling from his friends.

In fact, Jamie is the one interested in dressing up, rather than Claire. This trait emphasizes his modern metrosexual nature. Likewise, Jamie tells Claire that all the girls in Castle Leoch are jealous of her curly hair -- a comment that sounds like girl talk (*Outlander,* ch. 16). This sort of pride in appearance emphasizes his status as "new man" for readers; though it's not necessarily an anachronism, it seems modern.

> *Queer Eye* tells men that a new type of feminized labor must be incorporated into their understandings of masculinity. These include care of the self regimes, the constant maintenance of appearance through grooming techniques, and consuming and wearing appropriate (read: stylish) clothing. Such feminized aesthetic labor, like domestic labor, must be incorporated into men's constructions of self and masculinity, transforming them in the process. (Rosenberg 149-150).

While some men of the time, including Louis XV himself, dressed and groomed carefully to display wealth and status, Jamie is generally a ragged man living off the land in faded, practical clothes. Yet on occasion of status, he throws himself into preparing more than Claire does. The first of these moments appears on their wedding day. As he arrives in a "fine lawn shirt with tucked front, belled sleeves, and lace-trimmed wrist frills" (*Outlander,* ch. 14).

> According to *Queer Eye*, masculinity now requires similar expenditures of time and energy in order to produce docile bodies. Men on the show spend a great deal of time in front of mirrors and in salons, malls, and kitchens. Being a "successful" or "attractive" man, in other words, means policing one's body through daily rituals, that require participating in conspicuous consumption, so that one has the right accessories and accoutrements to "produce" and

> maintain this sensitive masculinity (Berila and Choudhuri 2005, 25)

His martyr complex is another sign of his sensitivity: In book two, he rips Claire's dress open in barbaric fashion to coerce John Grey into talking in order to save, as he thinks, his countrywoman from rape. After, Jamie has his own men beat him for carelessness in keeping watch.

> "I dinna ken exactly, Sassenach," he said finally. "Could be I thought I owed it to you. Or maybe to myself."
>
> I laid a light palm across the width of one shoulder blade, broad and flat, the edges of the bone clear-drawn beneath the skin. "Not to me."
>
> "Aye? Is it the act of a gentleman to unclothe his wife in the presence of thirty men?" His tone was suddenly bitter, and my hands stilled, pressing against him. "Is it the act of a gallant man to use violence against a captive enemy, and a child to boot? To consider doing worse?" (*Dragonfly* ch. 36)

His education, which John Grey later values so highly, also sets him apart from his barbaric time. Jamie's education is heavily literary, as he habitually quotes Greek, Latin, and classics. The books relate, "he had been schooled in the Classics at the Université in Paris, and – while disagreeing now and then with some of the Roman philosophers – regarded both Homer and Virgil as personal friends" (*The Drums of Autumn,* ch. 8). As Claire adds, "Jamie was a natural polygogue; he acquired languages and dialects with no visible effort, picking up idioms as a dog picks up foxtails in a romp through the fields" (*The Drums of Autumn,* ch. 8). This is certainly appropriate for his era and status – Gabaldon comments:

> A working knowledge of Latin and Greek and an appreciation for the major works of the ancient philosophers were hallmarks of a "man of worth" – a gentleman – in the eighteenth century. Jamie, grandson of a noble (even if

> illegitimate), and nephew of a clan chieftain, has certainly been well educated, and thus well versed in ancient languages and writings. Small wonder that he turns to these both as expressions of his love for Claire, and as tutoring for his beloved nephew Ian. (*Outlandish Companion* 523)

Yet by modern standards, Claire's education is more typically masculine, and his is more typically feminine. Claire knows far more science than Jamie, of course, as a nurse then later as a doctor (to say nothing of the twentieth-century upbringing). While Claire is seen trading her medical services for food and goods in the fourth book and after, Jamie uses his knowledge romantically, rather than practically, once again taking the role of aiding the family within the private sphere. He inscribes her wedding ring with

> "Then let amourous kisses dwell
> On our lips, begin and tell
> A Thousand and a Hundred score
> A Hundred and a Thousand more"

> "Da mi basia mille," he whispered, smiling. Give me a thousand kisses. It was the inscription inside my ring, a brief quotation from a love song by Catullus. I bent and gave him one back. "Dien mille altera," I said. Then a thousand more. (*The Drums of Autumn,* p. 153).

He was even trained by nuns, leading to his lack of vulgarity as well as an increased respect for opinionated women:

> "Perhaps we should send her to Ste. Anne, Dougal," offered one of the blank-faced figures squatting by the road. "I've not heard Jamie swear once since we left the coast, and he used to have a mouth on him would put a sailor to shame. Four months in a monastery must have had some effect. You do not even take the name of the Lord in vain anymore, do ye, lad?"
>
> "You wouldna do so either, if you'd been made to do penance for it by lying for three hours at midnight on the

> stone floor of a chapel in February, wearing nothin' but your shirt," answered my patient.
>
> The men all laughed, as he continued. "The penance was only for two hours, but it took another to get myself up off the floor afterward; I thought my…er, I thought I'd frozen to the flags, but it turned out just to be stiffness." (*Outlander,* ch.3)

Metaphorically, he's a character of the romantic past and he's tied there, as much as Bonnie Prince Charlie is. This also gives Claire more agency as Jamie cannot come to the future seeking her or offer to accompany her if she goes back – it's her choice whether to stay or return. She has the power in their relationship. When Claire chooses to stay, Jamie notes, "I wish I could have fought him for you…If I'd fought him man to man and won, ye'd not need to feel any regret over it" (*Outlander,* ch. 25). She points out it was her choice not his. Gabaldon explains:

> In answer to the assorted pleas I get for Jamie Fraser to find some way of traveling forward, because some people think it would be so neat to see him be amazed at microwave ovens and video games… sorry, not on your tintype. He's a man of his time, and I have more respect for his dignity than to try to circumvent the ways of nature for the sake of a lame joke. (*Outlandish Companion* 331)

Jamie is an anachronism so there must be substantial creativity to make more sensitive men to join his band. In book two, he adopts Fergus, who has talents with women's underwear and an intimate knowledge of their lives, as he was born in a house of prostitution:

> The last of the hairpins clinked on the table, and I slumped in the chair, eyes closed. Then I felt a touch again, and realized that he was brushing my hair, gently combing out the tangles.
>
> "You permit, milady?" he said, feeling it as I tensed in surprise. "The ladies used to say it helped them, if they were feeling worried or upset."

> I relaxed again under the soothing touch.
>
> "I permit," I said. "Thank you." After a moment, I said, "What ladies, Fergus?"
>
> There was a momentary hesitation, as of a spider disturbed in the building of a web, and then the delicate ordering of strands resumed.
>
> "At the place where I used to sleep, milady. I couldn't come out because of the customers, but Madame Elise would let me sleep in a closet under the stairs, if I was quiet. And after all the men had gone, near morning, then I would come out and sometimes the ladies would share their breakfast with me. I would help them with the fastening of their underthings – they said I had the best touch of anyone," he added, with some pride, "and I would comb their hair, if they liked."
>
> "Mm." The soft whisper of the brush through my hair was hypnotic. Without the clock on the mantel, there was no telling time, but the silence of the street outside meant it was very late indeed.
>
> "How did you come to sleep at Madame Elise's, Fergus?" I asked, barely suppressing a yawn.
>
> "I was born there, milady," he answered. The strokes of the brush grew slower, and his voice was growing drowsy. "I used to wonder which of the ladies was my mother, but I never found out." (*Dragonfly in Amber,* ch. 19)

Repeatedly, he is cast as a sensitive new man through his childhood in the all-women's community. Fergus is a lively shopping companion, advising Claire on colors of ribbon. He reveals in *Voyager* that he knows a great deal about pregnancy and childbirth as well. His French origin is blamed for many of his attitudes – he has sex with his wife while she's trying to start labor, something a cringing Jamie admits he couldn't do. As Claire concludes of his unorthodox methods, "Fergus has spent the first ten years of his life in the brothel where he'd been born. Consequently, he knew a great deal more about women – in some ways – than any other man I'd ever met" (*A Breath of Snow and Ashes,* ch. 35).

Roger too is a new man as Oxford professor, though he has his struggles with sensitivity. Like

Frank, he adopts his wife's child with suspect parentage and cares for both of them. He picks Brianna birth-control flowers, leaving her having children as her choice. He has no experience with manual labor and Claire discovers that his binocular vision will give him difficulty in war. Thus he must stick with indoor work and his ministry as he will never be a warrior – a job he leaves to Brianna.

Frank vs Jack Randall and the Love Triangle

> A vision of your own husband, turned into a monster – contrasted with a Scot so unconscionably handsome and virtuous that flirting with him seems both highly necessary and vaguely criminal? This is feminine fantasy, indeed. But after dozens upon dozens of male fantasies on the small and big screens, *Outlander* is a welcome relief. (Saraiya)

The most significant part of Frank in Claire's story is his reflection in sadistic villain Jack Randall. His actor, Tobias Menzies, notes: "There are some piquant, slightly chilling moments of seeing flashes of Frank in Jack and vice versa. We're having some fun with this unusual situation of them both having the same face" (Virtue).

Certainly, these are separate characters, yet this is a substitution fantasy – if the story is read as Claire leaving the real world for the magical one, Jack Randall is Frank's hidden face or true self, as in *The Wizard of Oz* the farmhands, traveling charlatan and cruel neighbor are revealed as trusted companions, wizard, and witch.

> The supporting characters around Claire are nothing if not wish-fulfilling – in the sense that they manifest the hopes and fears straight women have about men. Aside from the Scots who take her in and show her the ropes, she's immediately as caught between two men as she is between two worlds. (Saraiya)

The show emphasizes this as the movie does by

using the same actors. However, it also shows Frank unleashing his rage in "Both Sides Now" (108), pummeling an adversary nearly to death. The episode ends with Jamie demanding Jack Randall back away from his wife – given the alternating scenes of the episode, it feels like he's addressing Frank as well.

Black Jack is obsessed with Jamie of course. As he describes it in "The Garrison Commander" (105), he beat Jamie so much because he wouldn't break or cry out.

> The world suddenly narrowed down to my arm and his back, the whip connecting us both. The laughter changed, first to gasps, then to sobs. [crying] [all gasp] The crowd, they had to look away. They were horrified. [grunts] Blind fools. I think all they could see was the horror. I-I could see the beauty. I saw the truth. That boy and I... we were creating a masterpiece. An exquisite, bloody masterpiece. It was the most beautiful thing I've ever seen.

"With Jamie, this young man's body stands for all that is good and honourable about Scotland," says Menzies. "Jack's central drive is to colonise, so when he encounters a body that is able to endure more pain than he has ever administered before, it's the perfect foil for his particular proclivities. At times you could say it tips over into eroticism. Jack is a study in sadism" (Virtue). In their next showdown, he accepts Jamie's offer to let Randall rape and torture him. Claire thinks, "The attraction of a victim at once completely unwilling and completely compliant was irresistible" (ch. 35).

In the future, Frank is also obsessed with Jamie and discovers the truth of him, though he never divulges it to Claire. While Jamie was willing to release his wife to return home, Frank continues to hold on tightly:

> "Bree is mine, my daughter," he said, as though to himself. "The only child I'll ever have. I couldn't give her up." He gave a short laugh. "I couldn't give her up, but you couldn't see her without thinking of him, could you? Without that constant memory, I wonder – would you have forgotten him, in time?" (*Voyager,* ch. 19)

Disassociation is a major theme – on the show Claire barely remembers VE Day, which passed in a blur for her. She describes her second honeymoon with Frank as a "convenient masquerade... to get to know the people we'd become after five years apart" and mentions forgetting his laugh as she lay in her cot during the war. Claire notes, "In a way, burying himself in the distant past gave Frank an ability to escape the recent. While I was in the army, Frank had served in London in Intelligence, overseeing spies and running covert operations... He'd sent dozens of men behind the lines on secret missions. And most never came back. He didn't talk about it very often, but I knew it preyed on him" (101). Reading tea leaves, Mrs. Graham sees that Claire's husband is a stranger to her.

On the show, he's seen frantically searching for her, insisting over and over that she has not left him for another man. Though he rejects Mrs. Graham's theory of the standing stones, he finally rushes to them in a moment of pure faith and abandon. However, he fails to retrieve her. Balfe adds:

> And [what] we also felt really strongly about was that even though there was trouble in their marriage, in that they were disconnected slightly, there was still a lot there. She was very much in love with Frank. He was the first man in her life, and there is a lot of love there. And we also wanted to show how much, because the first half of the season, her drive is to get back to her husband and her own time, and if you don't have that strong thing, if you don't see what she's lost, then it doesn't really give it the momentum and the drive that it sort of needs. (Vineyard, "Caitriona Balfe")

In Claire's fantasy life as book one begins, Frank is the adversary (in fact, he has likely cheated on her and now plans to curtail her intellectual life as a housewife forevermore). It's unsurprising that she's literally and symbolically infertile around him. Jamie however offers her respect and admiration – he not only needs her as Frank does not, but offers her an entire world of ignorance and male stupidity where she can heal and teach as well as bashing sense into male heads.

Frank reveals in the third book that he truly is sterile, whereas Jamie is a literal source of creation (*Voyager,* ch. 19). It's also notable that Jamie believes her story of time travel, while Frank, for the most part, does not. On the show, Frank tells Mrs. Graham directly that he can't share her beliefs. Gabaldon adds, "Since he can't or won't admit the truth of her story, they can never discuss it fully, never resolve the situation; Jamie Fraser is always the ghost that haunts their marriage" (*Outlandish Companion* 375).

Jamie however lives in a culture of changelings and water horses, storytelling by the fire and legends of travelers through the stones. He has the sight, giving him literal and symbolic perception beyond others of his time.

> "I liked thinking about why Jamie would believe her and how he would take that news," Moore recalled. "What we talked about internally was the fact that Jamie, in episode three, said to Claire, 'I'm an educated man, but I did grow up in the Scottish Highlands.' And there were fairies and he was telling this story – so he comes from a world that actually is a little bit more accepting of this fantastical notion than we would be. They do still believe in witches, they do believe in strange mystical power. So the idea of traveling through the stones in another time is already like a myth to them. So it wasn't as big a leap for him to take, and also, he just believed that she wouldn't have lied about it. So it felt right that she could do it, and that he could believe, and that we could move the story." (Prudom, "Devil's Mark")

Claire begins her epic wholly rational, spying on the Circle Dancers like Frank and considering them anthropological curiosities. However, trained by Geillis and Jamie, as well as other companions, she grows more flexible. By the later books, Jamie's telling her about seeing Jem with this second sight, while she is advancing in her training of manipulating auras to heal. She studies with Master Raymond, then with the Native Americans – all training she never would have had in the rational present day.

> Her Scottish existence is neat allegory for what Claire would've experienced if she stayed in 1950s Britain: As a "modern" woman, she would've had access to electricity and penicillin, but like the women of the 18th century, she would've been expected to return to the home and bear children. "If she'd have stayed [in the '40s] and became the professor's wife in Oxford, I don't know what she would've done with that," Balfe explained. "She would've felt completely trapped." (Petersen)

When Jamie returns her to the stones, she stands poised between two worlds, deciding which one she will choose for herself. One is "her place," as Jamie calls it, the land of hot baths, technology, and her acquaintances. On the other is a fantastical adventure, danger, violence, and Jamie.

> "It was quite difficult for me, coming to that scene, because I didn't want to just be like, 'well, she's in love with Jamie so she's got to stay,' because that's not Claire," Balfe noted. "You had to think about an entire lifetime of a place and experience, versus a few months and a man. That's a big battle. The knowledge of the '40s and the ability for her as a woman to be surrounded by that kind of openness and possibility, versus this place where for saying too much or for mixing a few herbs together to heal people, you're almost been thrown in the fire. So for me, it was difficult to come up with her rationale." (Prudom, "Devil's Mark")

In stories of this sort, travel to the magical world indicates a journey to the subconscious, there to hear the voices of mentorship and hidden wisdom and grow through the journey. Girls visiting Oz and Narnia learn important lessons about themselves and their inner magic. Thus Jamie as well as Claire's new friends and teachers offer her the spiritual growth she's missed. She comments in the third book:

> My marriage to Jamie had been for me like the turning of a great key, each small turn setting in play the intricate fall of tumblers within me. Bree had been able to turn that key as well, edging closer to the unlocking of the door of myself. ... The door now was ajar, the light of an unknown future shining through its crack. But it would take more strength than I had alone to push it open. (ch. 36)

Claire chooses the world that is teaching her about her buried qualities, the one where she's encouraged to be strong and change history as well as herself. Brother Anselm even calls her a chosen one of a sort:

> "But it may also be regarded as a signal mark of God's favor," he went on, disregarding my interruption. The bright brown eyes regarded me speculatively.
>
> "I prayed for guidance, kneeling before the Blessed Sacrament," he went on, "and as I sat in the silence of the chapel, I seemed to see you as a shipwrecked traveler. And it seems to me that that is a good parallel to your present situation, is it not? Imagine such a soul, Madame, suddenly cast away in a strange land, bereft of friends and familiarity, without resources save what the new land can provide. Such a happening is disaster, truly, and yet may be the opening for great opportunity and blessings. What if the new land shall be rich? New friends may be made, and a new life begun."
>
> "Yes, but-" I began.
>
> "So" – he said authoritatively, holding up a finger to hush me – "if you have been deprived of your earlier life,

> perhaps it is only that God has seen fit to bless you with another, that may be richer and fuller." (ch. 40)

Claire spends much of her time comparing the two husbands and deciding which life she wants – spiritual and dangerous or comfortable and safe. Her husbands are opposites in everything – their surroundings and the physical and romantic lives they offer:

> In fact, it would be difficult to imagine a greater contrast. Frank was slender, lithe and dark, where Jamie was large, powerful and fair as a ruddy sunbeam. While both men had the compact grace of athletes, Frank's was the build of a tennis player, Jamie's the body of a warrior, shaped – and battered – by the abrasion of sheer physical adversity. Frank stood a scant four inches above my own five foot six. Face-to-face with Jamie, my nose fitted comfortably into the small hollow in the center of his chest, and his chin could rest easily on top of my head.
>
> Nor was the physical the only dimension where the two men varied. There was nearly fifteen years' difference in their ages, for one thing, which likely accounted for some of the difference between Frank's urbane reserve and Jamie's frank openness. As a lover, Frank was polished, sophisticated, considerate, and skilled. Lacking experience or the pretense of it, Jamie simply gave me all of himself, without reservation. And the depth of my response to that unsettled me completely. (ch. 16)

Frank offers her stability and propriety, while Jamie offers her unfettered passion. While Frank quietly cheats on Claire, Jamie is appalled by the suggestion of such a thing. He picks her up and tells her, "I mean to take ye to bed. Now. And keep ye there until you've learned just what claim I have on you" (*Outlander,* ch. 23). With Jamie, Claire discovers the healing power she can offer with sex, as he lies dying in book one.

Metaphorically, she leaves the magical world for the safe one to raise her child, which represents the most vulnerable new ideas of the creative self. At the same time, she becomes a doctor. For this quest, she leaves the dangerous war and perilous, demanding lover for the safe, reserved husband. Gabaldon notes: "When she goes back, pregnant and emotionally shattered, it's Frank who picks up the pieces and glues their life back together. ... This is pretty much the admirable behavior of an honorable man, and Claire both knows and appreciates it" (*Outlandish Companion* 375). Only after a safe period of complacency does Claire return to the dangerous world for more soul growth once her child and career have fully matured.

When Men Were Men...

Claire tries to explain to Jamie that the twentieth century is very different. He retorts, "If there's no need for as man to protect a woman, and care for her, then I think it will be a verra poor time!" (*Voyager,* ch. 42).

Claire's adventures with the Highlanders take her back to a romantic, primitive time when women wore skirts and men defended them with drawn swords. Seitz adds:

> As on *Thrones*, there are points where you cannot entirely defend the show's gender politics. (The core of its first few episodes is a captivity narrative involving a frequently shirtless Scottish hunk in a kilt who at one point tells the very feminist heroine, "I'll pick you up and throw you over my shoulder" – threat or promise?)

After the cattle raid, Claire notes, "Twenty-seven years of propriety were no match for several hundred thousand years of instinct. While my mind might object to being taken on a bare rock next to several sleeping soldiers, my body plainly considered itself the spoils of war and was eager to complete the formalities of surrender" (*Outlander,* ch. 18).

Jamie's savagery is the draw for Claire, as it is for heroines of *Gone with the Wind, Jane Eyre,* or

Wuthering Heights. These emphasize the transgressive nature of fantasy "Although the men in these texts may threaten social coherence by their 'hybrid' nature and their deceptive veneer of civilization, it often turns out to be the 'savage' nature and original taint of the women who love them that are the most profoundly disruptive" (Kaplan 163). To Claire, Jamie is a Viking warrior "ready to commit mayhem," especially as he stands before her hairy and naked on occasion, bristling in all directions. In the books and show, his heavy accent marks him as singularly Other, along with everyone else of his time.

There's also Jamie's ancestry: not only was he fostered with War Chief Dougal, but his grandfather Lord Lovat is a savage figure from Scottish history. Gabaldon reports:

> With Simon Fraser, Lord Lovat (the Old Fox), I played somewhat more loosely. Though I saddled him with a thoroughly fictitious illegitimate grandson, the general depiction of his personality as wily, sensual, and politically astute is based soundly on a good many accounts of his life and behavior – even though those accounts vary considerably in detail and reliability. (*Outlandish Companion* 138)

Simon Fraser of Beaufort (1667-1747) planned to gain the title of Lord Lovatby wedding the previous lord's daughter, age eleven. When she was moved from castle to castle to escape him, he finally claimed her mother, the dowager Lady Lovat, in the family mansion and married her by force while the bagpipes played in the next apartment to drown her screams. He fled to avoid rape charges, but soon returned with a colonel's commission in the Jacobite service. He played both sides as rebellion grew, ordering his troops to abandon the Jacobite cause in the first rising of 1715. When the English won, he received a royal pardon for his crimes and was finally awarded the estate of Lovat on 23rd August, 1716. He wed several more times, often violently, though his bastard son Brian (Jamie's father) was fictitious. Lovat invited Bonnie Prince Charlie to invade in 1740 but excused himself from following the impoverished prince when he finally arrived, giving his age and health as excuse. Nonetheless, his son rode with Prince Charlie. After Lord Lovat was executed by the English, though he managed to save his land for his son. She carefully weaves this historical Scottish character, more than any other except Prince Charlie himself, into her novels, exploring the graphic deeds that made him famous.

Clearly Jamie's rough background, hereditary and earned through campaigning in France and living rough in the Highlands, offers a female fantasy of the rogue or highwayman. Early in their acquaintance, Claire finds out he's a man on the run.

> "Obstruction, escape, and theft. You sound a right dangerous character," I said lightly, hoping to distract him from what I was doing.
>
> It worked at least slightly; one corner of the wide mouth turned up, and one dark blue eye glinted back over his shoulder at me.
>
> "Oh, I am that," he said. "A wonder you think yourself safe in the same room wi' me, and you an English lassie."
>
> "Well, you look harmless enough at the moment." This was entirely untrue; shirtless, scarred and blood-smeared, with stubbled cheeks and reddened eyelids from the long night ride, he looked thoroughly disreputable. And tired or not, he looked entirely capable of further mayhem, should the need arise. (*Outlander* ch. 4)

This is temporized of course by the fact that he was actually protecting his sister and is a very gentle and honorable man.

In addition, Claire's specific war experience has linked them – Frank managed intelligence from behind a desk in the war while Claire was at the front, watching the brutality in France. Jamie too has been on the front lines. Balfe notes:

> She sees his back for the first time, and that's quite a moment. When you see someone very scarred by war – and this is again where her experience comes into play. She has treated men like him, but never the same kind of situation. The story of what happens to his sister and also the way he tells it. Obviously there's a deep pain there, but he makes light of it. He really opens up to her in such an honest way, but it's without any self-pity. ...
>
> These are things that attract her to him. Here's a person who's endured so much pain but doesn't seem to have that bitterness or poison. His soul and spirit doesn't seem to be poisoned, and I think that's something that really intrigues her. It makes him a different type of person who's not hardened by what's happened to him. The fact that he opened to her has as much to do with her demeanor, too. She has the quality that makes him trust her right away. The fact that he does trust her and opens up to her, that deepens their bond. (Ng, "Caitriona Balfe on Claire")

She's struggling to find herself after World War II – she notes repeatedly that she's not the same sheltered woman who married Frank. Thus this soldier, much like the many she once doctored, seems a better fit than the intellectual Oxford professor.

Nonetheless, she grows frustrated with Jamie's hero act. Jamie plays the tough guy from their first meeting, as he stoically needs his dislocated shoulder fixed, then fails to mention he's been shot until he faints. Both times he insists he's all right and can ride, while Claire is aghast.

> "You are not all right, and it's no wonder," I snapped, venting my fear and irritation. "What sort of idiot gets himself knifed and doesn't even stop to take care of it? Couldn't you tell how badly you were bleeding? You're lucky you're not dead, tearing around the countryside all night, brawling and fighting and throwing yourself off horses...hold still, you bloody fool." (ch. 3)

Later Claire grows resentful again when Jamie insists she set all his broken bones without opium. "Will you stop being such a goddamned frigging hero!" she yells. "We all know what you've gone through, you don't have to prove how much you can stand! Or do you think we'll all fall apart if you're not in charge, telling everyone what to do every minute? Who in bloody hell do you think you are, frigging John Wayne?" (ch. 36). A few pages later she compares him to other "heroes" she treated in World War II, who tried to tough everything out but finally confided in someone. This Jamie finally does, to Claire's relief.

In true hero form, in the Rising, Jamie plans to ride down the English and sacrifice himself as "that would cause enough kerfuffle maybe for Claire to slip free" (*Dragonfly in Amber,* ch. 43). He turns himself over to the English to save the people of Lallybroch in book three. To aid Laoghire at Castle Leoch, on campaign for the Rising, in prison after, and when teaching Young Ian, he insists on being beaten or even severely whipped. While his teaching strategy appears to be guilting others into not repeating their crime, as they will have to watch Jamie be beaten for it, this certainly bears more than a trace of martyrdom.

More interestingly, his kinship with pain and over-courageous seeking of it is the flip side of Jack Randall. Menzies explains of Randall:

> I've always thought of the character as a study in sadism. And obviously for a sadist, someone who can withstand a lot of pain is of a bit of interest. [laughs] And I think that sort of piques his interest and it continues from there. I think the interaction between Jamie and Jack is less of the mental chess repartee and more a kind of meeting of, I don't know, a good and bad angel, really. I think Jack is interested by the genuine uprightness and moralness of Jamie. Not in a pompous way, not in a trained way, but he has an inherent,

> fundamental dignity which I think Jack is able to recognize even though it's something he himself may have lost. (Lutes)

Murtagh is a similar hero, traveling with Claire across the countryside seeking Jamie. He tells her if Wentworth Prison is impregnable, Dougal will be able to keep his promise and bury him and Claire beside Jamie, one on either side. When he thinks he's failed Jamie, he offers his life dramatically in penance and Jamie must find an excuse not to take it.

All the male characters participate in the Revolutionary War, Young Ian as a scout and Jamie as an officer. Even William Ransom joins the British Army, to his father's pride. When Dr. Denzell Hunter volunteers for a spy mission, Claire protests that he's too valuable to lose. Jamie replies, however, "He's a Quaker, Sassenach. But he's a man. If he was the sort of man who'd not fight for what he believes, he'd ha' stayed in his wee village and poulticed horses and looked after his sister. But he's not" (*An Echo in the Bone,* ch. 57).

In the Dismal Swamp, William Ransom and Ian Murray discuss Mohawks singing death songs and holding up under terrible torture then wonder if they could do the same. Several characters face what it means to be a man, especially in the army, as they struggle to discover their callings. Jamie tells Claire:

> When ye're a man, a good bit of what ye have to do is to draw up lines and fight other folk who come over them. Your enemies, your tenants, your children – your wife. Ye canna always just strike them or take a strap to them, but when ye can, at least it's clear to everyone who's in charge. ... And if ye're a man, you're in charge. It's you that keeps order, whether ye like it or not. (*A Breath of Snow and Ashes,* ch. 47)

While women should defend themselves, it's men who protect the clan.

Diana Gabaldon famously was watching the *Doctor Who* episode *War Games* while planning out her novel and was attracted by clever, likable Jamie McCrimmon in his Highland kilt. In fact, the teen hero was a companion alongside Zoe – an aggressive warrior-scientist from the future with more than a trace of Emma Peel, setting up the Jamie and Claire partnership on multiple levels. As Gabaldon explains more about the inspiring Jamie scene:

> In this particular scene, Jamie McCrimmon and Lady Jennifer, a WWI ambulance driver (hence demonstrably no one's delicate blossom) are somewhere with the TARDIS, but without the Doctor, who was presumably in considerable danger elsewhere/when. Jamie declares that he must go rescue the Doctor, tells Lady Jennifer to wait there, and heads for the TARDIS - followed closely by Lady Jennifer. When he perceives that she plans to come, too, he insists that she must stay behind, ostensibly because someone needs to tell their other companions what's going on. Lady Jennifer greets this piece of feeble persuasion with the scorn it deserves, demanding, "You just want me to stay behind because I'm a woman, isn't that right?" To which our courageous young Scotsman (who is considerably shorter than Lady Jennifer) replies, "Well, no, I - that is... you... I... well... yes!" Now, I found this demonstration of pig-headed male gallantry riveting.
>
> ...
>
> Jamie McCrimmon, from the eighteenth century and a culture in which women were respected, but not considered men's physical equals (for the excellent reason that they aren't), appears for the most part to accept the notion that the women with whom he has to do on his travels through time are in fact his equals and treats them that way - until now. When push comes to shove, and it's a matter of a woman taking on physical risk... he can't help it; he has to try to protect her, even though he accepts her as his intellectual and social equal. ("The Doctor's Balls" Kindle Locations 334-349).

Clearly, she was already prepared for the gendered partnership of Jamie and Claire.

Living in primitive times has other consequences

besides expectations. In one terribly controversial scene, Jamie beats Claire. Certainly, there's a cross-cultural lack of understanding, and his reasons as he explains them to Claire, are sound to him:

> "Ye dinna take things as serious as they are. Ye come from a place where things are easier, I think. 'Tis not a matter of life or death where ye come from, to disobey orders or take matters into your own hands. At worst, ye might cause someone discomfort, or be a bit of a nuisance, but it isna likely to get someone killed. It's the hard truth that a light action can have verra serious consequences in places and times like these – especially for a man like me" (ch.22)

He bears some responsibility for endangering the group as she does, because, to the men's eyes, he is responsible for his wife, as well as the rescue mission. As he adds, a man who had disobeyed orders and thus endangered the group as she did would "ha' likely had his ears cropped or been flogged, if not killed outright" (ch. 22). "In Jamie's mind it's about justice. It's about righting the scales of justice, in that time and place," Moore adds. "If you were a man [who put other lives in jeopardy], you'd be punished, and if you were a woman, this is how you'd be punished" (Vineyard, "Spanking").

> While Heughan understood why the spanking scene might've been shocking or repellent to modern audiences, he was able to rationalize Jamie's decision, given the time period and surroundings the Highlander was raised in. "He has to punish her, whether or not he believes in it. He says he doesn't, but he has to because otherwise the Highlanders won't protect her. She's in danger. There's a moral code, and it's the way he's been brought up, and he's now got responsibility, and he's trying to do everything that's right. He's trying to play that role and be responsible, and she keeps bloody messing with it," he laughed. "And obviously, out of that, he learns a very valuable lesson, and she does, and their relationship is yet again developed and moved forward. And if he hadn't, if he'd said, 'I won't punish you, it's okay – it's not the right thing to do, but you're very

naughty,' then they wouldn't have learned anything. And I think it's interesting, because this relationship is just developing, and it's like any marriage – it's taking on different forms. It's going to keep doing that. God knows where it's going to be in a year's time." (Prudom, "Spanking")

In the comic book adaptation, Dougal decides to whip Claire in public and only relents when Jamie insists it's meant to be his job. In any case, Claire puts up a fight.

"I will not allow you to beat me," I said firmly.

"Oh, you won't?" He raised his coppery brows. "Well, I'll tell ye, lass, I doubt you've much to say about it. You're my wife, like it or not. Did I want to break your arm or feed ye naught but bread and water or lock ye in cupboard for days – and don't think you don't tempt me either – I could do that, let alone warm your bum for you?"

"I'll scream!"

"Likely. If not before, certainly during. I expect they'll hear ye at the next farm; you've got good lungs." He grinned odiously and came across the bed after me.

He pried my fingers loose with some difficulty, and pulled firmly, hauling me to the side of the bed. I kicked him in the shins, but did no damage, not having shoes on. Grunting slightly, he managed to turn me facedown on the bed, twisting my arm to hold me there.

"I mean to do it, Claire! Now, if you'll cooperate wi' me, we'll call the account square with a dozen strokes."

"And if not?" I quavered. He picked up the strap and slapped it against his leg with a nasty thwapping sound.

"Then I shall put a knee in your back and beat you 'til my arm tires, and I warn ye, you'll tire of it long before I do."

I bounced off the bed and whirled to face him, fists clenched. "You barbarian! You...you sadist!" I hissed furiously. "You're doing this for your own pleasure! I'll never forgive you for this!" Jamie paused, twisting the belt.

He replied levelly, "I dinna know what's a sadist. And if I forgive you for this afternoon, I reckon you'll forgive me, too, as soon as ye can sit down again."

"As for my pleasure..." His lip twitched. "I said I would have to punish you. I did not say I wasna going to enjoy it." He crooked a finger at me.

"Come here."

In both, she does some damage to him (even more onscreen), but he overpowers her and spanks her repeatedly. The jaunty upbeat music of the episode is meant to comfort the audience, while focusing on the cat-and-mouse fight. "I wanted to say somewhere in there, 'You know what? It's going to be okay,'" Moore said. "This is a show that goes to dark places, but this is not one of them. This tells them, 'Relax. Enjoy it. It's kind of fun on a weird level. Just go there'" (Vineyard, "Spanking"). Gabaldon was pleased with the results, which demonstrated "the perfect balance between menace and comedy, anger and patience, and absolute balletic action. Riveting" (Vineyard, "Spanking").

Critics take several camps, from acceptance of the historical reality to an appalled reaction to any sort of wife-beating, no matter the circumstances. Gabaldon comments, "Some readers – particularly some female readers – often share her sense of indignation and outrage and start hopping up and down about, how dare Jamie? How dare I?" (Vineyard, "Spanking"). Jamie even admits he finds an exciting component to the proceedings. "There is a side to him that enjoys it," Heughan said, "but he's not doing it out of anger or hate. There is no malice" (Vineyard, "Spanking"). Gabaldon adds:

> The public response to this particular scene is fascinating. Most readers find it hilarious, erotic, or simply very entertaining. A few find it absolutely unacceptable – a "good" man, they argue, would never beat his wife, no matter what the circumstance!
>
> Well, but he would. Jamie Fraser is arguably a "good man," but he's an *eighteenth-century* good man, and he's acting not only from a completely different perception of the situation, but from a completely different set of assumptions as to what constitutes appropriate behavior.
>
> Those readers who object to this scene seem to respond in one of two ways: a) They simply can't sympathize with a man who resorts to violence, no matter

> what. Ergo, I should not have allowed him to do so! or b) Even if Jamie's behavior *is* historically appropriate, it's wrong for me to have shown it, because women who are in abusive relationships will read this and conclude that it is okay for their husbands to beat *them*! (*Outlandish Companion* 402)

There's also all Claire has undergone to consider. One critic notes: "The problem, then, is that he is beating a woman he loves, that he's risked life and limb for. He's beating a woman who has been threatened, defiled and assaulted multiple times within the last 48 hours. He's beating a woman that he's sworn to protect with his own body, his own life, if necessary" (Hill)

As Jamie reveals later, this is how he was brought up – with a father who would give him a chance to explain and would describe why the discipline was necessary in turn, but then would beat Jamie for his misdeeds. Jamie notes, "Once I told him I thought beating your son was a most uncivilized method of getting your own way. He said I'd about as much sense as the post I was standing next to, if as much. He said respect for your elders was one of the cornerstones of civilized behavior, and until I learned that, I'd better get used to looking at my toes while one of my barbaric elders thrashed my arse off" (ch. 22). Jamie and Claire revisit the argument in book six:

> "A man wouldna beat a woman, then, in your time? Not even for good cause?"
>
> And what was I to say to that? I couldn't lie, even if I wanted to; he knew my face much too well.
>
> "Some do," I admitted. "But it's not the same. There – then, I mean – a man who beat his wife would be a criminal. But," I added in fairness, "a man who beat his wife then would most often be using his fists."
>
> A look of astonished disgust crossed his face.
>
> "What sort of man would do that?" he asked incredulously.

> "A bad one."
>
> "So I should think, Sassenach. And ye dinna think there's a difference?" he asked. "Ye'd see it the same, if I were to smash your face, rather than only take a tawse to your bum?" (*A Breath of Snow and Ashes,* ch. 47)

She admits that she does see a difference, and that Jamie is correct to do so as well.

The wife of the time was treated as a minor. As such, the spanking scene can make more sense for Scottish readers – if a child had disobeyed a parent's commands and risked his own life and others in consequence, a spanking could certainly be justified.

> "I don't think she realizes what she's done by putting all the men in danger and what the repercussions of that are going to be, obviously," Balfe told *Variety*. "But the fight that her and Jamie have... sometimes when you're scared or when you've been hurt, you don't know what to do with all of this emotion, so you just lash out. And I think both of them are just giving it to each other and you really see them push each other's buttons, but it's coming from a place of fear. And it's like a parent who's like, 'Don't you ever do that again.' And it's incredible to watch them have this big thing, but then when he really shows her, 'it's because you scared me,' all of her defenses just melt and she's like, 'I'm so sorry, I'm so sorry.'" (Prudom, "Spanking")

More problematic is Tom Christie savagely beating his daughter Malva in the woods over and over, and Fergus taking his frustration out on wife, children, and himself. Both times Claire tries to intervene but can do little about the family arguments.

Though Brianna doesn't intend to use corporal punishment on her own children, in one of the late books, Jem neglects to lock up the henhouse and a wolf kills many of the chickens. Roger is advised to whip Jem hard to help him feel he's made amends for this savage sight – something that can never truly be fixed. Roger also jokes about wife beating and how much he wants to hit Brianna for time traveling without telling him, but doesn't actually do it. Gabaldon adds:

> Frankly, this is one of my favorite scenes in that particular book. It illustrates perfectly the cultural and personal clashes going on between these two characters – clashes in which each one is absolutely convinced that he or she has the right of it – and they both do!
>
> ...
>
> From Jamie's point of view, his wife has – for no apparent reason beyond stubbornness – flagrantly disobeyed instructions meant only to keep her safe, and has fatheadedly wandered into a situation endangering not only her and himself, but all the men with him. Beyond that, she's brought him into face-to-face contact with the man he most despises, caused him to reveal himself in a way that will ensure determined pursuit, and worst of all – allowed Jack Randall to assault her sexually. He's not only annoyed with her for her original thoughtless (he thinks) behavior, he's sexually outraged at its results, and – unable to deal properly with Randall – is strongly inclined to take it out on the available guilty party. Even so, he might not resort to violence, save for two things: his own history of physical discipline, which leads him to consider the punishment he intends inflicting not only reasonable, but quite moderate – and more important, his notions of the *Rightness* of things, (which includes, though less important, the moral pressure of his companions' opinion). (*Outlandish Companion* 401-402)

On the show, Jamie feels this way, but as Claire refuses to forgive him, he chooses flexibility. He tells Claire: "Wives obey their husbands. Husbands discipline them when they don't. Now, that's how it was with my father and his father on and on and on, back. But maybe for you and me it has to go a different way."

To make it up to her in the book, he tells her stories of his own floggings – matter-of-fact ones about his childhood, the humiliating one from when he was fifteen, and the shameful brutal experience at

Jack Randall's hands. Claire reflects that his sharing such personal stories is an expression of love: "I gave you justice, it said, as I was taught it. And I gave you mercy, too, so far as I could. While I could not spare you pain and humiliation, I make you a gift of my own pains and humiliations, that yours might be easier to bear" (ch. 22).

In both, Jamie formally swears on a dagger's cross-shaped hilt that she has his fealty and loyalty. "If ever my hand is raised against you in rebellion or anger, then I ask that this holy iron may pierce my heart" (ch. 22). Thus the matter is settled. However, this too is problematic. Only a few days ago, he insisted she must obey him because he was a soldier and she a civilian without the understanding of where danger was lurking. Now he's sworn to obey her orders? He did not beat her in "rebellion or anger" before – it was, as he tells her in the same conversation as the oath-taking, something he felt she deserved. While the oath settles things between them, and he keeps it, it would have been all-too-possible for another situation to appear in which the men would demand he discipline his wife. Would he simply tell them he'd sworn fealty to her?

On the more romantic side, it must be noted that Jamie never actually swears fealty to anyone, neatly sidestepping it (or sometimes not so neatly) in the case of his Fraser grandfather, his uncle Colum MacKenzie, and Bonnie Prince Charlie. While he's a very independent agent most of the time, his only true fealty is to his wife.

In both book and show, Jamie has the line "I mean to make you call me master." But also "Seems I canna possess your soul without losing my own." Claire calls him master, but both times keeps it a bit sarcastic and accompanied by a death threat to emphasize he will never truly own her.

> "Will you do me the honor of sharing my bed, O lord and master?" I asked politely.
>
> Obviously suspecting something, he considered a moment, then nodded, just as formally. "I will. Thank you." He was raising the reins to go when I stopped him.
>
> "There's just one more thing, master," I said, still polite.
>
> "Aye?"
>
> I whipped my hand from the concealed pocket in my skirt, and the dawn light struck sparks from the blade of the dagger pressed against his chest.
>
> "If," I said through my teeth, "you ever raise a hand to me again, James Fraser, I'll cut out your heart and fry it for breakfast!"

On the show, she holds his own knife to his throat during sex. "She really draws her boundary line," Balfe notes. "I think that that's her saying, 'Look, I will love you with every fiber of my being, but not more than I love myself, and as long as you respect me, then we're good'" (Prudom, "Spanking").

Though Jamie swears he won't spank her again, a few more problematic moments follow. Claire demands he beat her for unfaithfulness in the second book, thinking "Better violence than silence" (ch. 29). He refuses, pointing out that they have both hurt each other emotionally.

Later in book two, Jamie gags and ties Claire and strips half her dress off to provoke a young English officer who thinks she's a prisoner. After, Jamie tells her, "I thought perhaps ye might be willing to sacrifice your modesty to prevent my havin' to damage the lad, but under the circumstances, I hadna time to ask your permission. If I was wrong, then I'll ask your permission, lady" (ch. 36).

There are other rough characters and manly men in the series, of course. Young Ian especially develops a savage side. After his time with the Kahnyen'kehaka, he cuts off an enemy's ear, explaining it will be a useful talisman for their journey. Rescuing Claire and Brianna in *A Breath of*

Snow and Ashes, Ian, Jamie, and Roger burst onto the scene much like a war band, with pounding drums and loaded firearms. They rescue their women violently, and insist they will kill to protect them.

Jem grows up in the rural culture and it shows. He speaks Gaelic and accepts time travel as a matter of course much like Jamie with his flexible outlook to the supernatural. In school later he traps and kills a rat "to the admiration of his male classmates and the horror of the girls" (*An Echo in the Bone,* ch. 26). He goes off to live in Jamie's cave for a few days, fully aware of how to take care of himself in the wilderness.

In the civilized twentieth century, Roger proposes marriage to Brianna who turns him down. He worries that "Ye think ye cannot be satisfied with a boring historian – ye must have a – a – great passion, as she did for him, and you think I'll maybe not measure up?" (*The Drums of Autumn,* ch. 18) She assures him she means she doesn't want her feelings to change, as Claire's did for Frank. Nonetheless, Professor Roger Wakefield, minister's son, becomes the unkempt, primitive Roger MacKenzie, unwashed and covered in stubble. Roger arrives at the airport in "a white shirt and scruffy jeans." As Brianna thinks, "With his hair worn long enough to brush his collar, disheveled and beard-stubbled, he looked not only rakish but mildly dangerous" (ch. 3). In his kilt, he performs a rough Highland masculinity for her and she's enchanted. As he tells Brianna, "By day, mild-mannered historian Roger Wakefield is a harmless Oxford academic. but at night, he dons his secret tartan regalia and becomes the dashing – Roger MacKenzie" (*The Drums of Autumn,* ch. 3). After, he woos her in primitive times ... and succeeds. As they settle in the past, he has transformed from Brianna's Frank, courting her politely in modern Inverness, to her disreputable, passionate, woods-savvy Jamie.

Misogynists

As Claire notes, "Murtagh was one of those men who always looked a bit startled to find that women had voices, but he nodded politely enough." Murtagh insists women shouldn't learn knife fighting but only the use of poison (ch. 19). As he adds, "I've yet to see the auld woman believes in witches, nor the young one, neither. It's men think there must be ill-wishes and magic in women, when it's only the natural way of the creatures" (*Outlander,* ch. 31). Claire retorts that she sees why he never married.

As the priest Father Bain is described, "He takes the view that every woman since Eve is a born temptress who should be beaten daily by her husband to keep evil at bay." Later, he says, "I will not be ordered about by a woman" ("The Way Out," 103). In the book, Father Bain is horrified when Claire offers to treat him for dog bites. He babbles that a man of God cannot expose his personal parts to a woman and accuses her of immorality. Her warning that it will fester is taken as a curse.

Jack Randall is a sadist, apparently only able to rape women if they scream in terror. Jenny and Claire each defeat him by refusing to show fear, and he finds he can't perform. In a horrifying moment of the book, he interrogates Claire by punching her in the stomach and adds, "I trust you are not with child, Madam ... because if you are, you won't be for long" (ch. 12). Of course he tries to rape her and threatens to cut her savagely while interrogating her at Fort William. He offers to have Claire raped by a monstrous guard at Wentworth Prison. Clearly, he tortures women specifically along gender lines, twisting a British officer's expected gallantry into perversion. All this suggests he's treated other women just as badly.

Randall is obsessed with Jamie, and taunts him about Claire during the extended torture of book one. By asking for details of their marriage and pushing Jamie to say her name, Black Jack once again attacks the characters at the point of their vulnerability. On the show he taunts Jamie, "Oh, first she orders you to fire, now she orders you to flee. Who's the man in this marriage, Fraser?" ("The Reckoning," 109).

Dougal is introduced with the line, "I don't hold wi' rape, and we've not the time for it anyway" (ch. 3). His honor and practicality appear here, though his callous disregard for Claire, blended with lust for her, grows increasingly evident. His actor, Graham McTavish, notes:

> Dougal has a history of being interested in and pursuing strong women. He finds them attractive and Claire is a strong woman who has never been captured before. She represents, quite literally, the future. For him to encounter her makes him want to pursue her that much more, so in the coming episodes he gets pretty keen on her. At the same time Dougal's got many plates up in the air. While there's a part of him that finds her attractive, there's also a part that is mindful of his duty toward the clan, and over and above, to his duty toward the restoration of the Stuart monarchy. Always with Dougal, the superobjective is getting the Stuart back and everything else with Claire is beneath that. It would be great if he could date Claire. If he could take her over to the clan it'd be great, but [the Stuart monarchy is] the thing that he focuses on.
>
> His relationship with Claire is one of the most enjoyable aspects of the show for me – the push and pull between them and that he is determined to get her one way or another. In subsequent episodes, marriage is no barrier to him. It doesn't matter that he might arrange the marriage between Claire and Jamie. Hey, that's just a piece of paper. She says, that doesn't stop you from "sampling other pleasures." He's quite bold.
>
> That line sums up the character quite nicely. (Ng)

On the show, Dougal fantasizes about her especially in the wedding episode, and then disturbingly makes a pass at her, saying, "I commend you for doing your duty. But it needn't stop you from sampling other pleasures. I find you to be the most singular woman, Claire." This of course foreshadows his later proposal when they fear Jamie cannot be saved.

In the books, his obsession is more about cheating Captain Randall, and he only propositions Claire when he's drunk at the Gathering and when later he suspects Jamie's dead. In the latter, Claire decides he's more interested in the property than in her.

Though he's inappropriate, he also admires her, noting, "Now, she took a few blows at the hands of Randall and kept silent, which is a fair sight more than I'd expect of any ordinary woman." In the wedding episode, he gives much advice to Jamie, including that he should be standoffish

> Jamie: Aye, he said, "you never want to let a woman see "you're too eager to please her. Gives her too much power."
> Claire: Really? And what did you have to say to that?
> Jamie: I said I was completely under yer power and happy to be there.

The show gives a bit more insight into his marriage in the book, as he's torn by grief through the loss of his wife. He staggers about drunkenly, proclaiming, "Not even a blind man would think she was bonny... But she deserved better than me" ("By the Pricking of my Thumbs," 111).

In "The Search" (114), Dougal proposes to Claire, wanting to possess both her and Lallybroch. He tells Claire to stop acting like "an empty headed woman" and tells her, "You're being clever, not wise" and "You're blinded by love." He believes women shouldn't be mouthy but should be smart enough to preserve their lives by playing the game.

He ignores her gender-based challenges, such as "What's the matter? Are you scared you're not as good as him?"

Of course, the Jacobite cause comes first for him. In "Rent," he accuses Claire of "sowin' the seeds of doubt in our midst, working behind the cover of yer woman's skirts to undermine the cause." Likewise, at the end of the second book, his wariness of Claire and belief she's undermining the Jacobites combine in a sexist display:

> "I dinna blame ye, lad," he said. His voice was suddenly weary, and I remembered that he was a man in his fifties. "It isna your fault, Jamie. She's bewitched ye – anyone can see that." His mouth twisted as he looked again at me.
>
> "Aye, I ken weel enough how it's been for ye. She's worked the same sorcery on me, betimes." His eyes raked over me, burning. "A murdering, lying slut, would take a man by the cock and lead him to his doom, wi' her claws sunk deep in his balls. That's the spell that they lay on ye, lad – she and the other witch. Take ye to their beds and steal the soul from you as ye lie sleeping wi' your head on their breasts. They take your soul, and eat your manhood, Jamie."
>
> His tongue darted out and wetted his lips. He was still staring at me, and his hand tightened on the hilt of his sword.
>
> "Stand aside, laddie. I'll free ye of the sassenach whore." (*Dragonfly in Amber,* ch. 46)

His sexism doesn't come from nowhere – he may feel bitter at Geillis, a real witch, having seduced him to the Jacobite cause then abandoned him to face defeat beside his new chief.

Tom Christie from the sixth book is a similar character. He's revolted by Claire's outspoken attitudes and loose, curly hair. He warns his daughter Malva to beware of her notebook, which he fears is full of spells. He also regularly beats his daughter in the woods, worrying Claire. As Christie finally reveals, his own wife was a witch who committed adultery with his brother.

> "It was not his fault! Mona was a witch – an enchantress." His lips compressed at the expression on my face. "Ye don't believe me, I see. It is the truth; more than once, I caught her at it – working her charms, observing times – I came once to the roof o' the house at midnight, searching for her. I saw her there, stark naked and staring at the stars, standing in the center of a pentacle she'd drawn wi' the blood of a strangled dove, and her hair flying loose, mad in the wind." (ch. 97)

Whatever the truth of her behavior or powers, Tom decides that his brother wasn't responsible but enchanted by a wicked woman, laying all the blame on the female. He also extends the blame to Malva – the child of his wife and brother.

> "The girl ... she was nay more than five years old when I first saw her, but already she had it – the same slyness, the charm – the same darkness of soul."
>
> He had tried to the best of his ability to save Malva, as well – to beat the wickedness out of her, to constrain the streak of wildness, above all, to keep her from working her wiles upon men.
>
> "Her mither had that, too." His lips tightened at the thought. "Any man. It was the curse of Lilith that they had, the both of them." (ch. 97)

As he considers his five-year-old daughter a witch and regularly beats her, it's no surprise she turns defiant and strong-willed, until their family crumbles apart, with her father still blaming her for everything.

Many men treat women badly, though soldiers' attitudes towards prostitutes seem the worst. In the Lord John books, initiation into the Hellfire Club involves having sex with and then murdering a young woman from a poor family, considered disposable by the men in charge.

Men's Communities

In Hume's 1742 essay, "Of the Rise and Progress of the Arts and Sciences," he argues that male gallantry lies at the base of politeness, thus women civilize men through their presence.

> What better school for manners than the company of virtuous women; where the mutual endeavor to please must insensibly polish the mind, where the example of female softness and modesty must communicate itself to their admirers, and where the delicacy of that sex puts every one on his guard, lest he give offence by any breach of decency? (qtd. in Carr 50)

On the show, the garrison invites Claire to dinner and treats her courteously, plying her with wine and complimenting her beauty, exclaiming over and over how pleased they are to be in the presence of an English lady. She's flattered by their gallantry and enjoys being treated this way after the coarse Scots. Brigadier General Sir Oliver Lord Thomas says, "My word, Madam. If I were brave enough, I would commission you a colonel in one of my regiments. You do know how to order men about" ("The Garrison Commander," 106).

However, the soldiers prove themselves racist to the Scots and condescending to her as they note: "No doubt your time here has muddied your proper English thinking" and "My lord, I think the lady has lived among the savages too long."

When she insists, "Both sides have committed depredations they should both be ashamed of," one retorts, "Dog me, that's a woman's view for you if ever I heard one. That is why I make it a point never to discuss politics with a lady."

Even Jack Randall has his polite veneer. Claire notes in book two that he remains "as formal as ever and there was no trace of humanity on the hard, handsome features as he bowed to me and took his leave" (ch. 42). She takes advantage of this when necessary.

> "The hospitality of this house seems a trifle lacking by comparison with its appointments," I said, as haughtily as I could manage under the circumstances, which wasn't all that much. Still, Louise's example of great-ladydom had not been entirely in vain.
>
> The Duke laughed, a high, chittering sort of laugh, like a bat that has just heard a good one.
>
> "Your pardon, Madam. You're quite right; I should have thought to offer you refreshment before presuming to question you. Most thoughtless of me."
>
> He murmured something to the footman who appeared in answer to his ring, then waited calmly before the fire for the tray to arrive. I sat in silence, glancing around the room, occasionally stealing a look at my host. Neither of us was interested in making small talk. Despite his outward geniality, this was an armed truce, and both of us knew it. (*Dragonfly in Amber,* ch. 44)

By contrast, Dougal respects her and addresses her as a person. Moreover, when Captain Randall discards his gentlemanly façade and beats her, Dougal rushes to her rescue. Hume adds:

> As nature has given *man* the superiority above woman, by endowing him with greater strength both of mind and body; it is his part to alleviate that superiority, as much as possible, by the generosity of his behavior and by a studied deference and complaisance for all her inclinations and opinions. (qtd. in Carr 50)

Thus Hume takes this a step beyond politeness into a sort of *Noblesse oblige* –because man is superior, he should share his status with woman and elevate her out of generosity.

In the Enlightenment, refined gentlemen met in refined, homosocial spaces, which served to keep women from education and politics, at least to an extent. This ensured, to the male point of mind at the time, that women's influence would not extend too far (Carr 38). Societies included clubs, from university to scientific to purely social. Coffee houses, a recent innovation, joined this list, seen as less boisterous than taverns. The Lord John novels casually mention historical coffee houses like White's and Boodle's, along with literary salons. Claire adds that "the Philadelphia coffee houses tended to be male preserves of business, gossip, and politics" (*Written in My Own Heart's Blood,* ch. 112).

Debate, reading, and intellectual exercise were featured here, with the latest periodicals and books on the shelves. In Scotland, the Enlightenment and its gentlemanly society tended to be open to, as Melton puts it, "men and women with sufficient property and education to enjoy regular access to newspapers, novels and other products of eighteenth-century print culture" (Carr 54).

Lord John's club the Society for the Appreciation of the English Beefsteak appears to be fictional, though certainly a product of its time. Food and drink are central, but there are also gambling, political debate, and business meetings – all specifically help in the homosocial world. Lord John spends time with his male friends at the sale de arms, practicing fencing. He also travels to the infamous Lavender House and Hellfire Club, though he regrets both visits.

Jamie, courting Prince Charles's favor, must accompany him to a whorehouse. Upon seeing bites and scratches on her husband, Claire is furious, though Jamie insists they're "the scars of honorable combat, gained in defending]his] virtue" (*Dragonfly in Amber,* ch. 18). He also mentions that his companions have wives and mistresses as well, and all of them accept such behavior.

Male societies of course included the Freemasons. "Their aim was to foster social harmony by uniting different social, political, and religious groups. This was largely achieve through a lodge culture of male conviviality, primarily expressed through heavy drinking" (Carr 70).

Jamie is made a Freemason in prison to benefit the English officers, who need another member. He then makes all the prisoners join, to bind the Catholics and Protestants together. "Freemasons held as basic principles the notions of equality – gentleman, crofter, fisherman, laird; such distinctions were not taken account of in a lodge – and tolerance. No discussion of politics or religion among the brothers, that was the rule" (*Fiery Cross*, ch. 95). Jared and Roger reveal themselves as members in time, emphasizing a secret "boy's club," which continues on the Ridge.

Gendered social space in France includes the *lever,* King Louis's morning ritual. This, like the clubs, was an important place to put one's petition forward. In contrast is the female petitioner, who approaches the king in private and is required to sleep with him, often to advance her husband's political career.

Too, there is the duel. "In the context of Scottish Enlightenment gender ideology, violence was antithetical to male refinement, yet dueling and other forms of violent behavior continued among men whose gentlemanly status placed them as members of polite society" (Carr 143). The duel was a method of maintaining public reputation especially among other men. Jamie describes with chagrin fighting a duel over a young lady, only to have her swoon over the loser. In this case, while he may gain respect in the male community, he loses his goal, the woman.

Of course, this is a sign of manliness: "Jamie and Murtagh took each other on every two or three days to keep in practice, clashing and parrying and lunching up and down the garden, to the untrammeled delight of the servants, male and female alike, who all surged onto the balconies to watch" (*Dragonfly in Amber,* ch. 11).

On the show, the Duke of Sandringham and the Watch want Jamie to help them - the former in a duel and latter in a raid. This adds to the action of the show but also emphasizes the homosocial community and its violence. Quarry, leader of the Watch in the episode of that name, even considers Jamie an old soldier colleague from the army.

In "By the Pricking of my Thumbs" (110), Sandringham and the MacDonalds each fire a ceremonial shot, then Sandringham offers his apology for non-payment of debt, and honor is upheld. When the MacDonalds hurl insult after, however, the Duke withdraws, noting, "A duel is one thing, a common brawl quite another." Only one is technically worthy of a lord.

This male-only activity was regarded with ambivalence at the time - it was an honorable act for a man, but also uncivilized and rather selfish as it put his personal honor ahead of the community's. Jamie's duel in book two emphasizes this point of view, as doing so endangers his entire mission in France and thus all of Highland society. It also threatens Claire and her husband Frank. Nonetheless, Jamie succumbs, not only to settle his personal honor and drive for vengeance, but to avenge the injuries done to young Fergus.

Later on, Lord John and his brother fight in a series of duels. "The display of male honor through the duel provided an alternative to a gentlemanly refinement founded on inner sensibility and outward self-command" (Carr 150). While Lord John prides himself on politeness and control, the slurs against him grow so great that he must challenge them.

In *The Scottish Prisoner*, Jamie provokes Edward Twelvetrees to a duel after the man publically calls him and Lord John lovers. Jamie notes that

Twelvetrees hurled the accusation to discredit Lord John, who was accusing him of treason. Jamie insists on keeping the appointment, noting that his "honor as a man" is at stake (ch. 31). Jamie prepares to duel him, but knowing he's terribly out of practice, Lord John challenges the man for an earlier appointment. The customs of the duke appear, from the Second, whose duty it is to finish the fight on his friend's behalf, to the elaborate formality, as Twelvetrees brings a surgeon for his own use as well as his enemy's.

Male Hierarchy and Allegiance

Books one and two are filled with the issue of Jamie's oath of allegiance – which he never gives. Colum MacKenzie has ambivalent interest in appointing Jamie his heir, while Lord Lovat only wishes the status and wealth of Jamie's estate sworn to his service – so much that he tries to gain them by trickery. Jamie shrugs off the violence of Lord Lovat's clan towards himself, even when they hold him and punch him in the stomach.

> "It's only play-acting, Sassenach; ye shouldna worry."
>
> "Play-acting! Good God, Jamie!"
>
> "Have ye no seen a strange dog join a pack, Sassenach? The others sniff at him, and nip at his legs, and growl, to see will he cower or growl back at them. And sometimes it comes to biting, and sometimes not, but at the end of it, every dog in the pack knows his place, and who's leader. Old Simon wants to be sure I ken who leads this pack; that's all."
>
> "Oh? And do you?" I lay down, waiting for him to come to bed. He picked up the candle and grinned down at me, the flickering light picking up a blue gleam in his eyes.
>
> "Woof," he said, and blew out the candle. (*Dragonfly in Amber,* ch. 40)

There's also the matter of allegiance to Prince Charlie, which Jamie never actually swears, though he fights for the man. Jamie is a leader, not a follower, and is most often found charting his own course. He honors the men pledged to him, but makes no official pledge to those above him.

Jamie and Claire acknowledge Charlie's power as the king without a throne, but freely admit his helplessness and inexpert leadership. In their world of respect and hierarchy, not enough people can be convinced to follow him.

> "Bonnie Prince Charlie," I said softly to myself, looking over my reflection in the large pier glass. He was here, now, in the same city, perhaps not too far away. What would he be like? I could think of him only in terms of his usual historical portrait, which showed a handsome, slightly effeminate youth of sixteen or so, with soft pink lips and powdered hair, in the fashion of the times. Or the imagined paintings, showing a more robust version of the same thing, brandishing a broadsword as he stepped out of a boat onto the shore of Scotland.
>
> A Scotland he would ruin and lay waste in the effort to reclaim it for his father and himself. Doomed to failure, he would attract enough support to cleave the country, and lead his followers through civil war to a bloody end on the field of Culloden. Then he would flee back to safety in France, but the retribution of his enemies would be exacted upon those he left behind. (*Dragonfly in Amber,* ch. 7)

In war, he's even less effective, demonstrating his near-total lack of battle experience in wild plans and ill-thought out invasions, ending with the hopeless charge at Culloden. By insisting on a straightforward battle on the moors instead of guerrilla warfare, he loses his cause. As a leader, he falls short, throwing away the lives of so many pledged men in a useless charge while he flees. In fact, Prince Charlie "ran off so fast at the end of the battle that he left behind his sterling silver picnic set" (*Dragonfly in Amber,* ch. 4). As Claire comments:

> But do you know what's really funny? That poor, silly sot and his greedy, stupid helpers; and the foolish, honorable men who couldn't bring themselves to turn back...they had

> the one tiny virtue among them; they believed. And the odd thing is, that that's all that's endured of them – all the silliness, the incompetence, the cowardice and drunken vainglory; that's all gone. All that's left now of Charles Stuart and his men is the glory that they sought for and never found. (*Dragonfly in Amber,* ch. 47)

Jamie, by contrast, does everything possible to save his men's lives at Culloden, refusing to let another leader get them killed in his absence.

While this is Jamie's only time of leading the men of Lallybroch, his status as chief appears through the series. After Claire is attacked, Murtagh offers his blade to Jamie:

> "I've failed ye," the little man said quietly. "And I'll ask ye, as my chief, to take my life now, so I needna live longer wi' the shame of it."
>
> Jamie drew himself slowly upright, and I felt him push away his own tiredness as he brought his gaze to bear on his retainer. He was quite still for a moment, hands resting on his knees. Then he reached out and placed one hand gently over the purple knot on Murtagh's head.
>
> "There's nay shame to ha' fallen in battle, mo caraidh," he said softly. "The greatest of warriors may be overcome."
>
> But the little man shook his head stubbornly, black eye unwinking.
>
> "Nay," he said. "I didna fall in battle. Ye gave me your trust; your own lady and your child unborn to guard, and the wee English lassie as well. And I gave the task sae little heed that I had nay chance to strike a blow when the danger came. Truth to tell, I didna even see the hand that struck me down." (*Dragonfly in Amber,* ch. 19)

After discovering that in Murtagh's mind, Jamie is his chief as he swore an oath when Jamie was a baby, Jamie gives him a noble task to make up for his failure – he must find the men and take his vengeance.

Of course, Jamie's close male friendships are vital to the story. Hugh Munro saves Jamie and Claire, while Willie, Angus, and Rupert charge into Wentworth to rescue Jamie, along with the loyal

Murtagh. Ian is the responsible foster brother. While reckless Jamie is off having adventures, Ian cares for Lallybroch, from crops and rents to its tenants. He provides a safe haven for Jamie and remains the steadfast best friend as Jenny flies into tempers over some of Jamie's exploits.

In Ardsmuir Prison, Lord Jamie gets automatic homage from the other prisoners, though they haven't pledged an oath to him.

> He was a gentleman born, and had been both a laird and a fierce warrior; a man much respected among the Highlanders. The men deferred to him naturally, seeking his opinion, asking his judgment, and the weaker sheltering in his presence.
>
> "And that griped Tom Christie's arse like a saddle-gall," Kenny said, nodding wisely. "See, he'd got to thinking as how he was the biggest frog in the pond, aye? ... It wouldna have been so bad, maybe, save that half his wee band of salvationers started creepin' off from their prayers to hear Mac Dubh tell stories. But the main thing was the new governor."
>
> Bogle, the prison's original governor, had left, replaced by Colonel Harry Quarry. Quarry was a relatively young man, but an experienced soldier, who had fought at Falkirk and at Culloden. Unlike his predecessor, he viewed the prisoners under his command with a certain respect – and he knew Jamie Fraser by repute, regarding him as an honorable, if defeated, foe.
>
> "Quarry had Mac Dubh brought up to see him, soon after he took command at Ardsmuir. I couldna say what happened between them, but soon it was a matter of course; once a week, the guards would come and take Mac Dubh off to shave and wash himself, and he would go take a bit of supper with Quarry, and speak to him of whatever was needed."
>
> "And Tom Christie didn't like that, either," Roger guessed. (*The Fiery Cross*, ch. 95)

Jamie solves the problem by binding them all together as Masons ... though he remains in charge as lodgemaster. He in turn is invited to the lodge by Quarry as they need another member and as Quarry thinks, "A gentleman was a gentleman, after all, Jacobite or no."

When Jamie tells the story himself, he views the prisoners as his men, due all the protection of their chief. He takes a whipping for one, and bargains with the prison's governor for better treatment when some fall ill. This responsibility is one of the reasons he doesn't run away.

> "I had to go back," he said slowly. "For the sake of the men there, if for nothing else."
>
> "The men in the prison?" I said, surprised. "Were some of the Lallybroch men arrested with you?"
>
> He shook his head. The small vertical line that appeared between his brows when he thought hard was visible, even by starlight.
>
> "No. There were men there from all over the Highlands – from every clan, almost. Only a few men from each clan – remnants and ragtag. But the more in need of a chief, for all that."
>
> "And that's what you were to them?" I spoke gently, restraining the urge to smooth the line away with my fingers.
>
> "For lack of any better," he said, with the flicker of a smile.
>
> He had come from the bosom of family and tenants, from a strength that had sustained him for seven years, to find a lack of hope and a loneliness that would kill a man faster than the damp and the filth and the quaking ague of the prison.
>
> And so, quite simply, he had taken the ragtag and remnants, the castoff survivors of the field of Culloden, and made them his own, that they and he might survive the stones of Ardsmuir as well. Reasoning, charming, and cajoling where he could, fighting where he must, he had forced them to band together, to face their captors as one, to put aside ancient clan rivalries and allegiances, and take him as their chieftain.
>
> "They were mine," he said softly. "And the having of them kept me alive." (*Voyager,* ch. 33)

He's appalled when they're transported to the Colonies without him, and once he goes himself he tracks them down one by one to invite them to join his community. In the New World, though Christie can be a problematic tenant, the other men from Ardsmuir would do anything for him.

After his wife commits a terrible crime, Mr. Bug offers his life to Jamie and calls him his chieftain.

> One word, and we stood in Scotland. It was easy to see the difference in attitude between Jamie's new tenants and his Ardsmuir men – the difference of a loyalty of agreement and one of acknowledgment. This was different still: an older allegiance, which had ruled the Highlands for a thousand years. The oath of blood and iron. (*A Breath of Snow and Ashes,* ch. 33)

When Roger finds himself confronted by irate father Jamie, both men fight over Brianna, and giving in to his primitive instincts, Roger insists, "She's mine." When Roger moves in with them as Brianna's husband, Jamie roughs him up and threatens to feed his heart to the pigs if he hurts Brianna. Claire calls these exaggerated male displays "testosterone poisoning." In book five, Roger worries that he hasn't been given his hierarchical role as Jamie's second-in-command, but soon finds that he has. He becomes part of the family, lieutenant to "Himself," though never precisely his equal.

Fathers

Jamie does not get to be a dad, though Claire is incontrovertibly a mom. His son he sees intermittently, only when the young boy comes down for riding lessons, and of course, Jamie cannot tell him the truth or properly discipline him. However, William is lost on a picnic and Jamie goes and finds the boy. Carrying him after, he feels a burst of tenderness.

> To this point, he could not really have said that he loved William. Feel the terror of responsibility for him, yes. Carry thought of him like a gem in his pocket, certainly, reaching

> now and then to touch it, marveling. But now he felt the perfection of the tiny bones of William's spine through his clothes, smooth as marbles under his fingers, smelled the scent of him, rich with the incense of innocence and the faint tang of shit and clean linen. And thought his heart would break with love." (*The Scottish Prisoner,* ch. 39)

Likewise, Jamie has a flock of nieces, nephews, stepchildren, and other surrogates, as well as a daughter, but all are kept rather distant. Fergus, he adopts at age ten and must soon leave behind at Lallybroch – Jenny arguably is more of a presence in his life. While hiding in a cave, Jamie greets Jenny's children once a month or so for "sleepy kisses." He only has a few years to read little Marsali and Joan stories by the fire before he leaves for Edinburgh. Nonetheless, Marsali and Fergus both see him as her rightful father, legally and morally allowed to prohibit her marriage. In all these relationships, Jamie entertains the children or sweeps them away on marvelous, reckless adventures, but doesn't stay day by day to wipe up messes and teach life lessons. It's a fantasy of fatherhood, not a reality.

When Jamie insists he sees his nephew Young Ian as a son, Ian challenges him on it. Ian finally insists that Jamie be more than the fun, danger-seeking uncle and provide the discipline. "Ye've said often enough ye care for him as though he were your son. ... Well, I'll tell ye, Jamie – it's no that easy to be his Da; best ye go and find that out now, aye?" (*Voyager,* ch. 32). Jamie is ordered to take the boy out and strap him.

While Jamie tries to perform his fatherly responsibilities for Brianna, most notably finding her a husband, she resists his efforts. Frank and Jamie can both be old fashioned about Brianna – Frank thinks she'll look cheap if she pierces her ears, and Jamie is disturbed by a photo of Brianna in a bikini, kicking water at a teenage boy. Claire has difficulty explaining to Jamie, not only about the bikini but that "Bree's a grown woman; she'll marry when and as she likes, not when someone arranges it for her. She doesn't *need* to marry for that matter. She's having a good education; she can earn her own living" (*Voyager,* ch. 42).

While this concept doesn't fully register, Jamie takes her hunting, telling her to wear her breeks and admiring her skill at shooting his rifle. He has her do the surveying on Fraser's Ridge and welcomes her improvements to his saddlebags. As he works with her on engineering projects, he raises no objection to her "unwomanly" behavior,

Meanwhile, Jamie regards his own father, Brian, as wonderful. Calm and competent, he whipped Jamie in public, so his tenants could see he wasn't above them. "The tenants would know I understood justice, at least from the receiving end," Jamie quips (*Dragonfly in Amber,* ch. 31). Further, Brian always offered Jamie the opportunity to explain his actions. As Jamie notes, "It's no so common for a man to show his feelings for his sons...his own father was nothing like him, so I thought as how he must have made up his mind to do it all differently, once he had the chance" (*Dragonfly in Amber,* ch. 40). Brian tries to save Jamie from the second whipping, but instead dies of shock as he fears his son has been killed before his eyes. He is so much the father of the story that fatherhood finally kills him.

In his "Inside the Episode" talks, Ron Moore describes "the complications of stepping into his dead father's shoes" as the story arc of "Lallybroch" (112), as Jamie wears his father's coat and tries to run the estate as his father would have. It's Claire who must tell him that he's losing his personality in this persona of Laird.

Jamie tells Young Ian as they prepare for war that his father and male mentors often come to him before a battle, though he carries his women into battle with him: "They're the root of your strength" (*Written in My Own Heart's Blood,* ch. 66). Ian appears to save Young Ian in battle, and Jamie senses Dougal and Murtagh as well as Brian.

Roger learns to be a responsible father, from diapers to a single whipping, after Jem's carelessness leads to a slaughter of chickens. He commits entirely to fatherhood, despite the question of Jem's paternity. When Jem is beaten in school for speaking Gaelic, Roger comforts Jem with sensitivity, and then transforms the school system to one of tolerance by teaching Gaelic to all the children. Finally, he risks his life seeking Jem through the stones, uncertain where he'll arrive but unwilling to ever give up the search.

There are some wicked fathers, like the abusive Robbie MacNab in the first book and Tom Christie in the sixth. "Lord John and the Haunted Soldier" introduces the Reverend Mr. Thackeray, who casts out his pregnant daughter, as he "cannot be seen to suffer licentiousness and lewd behavior." He worries about the example he sets for his congregation far more than his penniless child and grandchild.

Lord John becomes a stepfather to Willie and is seen doing an admirable job, raising a brave, courteous, and helpful young man. John loves Willie of course. He says, "Were any man to impugn my affection for him, or to say he is not my son, I would call him out on the instant for it" (*The Drums of Autumn,* ch. 63). His brother Hal, an adult when they lost their father, cares for John as more father than brother, though both feel their real father's loss.

> "I was twenty-one when my father died," Hal remarked out of the blue. "Grown. Had my own life, had a wife – " He broke off abruptly, his mouth twisting. "Didn't think I needed him at all, until he suddenly wasn't there."

> "What could he have done for you?" I asked, sitting down again.
>
> ...
>
> "Been there," he said simply. "Listened. Perhaps ... approved of what I was doing." The last few words came low, barely audible. "Or maybe not. But ... been there." (*Written in My Own Heart's Blood,* ch. 12).

The pair spend *Lord John and the Brotherhood of the Blade* investigating their father's murder and clearing his name, out of pride as well as love.

Hal has three sons and a daughter. He spends book eight combing America for one son and tending to another, even while dealing with his daughter's less-than-perfect engagement. He tells Claire: "You'd die for them, happily. Your family. But at the same time you think, Christ, I can't die! What might happen to them if I weren't here? ... And you know bloody well that you mostly can't help them anyway; they've got to do it – or not – themselves" (*Written in My Own Heart's Blood,* ch. 12).

Another father who deserves credit is Claire's Uncle Lamb, a traveling archeologist suddenly saddled with a dependent. Upon finding her a nice boarding school, she cries and clings to him.

> Uncle Lamb, who hated personal conflict of any kind, had sighed in exasperation, then finally shrugged and tossed his better judgment out the window along with my newly purchased round straw boater. "Ruddy thing," he muttered, seeing it rolling merrily away in the rearview mirror as we roared down the drive in high gear. "Always loathed hats on women, anyway." (ch. 1)

He takes her on digs around the world and teaches her skills from book learning to living rough. Claire adds, "Casual as his own life had been – he always was there. I'd felt his loss acutely when he died, but I'd been married then" (*Written in My Own Heart's Blood,* ch. 12). Before he's killed in the Blitz, he makes certain she'll be cared for.

Roger's Reverend Wakefield, another bachelor uncle suddenly father to a small child, raises Roger with love and compassion. All Roger's memories are positive, as he thinks of the stable love he received and the excellent education in the old and new traditions of the Highlands. Both foster parents make an effort to keep photos and records of the children's parents, so the children can connect with their heritages.

Conclusion

> With a second season already in pre-production, and seven further novels to adapt, the Outlander universe will continue to expand. How would Moore tease the future of his show set in the past? "We're following the shape of the books, so in season two suddenly the action moves to Paris in the 18th century. We'll have a completely different look and tone," he says. "It kinda becomes a war story; we get more involved in the Jacobite rebellion and Bonnie Prince Charlie turns up." (Virtue)

Readers are looking forward to many book characters and events, as well as the touching romantic moments. While the books have their devoted core audience, the Starz show is collecting a new army of fans, inspiring them to love this epic of the Highlands and its heroes, Claire and Jamie. As it does so, it subtly opens people's minds to the ongoing politics of gender, in the past as well as today.

Reading Order

Outlander (1743, 1945)
Dragonfly in Amber (1743-1745, 1968)
Voyager (1746-1767, 1968)
The Drums of Autumn (1767-1770, 1968-1971)
The Fiery Cross (1770-1772)
A Breath of Snow and Ashes (1773-1776, 1978)
An Echo in the Bone (1776-1778, 1978-1980)
"The Space Between" (March 1778) [short story]
"A Leaf on the Wind of All Hallows" (Oct. 1941, 1739) [short story]
Written In My Own Heart's Blood (1739, 1778-1779, 1980)

These can be read at any point and provide additional backstory for book one
"Virgins" (Oct. 1740) [short story]
The Exile (1743) [graphic novel]

These take place within Jamie's Helwater years in *Voyager* and should be read before *An Echo in the Bone,* where characters begin to cross over.

Lord John and the Hand of Devils [collection]
Lord John and the Hellfire Club (1756)
Lord John and the Succubus (Sept. 1757)
Lord John and the Haunted Soldier (Nov. 1758)
Lord John and the Private Matter (June 1757-Aug. 1757)
Lord John and the Brotherhood of the Blade (Jan. 1758-Oct. 1758)
"The Custom of the Army" (1759) [short story]
The Scottish Prisoner (1760)
"Lord John and the Plague of Zombies" (1761?)

Episode Guide

Season One

1	101	09/Aug/14	Sassenach
2	102	16/Aug/14	Castle Leoch
3	103	23/Aug/14	The Way Out
4	104	30/Aug/14	The Gathering
5	105	06/Sep/14	Rent
6	106	13/Sep/14	The Garrison Commander
7	107	20/Sep/14	The Wedding
8	108	27/Sep/14	Both Sides Now
9	109	04/Apr/15	The Reckoning
10	110	11/Apr/15	By the Pricking of My Thumbs
11	111	18/Apr/15	The Devil's Mark
12	112	25/Apr/15	Lallybroch
13	113	02/May/15	The Watch
14	114	09/May/15	The Search
15	115	16/May/15	Wentworth Prison
16	116	30/May/15	To Ransom a Man's Soul

Cast

Producer/Showrunner Ron Moore
Costume Designer Terry Dresbach
Caitriona Balfe as Claire Beauchamp Fraser
Sam Heughan as James (Jamie) Alexander Malcolm MacKenzie Fraser
Tobias Menzies in the dual roles of Frank Randall and Jonathan (Black Jack) Randall.
Stephen Walters as Angus Mhor
Grant O'Rourke as Rupert MacKenzie
Annette Badland as Mrs. FitzGibbons
Graham McTavish as Dougal MacKenzie
Gary Lewis as Colum MacKenzie
Duncan Lacroix as Murtagh Fraser
Lotte Verbeek as Geillis Duncan
Bill Paterson as Ned Gowan
Finn Den Hertog as Willie
John Heffernan as Brigadier General Lord Oliver Thomas
Roderick Gilkison as Young Hamish MacKenzie
James Fleet as the Reverend Wakefield
Laura Donnelly as Jenny Fraser Murray
Steven Cree as Ian Murray
Nell Hudson as Laoghaire MacKenzie
Kathryn Howden as Mrs. Baird
Tracey Wilkinson as Mrs. Graham
Liam Carney as Auld Alec
Aislin McGuckin as Colum's wife, Letitia
Prentis Hancock as Uncle Lamb
Simon Callow as the Duke of Sandringham
Douglas Henshall as Taran MacQuarrie
James Fleet as Rev. Dr. Reginald Wakefield
Aislín McGuckin as Letitia MacKenzie
Tim McInnerny as Father Bain
Simon Meacock as Hugh Munro
Lochlann O'Mearain as Horrocks

Works Cited

Dresbach, Terry. *Terry Dresbach: An 18th Century Life.* 2014. Blog. http://terrydresbach.com.

Friedlander, Whitney. "'Outlander' Costume Designer on Wedding Dresses, Kilts and Corsets." *Variety* 20 Sept 2014. http://variety.com/2014/artisans/news/outlander-wedding-costume-designer-1201309495.

Gabaldon, Diana. *A Breath of Snow and Ashes.* New York: Random House, 2005.

–. "A Breath of Snow and Ashes." *Scattered Paper* 7 April 2010. Blog Post. http://scatteredpaper.blogspot.com/2010/04/breath-of-snow-and-ashes.html

–. *Books and Writers Community.* Compuserve forums September 2011 Board Post http://forums.compuserve.com/discussions/Books_and_Writers_Community/_/_/ws-books/72364.1

–. *Dragonfly in Amber.* New York: Random House, 1992.

–. "The Doctor's Balls." *Chicks Unravel Time: Women Journey Through Every Season of Doctor Who.* Edited by Deborah Stanish and L.M. Myles. USA: Mad Norwegian Press, 2012. Kindle Edition.

–. *The Drums of Autumn.* New York: Random House, 1996.

–. *An Echo in the Bone.* New York: Random House, 2009.

–. The Exile: An Outlander Graphic Novel. New York: Del Ray, 2010.

–. *The Fiery Cross.* New York: Random House, 2001.

–. "A Leaf on the Wind of All Hallows." *Songs of Love and Death,* eds. George R. R. Martin and Gardner Dozois, USA: Gallery Books, 2010. 429-468.

–. *Lord John and the Brotherhood of the Blade.* New York: Random House, 2011.

–. "Lord John and the Plague of Zombies" *Down*

These Strange Streets. Ed. George R.R. Martin and Gardner Dozois. New York: Penguin, 2011.
– . "Lord John and the Succubus." *Lord John and the Hand of Devils*. New York: Random House, 2007. 45-156.
– . *Outlander*. New York: Bantam Dell, 1992.
– . "Outlander Reread Thoughts." *Books and Writers Community. Compuserve*. November 2010. Board Post. http://forums.compuserve.com/discussions/Books_and_Writers_Community/Diana_Gabaldon/Outlander_reread_thoughts/ws-books/69201.1?nav=messages#a1
– . *The Outlandish Companion*. New York: Delacorte Press, 1999.
– . *The Scottish Prisoner*. New York: Random House, 2011.
. "The Space Between." *The Mad Scientist's Guide to World Domination: Original Short Fiction for the Modern Evil Genius*. Ed. John Joseph Adams. New York: Tor, 2013. 161-243.
– . *Voyager*. New York: Random House, 1993.
Lutes, Alicia. "*Outlander*'s Sam Heughan and Tobias Menzies on that Black Jack Randall Reveal." *The Nerdist*. 27 April 2015. https://nerdist.com/outlander-interview-sam-heughan-tobias-menzies-black-back.
McCreary, Bear. "By the Pricking of My Thumbs" and "The Devil's Mark." *Bear McCreary Official Site* April 2015. http://www.bearmccreary.com/blog/blog/outlander-by-the-pricking-of-my-thumbs-the-devils-mark/#blog/blog/outlander-by-the-pricking-of-my-thumbs-the-devils-mark/
– . "Comic Con 2014 Highlights." *Bear McCreary Official Site* 29 July 2014. http://www.bearmccreary.com/#blog/blog/films/comic-con-2014-highlights.

– . “Outlander: The Garrison Commander, The Wedding, Both Sides Now.” *Bear McCreary Official Site* 28 Sept 2014. http://www.bearmccreary.com/#blog/blog/outlander-the-garrison-commander-the-wedding-both-sides-now.

–. “Outlander: Sassenach.” *Bear McCreary Official Site* 29 July 2014. http://www.bearmccreary.com/#blog/blog/outlander-sassenach.

Moore, Ron. “Inside the World of Outlander.” Episodes 101-108. *Starz Extras. Starz.com.*

Nemiroff, Perri “*Outlander* Cast on Sex and Nudity in Historical Scotland.” *Collider* 11 April 2015. http://collider.com/outlander-cast-on-sex-and-nudity-in-historical-scotland/

Ng, Philiana. “*Outlander*: Graham McTavish on Dougal’s ‘Superobjective,’ Claire and Rewriting History.” *Hollywood Reporter* 6 Sept 2014 http://www.hollywoodreporter.com/live-feed/outlander-graham-mctavish-dougal-729642

– . “*Outlander*: Caitriona Balfe on Claire and Jamie’s Steamy Connection (Q&A).” *Hollywood Reporter* 16 Aug 2014. http://www.hollywoodreporter.com/live-feed/outlander-caitriona-balfe-claire-jamies-725840

Prudom, Laura. “*Outlander* Stars Break Down Claire and Jamie’s First Fight, That Spanking Scene.” *Variety* 5 April 2015 http://variety.com/2015/tv/news/outlander-jamie-claire-spanking-fight-reckoning-1201466598

– . “*Outlander* Stars Talk Claire’s Choice, Geillis’ Sacrifice in ‘The Devil’s Mark’” *Variety* 18 April 2015. http://variety.com/2015/tv/news/outlander-claire-tells-jamie-the-truth-chooses-to-stay-

1201475259/
Schwartz, Terri. "Outlander's Naked Black Jack: Tobias Menzies Confirms, 'It's all me.'" *Zap2It* 27 Apr 2015. http://www.zap2it.com/blogs/outlander_tobias_menzies_black_jack_naked-2015-04
Vineyard, Jennifer. *Outlander*'s Caitriona Balfe on Feminism, Fans, and Love Triangles." Vulture 28 Aug 2014. http://www.vulture.com/2014/08/caitriona-balfe-outlander-claire-chat.html
–. "Why Fans Clapped During *Outlander*'s Spanking Scene." *Vulture* 5 April 2-15 http://www.vulture.com/2015/04/outlander-spanking-scene-premiere.html

Secondary

Bell, Robert Fitzroy, ed. *Memorials of John Murray of Broughton Sometime Secretary to Prince Charles Edward.* Edinburgh: Edinburgh University Press, 1898. http://www.electricscotland.com/history/charles/
Brownmiller, Susan. *Against Our Will: Men, Women, and Rape.* New York: Bantam, 1976.
Burgin, Victor James Donald, and Cora Kaplan, eds. *Formations of Fantasy.* London: Methuen, 1986.
Carr, Rosalind. *Gender and Enlightenment Culture in Eighteenth Century Scotland.* Edinburgh, Edinburgh University Press, 2014.
Chaudhuri, Shohini. *Feminist Film Theorists.* New York: Routledge, 2006.
Clover, Carol J. "Her Body, Himself: Gender in the Slasher Film" Thornham 234-250.
Condren, Mary. *The Serpent and the Goddess.* San Francisco: Harper & Row, 1989.
De Beauvoir, Simone. *The Second Sex.* Trans. H. M. Parshley. London: David Campbell, 1993.

Doane, Mary Ann. *Femme Fatales: Feminism, Film Theory, Psychoanalysis.* New York, Routledge, 1991.

Frankel, Valerie Estelle. *From Girl to Goddess: The Heroine's Journey in Myth and Legend.* Jefferson, NC: McFarland and Co., 2010.

--. *The Symbolism and Sources of Outlander* Jefferson, NC: McFarland, 2015.

Glover, Katharine. *Elite Women and Polite Society in Eighteenth-Century Scotland.* Woodbridge: Boydell Press, 2011.

Glynn, Basil. "The Conquests of Henry VIII: Masculinity, Sex, and the National Past in The Tudors." Glynn, Basil, James Aston, and Beth Johnson, eds. *Television, Sex, and Society: Analyzing Contemporary Representations.* New York: Continuum, 2012. 157-173.

Goodman, Philomena. *Women, Sexuality, and War.* New York: Palgrave, 2002.

Hale, Mike. "A Highland Fling Would Not Be Unexpected Here." *The New York Times* 1 Aug 2014. http://www.nytimes.com/2014/08/02/arts/television/outlander-a-starz-series-adapted-from-the-novels.html

Haskell, Molly. "The Woman's Film." Thornham 20-31.

Hill, Libby. "*Outlander* Recap: The Show Takes a New Point of View." Arts Beat. *The New York Times.* 4 April 2015. http://artsbeat.blogs.nytimes.com/2015/04/04/outlander-recap-season-1-episode-9-reckoning/?_r=1

Hughes, Sarah. "*Outlander* is Billed as the Feminist *Game of Thrones* - so What's the Secret of its Success?" *The Independent* 26 April 2015. http://www.independent.co.uk/arts-entertainment/tv/features/outlander-is-billed-as-

the-feminist-game-of-thrones – so-whats-the-secret-of-its-success-10101972.html
Ibson, John. "Sensitive Male." *American Masculinities: A Historical Encyclopedia.* Ed. Bret Carroll. USA: Sage Publications, 2013.
Kaplan, Cora. "The Thorn Birds: Fiction, Fantasy, Femininity." Burgin, Donald, and Kaplan 142-166.
Kuhn, Annette. "Women's Genres: Melodrama, Soap Opera and Theory." Thornham 146-156.
Kutulas, Judy. "Liberated Women and New Sensitive Men: Reconstructing Gender in the 1970s Workplace Comedies." *The Sitcom Reader: America Viewed and Skewed.* Ed. Mary M. Dalton. USA: SUNY Press, 2005.
Landay, Lori. *Madcaps, Screwballs, and Con Women: The Female Trickster in American Culture.* Pennsylvania: University of Pennsylvania Press, 1998.
Lewallen, Avis. "Lace: Pornography for Women?" *The Female Gaze.* Ed. Lorraine Gamman and Margaret Marshment. Seattle: Real Comet Press, 1989. 86-101.
Prior, Mary. "Women and the Urban Economy: Oxford, 1500-1800" *Women in English Society 1500-1800.* Ed. Mary Prior. London: Routledge,1985.
Maerz, Melissa. "Let's Talk about that 'Outlander' Sex Scene." *EW* 11 Aug 2014. http://insidetv.ew.com/2014/08/11/outlander-sex-scene/
Marshall, Rosalind K. *Virgins and Viragos.* Academy Chicago Ltd: Chicago, 1983
Martin, Michael. "Anna Paquin." *Interview Magazine* 2013. http://www.interviewmagazine.com/film/anna-paquin-true-blood.
McNamara, Mary. "HBO, You're Busted." *Los Angeles*

Times 3 July 2013. http://articles.latimes.com/2011/jul/03/entertainment/la-ca-hbo-breasts-20110703.

Mulvey, Laura. "Visual Pleasure and Narrative Cinema," *Screen* 16.3 Autumn 1975 pp. 6-18. http://www.scribd.com/doc/7758866/laura-mulvey-visual-pleasure-and-narrative-cinema

Petersen, Anne Helen. "Outlander Is The Feminist Answer To Game Of Thrones — And Men Should Be Watching It." *BuzzFeed* 4 Aug 2014. http://www.buzzfeed.com/annehelenpetersen/watch-outlander

Pollitt, Katha. "The Smurfette Principle." *The New York Times* 7 Apr 1991. http://www.nytimes.com/1991/04/07/magazine/hers-the-smurfette-principle.html

Radway, Janice A. *Reading the Romance: Women, Patriarchy, and Popular Literature.* North Carolina: University of North Carolina Press, 1991.

Ramsdell, Kristin. *Romance Fiction: A Guide To the Genre.* California State University, Hayward 1999. Libraries Unlimited, Inc.

Riviére, Joan. "Womanliness as Masquerade." Burgin, Donald, and Kaplan 35-44.

Rosenberg, Buck Clifford "Masculine Makeovers: Lifestyle Television, Metrosexuals and Real Blokes." *Exposing Lifestyle Television: The Big Reveal.* Ed. Gareth Palmer. Ashgate, Aldershot, 2008,

Saraiya, Sonia. "*Outlander* is Letter-Perfect Historical Fantasy." *AV Club* 8 August 2014. http://www.avclub.com/review/outlander-letter-perfect-historical-fantasy-207758

Schama, Chloe. "Show Some Spine." Sunday Book Review. *The New York Times* 30 June 2013.

Seitz, Matt Zoller. "*Outlander* Is No *Game of Thrones*, But That's a Good Thing." *Vulture* 7 August 2014.

http://www.vulture.com/2014/08/tv-review-ron-d-moores-outlander.html

Silverman, Kaja. "Lost Objects and Mistaken Subjects." Thornham 131-145.

Thornham, Sue. *Feminist Film Theory.* Edinburgh: Edinburgh University Press, 1999.

Varner, Gary R. *Menhirs, Dolmen and Circles of Stone: The Folklore and Mythology of Sacred Stone.* USA: Algora Pub, 2004.

Virtue, Graeme. "*Outlander: Game Of Thrones* Helped Open the Door for Us." *The Guardian* 21 Mar 2015. http://www.theguardian.com/tv-and-radio/2015/mar/21/ronald-d-moore-outlander.

Walker, Barbara G. *The Crone.* San Francisco: Harper San Francisco, 1985.

Index

About the Author

Valerie Estelle Frankel is the author of many books on pop culture, including *Doctor Who - The What, Where, and How, History, Sherlock: Every Canon Reference You May Have Missed in BBC's Series 1-3, Homages and the Highlands: An Outlander Guide,* and *How Game of Thrones Will End.* Many of her books focus on women's roles in fiction, from her heroine's journey guides *From Girl to Goddess* and *Buffy and the Heroine's Journey* to books like *Women in Game of Thrones* and *The Many Faces of Katniss Everdeen.* Once a lecturer at San Jose State University, she's a frequent speaker at conferences. Come explore her research at www.vefrankel.com.

31575134R00162

Made in the USA
Middletown, DE
04 May 2016